NNG™ Reference Manual

Garrett D'Amore

Second Edition

Thank you for purchasing this book! Purchases of this book help fund continued development NNG™. For updates, additional formats, errata, and more information, please visit it's homepage at http://staysail.tech/books/nng_reference.

NNG™ and nanomsg™ are trademarks of Garrett D'Amore.

ISBN 978-1-7324234-4-2
Second edition (paperback), November 2018.

For Jenichka —

The sun always shines when you are home.

Contents

Preface

At the time of this writing, we are wrapping up NNG for its formal 1.0.0 release. It's a good time for reflection on the road that we took to get here. Like the road on the cover of this book, it was windy (if quite a bit longer), but what we find at the end has made the journey worthwhile.

Originally the NNG project was conceived as a relatively modest effort to rewrite nanomsg based on threads, with a more readily extensible internal architecture so that we could more easily undertake projects like the ZeroTier and TLS transports.

It would not be incorrect to say that the initial NNG effort was started in "anger", as we were frustrated with nanomsg's very complex internal state machines. Looking back on it now, those complex state state machines don't seem nearly as insane as they did just a year ago.

The simple, naïve, approach we would have preferred, and the one we originally started with, involved significant use of threads, inspired by the work we did in mangos, which uses Go's goroutines heavily. Goroutines are excellent. Threads, it turns out, are not. Scalable, asynchronous, *portable* I/O is a lot harder than it looks.

> Our experience with in-kernel threads on illumos and Solaris spoiled us, and left us utterly unprepared for cesspool that really is large amounts of userspace programming.

Instead, we have created our own, completely asynchronous core, giving us advanced multiprocessing and concurrency capabilities, without either sacrificing portability or settling for some unhappy least common denominator. This core is a robust foundation for NNG and handling the "Scalability Protocols", but if we're being completely honest, we think this core has braod applicability for beyond just the Scalability Protocols. It will be interesting to see if others come to the same conclusion.

Builting upon this robust foundation, we have engineered a substantial project, with capabilities far in exceess of the original nanomsg, while still preserving compatibility with the the network protocols that form the backbone of the nanomsg ecosystem, and even a compatible programming interface for nanomsg library users. In addition to compatibility with nanomsg, we find that NNG has greatly increased scalability, reliability, and usability (especially when developing concurrent applications).

NNG also has complete HTTP server and client implementations, support for TLS, and a plethora of other capabilities. Much of this is made possible by a the aforementioned asynchronous I/O framework.

We've tried to stay true to the core nanomsg goals about being light-weight, liberally licensed, and implemented in C. (After all, those were the things that drew us to nanomsg in the first place!) In addition we added a couple of new ones. Specifically, reliability, performance, and extensibility (in that order) were added as core goals for the project.

We believe that NNG represents a substantial step forward over other messaging frameworks, and have enjoyed creating it. We hope you find it useful. There is still a lot more we want to do, and future release of NNG will continue to expand it's capabilities. We're just getting started.

— *Garrett D'Amore*, May 30, 2018

Acknowledgements

We would like to thank Janjaap Bos, at Capitar IT Group BV. Without his patronage, neither NNG nor this book would be possible.

We would also like thank Martin Sústrik for creating the original nanomsg project, the foundation upon which all of this work is based.

And certainly not least of all, we would like to thank the various members of the community who have followed and supported the NNG project in so many different ways.

Colophon

This book was created using a combination of the excellent Asciidoctor program and homegrown scripts. The image on the cover is of the Phare du Petit Minou located in Plouzané, France, and was captured by William Bout.

About This Book

This reference manual documents the Application Programming Interface (API) provided by NNG version 1.1.

Audience

This book contains reference pages describing the C language programming interface to NNG version 1.1. It is intended to serve as a desk reference for developers working in the C language using that API.

Developers working with NNG from other languages may find this book useful as well, particularly when debugging programs.

About NNG

NNG is a communications library, implemented in C99, to facilitate developing distributed applications using common communications patterns (such as publish and subscribe, request and reply, and surveyor and respondent) with a minimum of fuss.

It is a follow-on to the nanomsg project, and like that project is brokerless (consisting only of a library). It remains compatible with nanomsg at the network level, as well as other projects implementing the Scalability Protocols.

More information can be found at nanomsg.org.

Organization

This book is organized into major parts called "Sections". This organization is derived from a historical practice dating back to AT&T UNIX, where the programmer's reference for that operating system was divided into major sections, such as a section for command line interfaces and another section for system calls, and another section for library functions.

We've used a similar section numbering system, where Section 1 is for the command line program, Section 3 is for the main programming interface, Section 5 is for types and macros, and Section 7 is for protocols and transports. Furthermore, there are some supplemental Sections that are subgroups of Section 3, such as Section 3http, which is for HTTP specific functions.

Generally most NNG programs can be written with only the functions documented in Section 3.

Within the sections are "pages" for each major function or other high level topic. For example, a single "page" exists for the nng_close(3) function.

Within each page there are common sections for the synopsis and description, as well as return values and any errors that may be relevant.

Conventions

Throughout this book there are occasional warnings, notices, and tips. These are visually distinguished as follows:

Tips are things that the reader may find useful, such as suggestions for use or tim saving hints.

Notes are things that the reader should be aware of, and provide additional information or context that may aid in the understanding or use of the topic.

Warnings are used to denote important cautionary advice, which should be carefully heeded. Ignoring such advice may lead to crashes, unexpected behavior, loss of revenue, or other undesirable conditions.

New in the 1.1 Release

This edition of the *NNG Reference Manual* includes numerous corrections, and bug fixes, a number of which were contributed by community members. It also documents some of the new features available in 1.1, which include new properties, new functions to make working with HTTP easier, and new functions for obtaining operational statistics.

Section 1

Commands and Utilities

NAME

nngcat - command line access to Scalability Protocols

SYNOPSIS

nngcat --help

nngcat --version

nngcat [*OPTION*]...

DESCRIPTION

The *nngcat* utility provides command line access to the Scalability Protocols, making it possible to write shell scripts that interact with other peers in a Scalability Protocols topology, by both sending and receiving messages.

OPTIONS

The possible values for *OPTION* are described below.

> 💡 The *nngcat* utility accepts shortened versions of these options, as long as the supplied option is unambiguous. For example --comp can be used in lieu of --compat, but --re may not be used for anything because it could mean any of --req, --rep, or --respondent.

When using the long form of an option (names prefixed with with --), if the option takes a value then the value may be supplied by appending the option with an equals sign and the value (e.g. --subscribe=times), by appending the option with a colon and the value (e.g. --subscribe:tribune) or by providing the data as the next program argument (e.g. --subscribe herald).

When using short form options (a single letter prefixed with a -), if the option takes a value it may either be immediately appended to the value (e.g. -L5678) or provided as the next program argument (e.g. -L 5678).

POSIX style option clustering of single letter options is not supported; each option must be presented as a separate argument to the program.

Generic Options

-h, --help
    Get usage help.

-V, --version
    Print the version and exit.

-v, --verbose
    Select verbose operation.

-q, --silent
    Select silent operation.

--compat

Compatible mode. This cause *nngcat* to behave more like the legacy *nanocat* application. In this mode connections are made asynchronously, and the **--pair** option selects version 0 of the *pair* protocol instead of version 1.

--subscribe=*TOPIC*

Subscribe to *TOPIC*. This option can only be used with the *sub* protocol. The *TOPIC* is checked against the first bytes of messages received, and messages are discarded if they do not match. This may be specified multiple times to subscribe to multiple topics. If not specified at all, then a default subscription to everything is assumed.

--count==*COUNT*

Limit the number of iterations when looping to *COUNT* iterations. For protocols that only send, this will only send *COUNT* messages before exiting. For protocols that only receive, this will only receive *COUNT* messages before exiting. For protocols that involve a full exchange, this will only perform *COUNT* exchanges (each exchange is characterized by at most a single send, and one or more receives.) If *COUNT* is zero, then an infinite number of iterations is performed.

Protocol Selection Options

ℹ️   At least one protocol must be selected.

--bus, --bus0

Select the *bus* version 0 protocol. This protocol can send and receive messages to and from other *bus* version 0 peers.

--req, --req0

Select the *req* version 0 protocol. This protocol sends messages to *rep* version 0 peers and receives replies from them.

--rep, --rep0

Select the *rep* version 0 protocol. This protocol receives messages from *req* version 0 peers and can send replies to them.

--pub, --pub0

Select the *pub* version 0 protocol. This protocol sends messages to *sub* version peers.

--sub, --sub0

Select the *sub* version 0 protocol. This protocol receives messages from *pub* version 0 peers, and filters them based on subscriptions set with **--subscribe**.

--push, --push0

Select the *push* version 0 protocol. This protocol sends messages to *pull* version 0 peers. A given message is normally only delivered to a single peer.

--pull, --pull0

Select the *pull* version 0 protocol. This protocol receives messages from *push* version 0 peers.

--pair0

Select the *pair* version 0 protocol. This protocol can send and receive messages with one connected *pair* version 0 peer.

--pair1

Select the *pair* version 1 protocol. This protocol can send and receive messages with one connected *pair* version 1 peer. It is not supported in **--compat** mode. (Polyamorous mode is not supported in *nngcat*, although peers may be using polyamorous mode.)

--pair

Acts as an alias for **--pair1**, unless **--compat** mode is selected, in which case it acts as an alias for **--pair0**.

--surveyor, --surveyor0

Select the *surveyor* version 0 protocol. This protocol sends a survey request to *respondent* version 0 peers, and then receives replies from them.

--respondent, --respondent0

Select the *respondent* version 0 protocol. This protocol receives survey requests from *surveyor* version 0 peers, and can send a reply to them.

Peer Selection Options

At least one peer address must be selected.

While legacy *nanocat* only supported one peer, *nng* can support more than one peer on a given connection.

--connect, --dial=*URL*

Connect to the peer at the address specified by *URL*.

--bind, --listen=*URL*

Bind to, and accept connections from peers, at the address specified by *URL*.

-x, --connect-ipc=*PATH*

Connect to the IPC path specified by *PATH*. This is the same as **--connect**=ipc://*PATH*.

-X, --bind-ipc=*PATH*

Bind to the IPC path specified by *PATH*. This is the same as **--bind**=ipc://*PATH*.

-l, --connect-local=*PORT*

Connect to localhost at the TCP port specified by *PORT*. This is the same as **--connect**=tcp://127.0.0.1:*PORT*.

-L, --bind-local=*PORT*

Bind to the TCP port specified by *PORT*. This is the same as **--bind**=tcp://127.0.0.1:*PORT*.

Receive Options

Data messages received can be formatted in different ways. These options can only be specified when using a protocol that receives messages.

-A, --ascii

The same as specifying **--format**=ascii.

-Q, --quoted

   The same as specifying **--format**=quoted.

--hex

   The same as specifying **--format**=hex.

--msgpack

   The same as specifying **--format**=msgpack.

--raw

   The same as specifying **--format**=raw.

--receive-timeout=*SEC*

   Give up receiving messages after *SEC* seconds pass without any received messages.

--recv-maxsz=*COUNT*

   Set the maximum message size socket will accept to *COUNT* bytes. Messages larger than this will be discarded. The default is 1048576 (1 MB). To eliminate any restriction, use 0.

--format=*FORMAT*

   Format data as indicated. The *FORMAT* can be any of:

   no

      No output at all.

   raw

      Raw output, every byte received is sent to standard output.

   ascii

      ASCII safe, printable ASCII is emitted verbatim, with other bytes substituted with . (period).

   quoted

      Messages are printed as quoted strings, using C language conventions.

   hex

      Messages are printed as quoted strings, with every byte appearing as an escaped hexadecimal value, such as \x2E.

   msgpack

      Messages are emitted as MessagePack [https://msgpack.org] "bin format" (byte arrays).

Transmit Options

Protocols that support sending data can use these options to select the data.

-D, --data=*DATA*

   Use *DATA* for the body of outgoing messages.

-F, --file=*FILE*

   Use *FILE* for the body of outgoing messages.

-i, --interval=*SEC*

> For protocols that send unsolicited data (as opposed to those that send data only in response to received messages), this will resend the outgoing message at repeating intervals of *SEC* seconds.

-d, --delay=*SEC*

> Wait *SEC* seconds before sending the first outgoing message. This is useful to let connections establish before sending data, thereby avoiding message loss.

--send-timeout=*SEC*

> Give up trying to send a message after *SEC* seconds.

TLS Options

These options are only present if TLS is configured; they are ignored when using addresses that are not secured with TLS.

-k, --insecure

> Skip peer validation.

-E, --cert=*FILE*

> Load own certificate from *FILE*.

--key=*FILE*

> Load own key from *FILE*. Should be used in conjunction with **--cert**. If not specified, and **--cert** is specified, then a single file containing both the private key and the associated certificate is assumed.

--cacert=*FILE*

> Load CA certificates from *FILE*. These CAs ("Certificate Authorities") are used as trust roots when validating certificates presented by peers.

ZeroTier Options

These options are only present if ZeroTier is configured; they are ignored otherwise.

--zt-home=*DIRECTORY*

> Directory for persistent ZeroTier node (key material, etc.) This directory must already exist. Only one program may use a ZeroTier node at a time; file locking is used to prevent this.

EXAMPLES

Echo service using request/reply.

```
$ addr="tcp://127.0.0.1:4567"
$ nngcat --rep --listen=${addr} --data="42" --quoted &
$ nngcat --req --dial=${addr} --data="what is the answer?" --quoted
"what is the answer?"
"42"
```

Send a chime every hour (3600 seconds).

```
$ addr=ipc:///grandpa_clock
$ nngcat --pub --listen=${addr} --data "cuckoo" --interval 3600 &
$ nngcat --sub --dial=${addr} --quoted &
"cuckoo"
```

SEE ALSO

libnng(3), nng(7), nng_bus(7), nng_pair(7), nng_pub(7), nng_pull(7), nng_push(7), nng_sub(7), nng_rep(7), nng_req(7), nng_respondent(7), nng_surveyor(7)

Section 3

Library Functions

NAME

libnng - nanomsg next generation library

SYNOPSIS

cc [*flags*] *files* **-lnng** [*libraries*]

DESCRIPTION

The *nng* library provides a common messaging framework intended to solve common communication problems in distributed applications.

It provides a C language API.

Common Functions

The following common functions exist in *libnng*.

nng_alloc()	allocate memory
nng_free()	free memory
nng_strdup()	duplicate string
nng_strerror()	return an error description
nng_strfree()	free string
nng_version()	report library version

Socket Functions

The following functions operate on sockets.

nng_close()	close socket
nng_dial()	create and start dialer
nng_getopt()	get socket option
nng_listen()	create and start listener
nng_recv()	receive data
nng_send()	send data
nng_setopt()	set socket option
nng_socket_id()	get numeric socket identifier

Connection Management

The following functions are used with either listeners, or dialers. Listeners accept incoming connection requests, and dialers make them.

nng_dial()   create and start dialer

nng_dialer_close()   close dialer

nng_dialer_create()   create dialer

nng_dialer_getopt()   get dialer option

nng_dialer_id()   get numeric dialer identifier

nng_dialer_setopt()   set dialer option

nng_dialer_start()   start dialer

nng_listen()   create and start listener

nng_listener_close()   close listener

nng_listener_create()   create listener

nng_listener_getopt()   get listener option

nng_listener_id()   get numeric listener identifier

nng_listener_setopt()   set listener option

nng_listener_start()   start listener

nng_pipe_close()   close pipe

nng_pipe_dialer()   return dialer that created pipe

nng_pipe_getopt()   get pipe option

nng_pipe_id()   get numeric pipe identifier

nng_pipe_listener()   return listener that created pipe

nng_pipe_notify()   register pipe notification callback

nng_pipe_socket()   return owning socket for pipe

Message Handling Functions

Applications desiring to use the richest part of *libnng* will want to use the message API, where a message structure is passed between functions. This API provides the most power support for zero-copy.

Messages are divided into a header and body, where the body generally carries user-payload and the header carries protocol specific header information. Most applications will only interact with the body.

nng_msg_alloc()   allocate a message

nng_msg_append()   append to message body

nng_msg_body()   return message body

nng_msg_chop()   remove data from end of message body

nng_msg_clear()   clear message body

nng_msg_dup()   duplicate a message

nng_msg_free()	free a message
nng_msg_get_pipe()	get pipe for message
nng_msg_insert()	prepend to message body
nng_msg_len()	return the message body length
nng_msg_realloc()	reallocate a message
nng_msg_set_pipe()	set pipe for message
nng_msg_trim()	remove data from start of message body
nng_recvmsg()	receive a message
nng_sendmsg()	send a message

Message Header Handling

💡   Few applications will need these functions, as message headers are only used to carry protocol-specific content. However, applications which use raw mode may need to access the header of messages.

nng_msg_header()	return message header
nng_msg_header_append()	append to message header
nng_msg_header_chop()	remove data from end of message header
nng_msg_header_clear()	clear message header
nng_msg_header_insert()	prepend to message header
nng_msg_header_len()	return the message header length
nng_msg_header_trim()	remove data from start of message header

Asynchronous Operations

Most applications will interact with *nng* synchronously; that is that functions such as nng_send() will block the calling thread until the operation has completed.

ℹ️   Synchronous operations which send messages may return before the message has actually been received, or even transmitted. Instead, These functions return as soon as the message was successfully queued for delivery.

Asynchronous operations behave differently. These operations are initiated by the calling thread, but control returns immediately to the calling thread. When the operation is subsequently completed (regardless of whether this was successful or not), then a user supplied function ("callback") is executed.

A context structure, an nng_aio, is allocated and associated with each asynchronous operation. Only a single asynchronous operation may be associated with an nng_aio at any time.

The following functions are used in the asynchronous model:

nng_aio_abort()	abort asynchronous I/O operation

nng_aio_alloc()	allocate asynchronous I/O handle
nng_aio_begin()	begin asynchronous I/O operation
nng_aio_cancel()	cancel asynchronous I/O operation
nng_aio_count()	return number of bytes transferred
nng_aio_defer()	defer asynchronous I/O operation
nng_aio_finish()	finish asynchronous I/O operation
nng_aio_free()	free asynchronous I/O handle
nng_aio_get_input()	return input parameter
nng_aio_get_msg()	get message from an asynchronous receive
nng_aio_get_output()	return output result
nng_aio_result()	return result of asynchronous operation
nng_aio_set_input()	set input parameter
nng_aio_set_iov()	set scatter/gather vector
nng_aio_set_msg()	set message for an asynchronous send
nng_aio_set_output()	set output result
nng_aio_set_timeout()	set asynchronous I/O timeout
nng_aio_stop()	stop asynchronous I/O operation
nng_aio_wait()	wait for asynchronous I/O operation
nng_recv_aio()	receive message asynchronously
nng_send_aio()	send message asynchronously
nng_sleep_aio()	sleep asynchronously

Protocols

The following functions are used to construct a socket with a specific protocol:

nng_bus_open()	open a bus socket
nng_pair_open()	open a pair socket
nng_pub_open()	open a pub socket
nng_pull_open()	open a pull socket
nng_push_open()	open a push socket
nng_rep_open()	open a rep socket
nng_req_open()	open a req socket
nng_respondent_open()	open a respondent socket
nng_sub_open()	open a sub socket

nng_surveyor_open()   open a surveyor socket

Transports

The following functions are used to register a transport for use.

nng_inproc_register()   register inproc transport

nng_ipc_register()   register IPC transport

nng_tcp_register()   register TCP transport

nng_tls_register()   register TLS transport

nng_ws_register()   register WebSocket transport

nng_wss_register()   register WebSocket Secure transport

nng_zt_register()   register ZeroTier transport

Protocol Contexts

The following functions are useful to separate the protocol processing from a socket object, into a separate context. This can allow multiple contexts to be created on a single socket for concurrent applications.

nng_ctx_close()   close context

nng_ctx_getopt()   get context option

nng_ctx_id()   get numeric context identifier

nng_ctx_open()   create context

nng_ctx_recv()   receive message using context asynchronously

nng_ctx_send()   send message using context asynchronously

nng_ctx_setopt()   set context option

Statistics

The following functions provide access to statistics which can be used to observe program behaviors and as an aid in troubleshooting.

nng_stat_child()   get child statistic

nng_stat_name()   get statistic description

nng_stat_name()   get statistic name

nng_stat_next()   get next statistic

nng_stat_string()   get statistic string value

nng_stat_timestamp()   get statistic timestamp

nng_stat_type()   get statistic type

nng_stat_unit()	get statistic unit
nng_stat_valueg()	get statistic value
nng_stats_free()	free statistics
nng_stats_get()	get statistics

URL Object

Common functionality is supplied for parsing and handling universal resource locators (URLS).

nng_url_clone()	clone URL structure
nng_url_free()	free URL structure
nng_url_parse()	create URL structure from string

Supplemental API

These supplemental functions are not intrinsic to building network applications with *NNG*, but they are made available as a convenience to aid in creating portable applications.

nng_clock()	get time
nng_cv_alloc()	allocate condition variable
nng_cv_free()	free condition variable
nng_cv_until()	wait for condition or timeout
nng_cv_wait()	wait for condition
nng_cv_wake()	wake all waiters
nng_cv_wake1()	wake one waiter
nng_msleep()	sleep for milliseconds
nng_mtx_alloc()	allocate mutex
nng_mtx_free()	free mutex
nng_mtx_lock()	lock mutex
nng_mtx_unlock()	unlock mutex
nng_opts_parse()	parse command line options
nng_random()	get random number
nng_thread_create()	create thread
nng_thread_destroy()	reap thread

HTTP Support

The library may be configured with support for HTTP, and this will be the case if WebSocket support is configured as well. In this case, it is possible to access functionality to support the creation of HTTP (and HTTP/S if TLS support is present) servers and clients.

Common HTTP Functions

The following functions are used to work with HTTP requests, responses, and connections.

nng_http_conn_close()	close HTTP connection
nng_http_conn_read()	read from HTTP connection
nng_http_conn_read_all()	read all from HTTP connection
nng_http_conn_read_req()	read HTTP request
nng_http_conn_read_res()	read HTTP response
nng_http_conn_write()	write to HTTP connection
nng_http_conn_write_all()	write all to HTTP connection
nng_http_conn_write_req()	write HTTP request
nng_http_conn_write_res()	write HTTP response
nng_http_req_add_header()	add HTTP request header
nng_http_req_alloc()	allocate HTTP request structure
nng_http_req_copy_data()	copy HTTP request body
nng_http_req_del_header()	delete HTTP request header
nng_http_req_free()	free HTTP request structure
nng_http_req_get_data()	get HTTP request body
nng_http_req_get_header()	return HTTP request header
nng_http_req_get_method()	return HTTP request method
nng_http_req_get_uri()	return HTTP request URI
nng_http_req_get_version()	return HTTP request protocol version
nng_http_req_reset()	reset HTTP request structure
nng_http_req_set_data()	set HTTP request body
nng_http_req_set_header()	set HTTP request header
nng_http_req_set_method()	set HTTP request method
nng_http_req_set_uri()	set HTTP request URI
nng_http_req_set_version()	set HTTP request protocol version
nng_http_res_add_header()	add HTTP response header
nng_http_res_alloc()	allocate HTTP response structure
nng_http_res_alloc_error()	allocate HTTP error response
nng_http_res_copy_data()	copy HTTP response body
nng_http_res_del_header()	delete HTTP response header
nng_http_res_free()	free HTTP response structure

nng_http_res_get_data()	get HTTP response body
nng_http_res_get_header()	return HTTP response header
nng_http_res_get_reason()	return HTTP response reason
nng_http_res_get_status()	return HTTP response status
nng_http_res_get_version()	return HTTP response protocol version
nng_http_res_reset()	reset HTTP response structure
nng_http_res_set_data()	set HTTP response body
nng_http_res_set_header()	set HTTP response header
nng_http_res_set_reason()	set HTTP response reason
nng_http_res_set_status()	set HTTP response status
nng_http_res_set_version()	set HTTP response protocol version

HTTP Client Functions

These functions are intended for use with HTTP client applications.

nng_http_client_alloc()	allocate HTTP client
nng_http_client_connect()	establish HTTP client connection
nng_http_client_free()	free HTTP client
nng_http_client_get_tls()	get HTTP client TLS configuration
nng_http_client_set_tls()	set HTTP client TLS configuration
nng_http_client_transact()	perform one HTTP transaction
nng_http_conn_transact()	perform one HTTP transaction on connection

HTTP Server Functions

These functions are intended for use with HTTP server applications.

nng_http_handler_alloc()	allocate HTTP server handler
nng_http_handler_collect_body()	set HTTP handler to collect request body
nng_http_handler_free()	free HTTP server handler
nng_http_handler_get_data()	return extra data for HTTP handler
nng_http_handler_set_data()	set extra data for HTTP handler
nng_http_handler_set_host()	set host for HTTP handler
nng_http_handler_set_method()	set HTTP handler method
nng_http_handler_set_tree()	set HTTP handler to match trees
nng_http_hijack()	hijack HTTP server connection

nng_http_server_add_handler()	add HTTP server handler
nng_http_server_del_handler()	delete HTTP server handler
nng_http_server_get_tls()	get HTTP server TLS configuration
nng_http_server_hold()	get and hold HTTP server instance
nng_http_server_release()	release HTTP server instance
nng_http_server_set_error_file()	set custom HTTP error file
nng_http_server_set_error_page()	set custom HTTP error page
nng_http_server_set_tls()	set HTTP server TLS configuration
nng_http_server_res_error()	use HTTP server error page
nng_http_server_start()	start HTTP server
nng_http_server_stop()	stop HTTP server

TLS Configuration Objects

The following functions are used to manipulate transport layer security (TLS) configuration objects.

> **ℹ** These functions will only be present if the library has been built with TLS support.

nng_tls_config_alloc()	allocate TLS configuration
nng_tls_config_auth_mode()	set authentication mode
nng_tls_config_ca_chain()	set certificate authority chain
nng_tls_config_ca_file()	load certificate authority from file
nng_tls_config_cert_key_file()	load own certificate and key from file
nng_tls_config_own_cert()	set own certificate and key
nng_tls_config_free()	free TLS configuration
nng_tls_config_server_name()	set remote server name

SEE ALSO

nng_compat(3compat), nng(7)

NAME

nng_aio_abort - abort asynchronous I/O operation

SYNOPSIS

```
#include <nng/nng.h>

void nng_aio_abort(nng_aio *aio, int err);
```

DESCRIPTION

The nng_aio_abort() function aborts an operation previously started with the handle *aio*. If the operation is aborted, then the callback for the handle will be called, and the function nng_aio_result() will return the error *err*.

This function does not wait for the operation to be fully aborted, but returns immediately.

If no operation is currently in progress (either because it has already finished, or no operation has been started yet), then this function has no effect.

RETURN VALUES

None.

ERRORS

None.

SEE ALSO

nng_aio_alloc(3), nng_aio_cancel(3), nng_aio_result(3), nng_aio(5), nng(7)

NAME

nng_aio_alloc - allocate asynchronous I/O handle

SYNOPSIS

```
#include <nng/nng.h>

int nng_aio_alloc(nng_aio **aiop, void (*callb)(void *), void *arg);
```

DESCRIPTION

The nng_aio_alloc() function allocates a handle for asynchronous I/O operations, and stores a pointer to it in *aiop*. The handle is initialized with a completion callback of *callb*, which will be executed when an associated asynchronous operation finishes. It will be called with the argument *arg*.

> ℹ️ The callback *callb* must not perform any blocking operations, and must complete its execution quickly. If *callb* does block, this can lead ultimately to an apparent "hang" or deadlock in the application.

Asynchronous I/O operations all take an nng_aio handle such as allocated by this function. Such operations are usually started by a function that returns immediately. The operation is then run asynchronously, and completes sometime later. When that operation is complete, the callback supplied here is called, and that callback is able to determine the result of the operation using nng_aio_result(), nng_aio_count(), and nng_aio_get_output().

It is possible to wait synchronously for an otherwise asynchronous operation by using the function nng_aio_wait(). In that case, it is permissible for *callb* and *arg* to both be NULL. Note that if these are NULL, then it will not be possible to determine when the operation is complete except by calling the aforementioned nng_aio_wait().

RETURN VALUES

This function returns 0 on success, and non-zero otherwise.

ERRORS

NNG_ENOMEM   Insufficient free memory to perform the operation.

SEE ALSO

nng_aio_abort(3), nng_aio_cancel(3), nng_aio_count(3), nng_aio_free(3), nng_aio_get_input(3), nng_aio_get_msg(3), nng_aio_get_output(3), nng_aio_result(3), nng_aio_set_input(3), nng_aio_set_iov(3), nng_aio_set_msg(3), nng_aio_set_timeout(3), nng_aio_stop(3), nng_aio_wait(3), nng_strerror(3), nng_aio(5), nng(7)

NAME

nng_aio_begin - begin asynchronous I/O operation

SYNOPSIS

```
#include <nng/nng.h>

bool nng_aio_begin(nng_aio *aio);
```

DESCRIPTION

The `nng_aio_begin()` function is called by the I/O provider to indicate that it is going to process the operation.

The function may return `false`, indicating that the *aio* has been closed by the caller asynchronously. In this case the provider should abandon the operation and do nothing else.

This operation should be called at the start of any I/O operation, and must be called not more than once for a given I/O operation on a given *aio*.

Once this function is called, if `true` is returned, then the provider MUST guarantee that `nng_aio_finish()` is called for the *aio* exactly once, when the operation is complete or canceled.

> ⓘ   This function is only for I/O providers (those actually performing the operation such as HTTP handler functions or transport providers); ordinary users of the *aio* should not call this function.

RETURN VALUES

`true`	The operation has been started.
`false`	The operation cannot be started.

ERRORS

None.

SEE ALSO

nng_aio_alloc(3), nng_aio_cancel(3), nng_aio_defer(3), nng_aio_finish(3), nng_aio_result(3), nng_aio(5), nng(7)

NAME

nng_aio_cancel - cancel asynchronous I/O operation

SYNOPSIS

```
#include <nng/nng.h>

void nng_aio_cancel(nng_aio *aio);
```

DESCRIPTION

The `nng_aio_cancel()` function aborts an operation previously started with the handle *aio*. If the operation is aborted, then the callback for the handle will be called, and the function `nng_aio_result()` will return the error `NNG_ECANCELED`.

This function does not wait for the operation to be fully aborted, but returns immediately.

If no operation is currently in progress (either because it has already finished, or no operation has been started yet), then this function has no effect.

> 🛈   This function is the same as calling `nng_aio_abort()` with the error `NNG_ECANCELED`.

RETURN VALUES

None.

ERRORS

None.

SEE ALSO

nng_aio_abort(3), nng_aio_alloc(3), nng_aio_result(3), nng_aio(5), nng(7)

NAME

nng_aio_count - return number of bytes transferred

SYNOPSIS

```
#include <nng/nng.h>

size_t nng_aio_count(nng_aio *aio);
```

DESCRIPTION

The `nng_aio_count()` returns the number of bytes transferred by the asynchronous operation associated with the handle *aio*.

Some asynchronous operations do not provide meaningful data for this function; for example operations that establish connections do not transfer user data (they may transfer protocol data though) — in this case this function will generally return zero.

This function is most useful when used with operations that make use of of a scatter/gather vector (set by `nng_aio_set_iov()`).

> **ⓘ** The return value from this function is undefined if the operation has not completed yet. Either call this from the handle's completion callback, or after waiting for the operation to complete with `nng_aio_wait()`.

RETURN VALUES

The number of bytes transferred by the operation.

ERRORS

None.

SEE ALSO

nng_aio_alloc(3), nng_aio_result(3), nng_aio_set_iov(3), nng_aio_wait(3), nng_strerror(3), nng_aio(5), nng(7)

NAME

nng_aio_defer - defer asynchronous I/O operation

SYNOPSIS

```
#include <nng/nng.h>

typedef void (*nng_aio_cancelfn)(nng_aio *aio, void *arg, int err);

void nng_aio_defer(nng_aio *aio, nng_aio_cancelfn fn, void *arg);
```

DESCRIPTION

The nng_aio_defer() function marks operation associated with *aio* as being deferred for asynchronous completion, and also registers a cancellation function *fn* and associated argument *arg*, thereby permitting the operation to be canceled.

If the *aio* is being canceled, the cancellation routine *fn* will be called with the *aio*, the *arg* specified by nng_aio_defer(), and an error value in *err*, which is the reason that the operation is being canceled.

The operation may not be cancelable; for example it may have already been completed, or be in a state where it is no longer possible to unschedule it. In this case, the *cancelfn* should just return without making any changes.

If the cancellation routine successfully canceled the operation, it should ensure that nng_aio_finish() is called, with the error code specified by *err*.

⚠ It is mandatory that I/O providers call nng_aio_finish() **EXACTLY ONCE** when they are finished with the operation.

ℹ This function is only for I/O providers (those actually performing the operation such as HTTP handler functions or transport providers); ordinary users of the *aio* should not call this function.

ℹ Care must be taken to ensure that cancellation and completion of the routine are multi-thread safe; this will usually involve the use of locks or other synchronization primitives.

💡 For operations that complete synchronously, without any need to be deferred, the provider should not bother to call nng_aio_defer(), although it is harmless if it does.

RETURN VALUES

None.

ERRORS

None.

SEE ALSO

nng_aio_alloc(3), nng_aio_cancel(3), nng_aio_finish(3), nng_aio_result(3), nng_aio(5), nng(7)

NAME

nng_aio_finish - finish asynchronous I/O operation

SYNOPSIS

```
#include <nng/nng.h>

void nng_aio_finish(nng_aio *aio, int err);
```

DESCRIPTION

The nng_aio_finish() function marks operation associated with *aio* as complete, with the status *err*. This will be the result returned by nng_aio_result().

This function causes the callback associated with the *aio* to called.

> ⚠ It is mandatory that operation "providers" call this function **EXACTLY ONCE** when they are finished with the operation. After calling this function they **MUST NOT** perform any further accesses to the *aio*.

> ℹ This function is only for I/O providers (those actually performing the operation such as HTTP handler functions or transport providers); ordinary users of the *aio* should not have any need for this function.

RETURN VALUES

None.

ERRORS

None.

SEE ALSO

nng_aio_alloc(3), nng_aio_begin(3), nng_aio_cancel(3), nng_aio_defer(3), nng_aio_result(3), nng_aio(5), nng(7)

NAME

nng_aio_free - free asynchronous I/O handle

SYNOPSIS

```
#include <nng/nng.h>

void nng_aio_free(nng_aio *aio);
```

DESCRIPTION

The nng_aio_free() function frees an allocated asynchronous I/O handle. If any operation is in progress, the operation is canceled, and the caller is blocked until the operation is completely canceled, to ensure that it is safe to deallocate the handle and any associated resources. (This is done by implicitly calling nng_aio_stop().)

RETURN VALUES

None.

ERRORS

None.

SEE ALSO

nng_aio_alloc(3), nng_aio_stop(3), nng_aio(5), nng(7)

NAME

nng_aio_get_input - return input parameter

SYNOPSIS

```
#include <nng/nng.h>

void *nng_aio_get_input(nng_aio *aio, unsigned int index);
```

DESCRIPTION

The nng_aio_get_input() function returns the value of the input parameter previously set at *index* on *aio* with the nng_aio_set_input() function.

The valid values of *index* range from zero (0) to three (3), as no operation currently defined can accept more than four parameters. (This limit could increase in the future.) If the index supplied is outside of this range, or of the input parameter was not previously set, then NULL is returned.

RETURN VALUES

Value previously set, or NULL.

ERRORS

None.

SEE ALSO

nng_aio_alloc(3), nng_aio_get_output(3), nng_aio_set_input(3), nng_aio_result(3), nng_aio(5), nng(7)

NAME

nng_aio_get_msg - get message from asynchronous receive

SYNOPSIS

```
#include <nng/nng.h>

nng_msg *nng_aio_get_msg(nng_aio *aio);
```

DESCRIPTION

The `nng_aio_get_msg()` function gets any message stored in *aio* as either a result of a successful receive (see `nng_recv_aio()`) or that was previously stored with `nng_aio_set_msg()`.

⚠️   The `nng_aio` must not have an operation in progress.

RETURN VALUES

None.

ERRORS

None.

SEE ALSO

nng_aio_set_msg(3), nng_recv_aio(3), nng_aio(5), nng_msg(5), nng(7)

NAME

nng_aio_get_output - return output result

SYNOPSIS

```
#include <nng/nng.h>

void *nng_aio_get_output(nng_aio *aio, unsigned int index);
```

DESCRIPTION

The nng_aio_get_output() function returns the output result at *index* resulting from the asynchronous operation associated with *aio*.

The type and semantics of output parameters are determined by specific operations.

> ❶ If the *index* does not correspond to a defined output for the operation, or the operation did not succeed, then the return value will be NULL.

> ⚠ It is an error to call this function while the *aio* is currently in use by an active asynchronous operation, or if no operation has been performed using the *aio* yet.

RETURN VALUES

The *index*th result of the operation, or NULL.

ERRORS

None.

SEE ALSO

nng_aio_alloc(3), nng_aio_get_output(3), nng_aio_set_input(3), nng_aio_result(3), nng_aio(5), nng(7)

NAME

nng_aio_result - return result of asynchronous operation

SYNOPSIS

```
#include <nng/nng.h>

int nng_aio_result(nng_aio *aio);
```

DESCRIPTION

The nng_aio_result() returns the result of the operation associated with the handle *aio*. If the operation was successful, then 0 is returned. Otherwise a non-zero error code is returned.

> ℹ The return value from this function is undefined if the operation has not completed yet. Either call this from the handle's completion callback, or after waiting for the operation to complete with nng_aio_wait().

RETURN VALUES

The result of the operation, either zero on success, or an error number on failure.

ERRORS

NNG_ETIMEDOUT	The operation timed out.
NNG_ECANCELED	The operation was canceled.

Various other return values are possible depending on the operation.

SEE ALSO

nng_aio_abort(3), nng_aio_alloc(3), nng_aio_wait(3), nng_strerror(3), nng_aio(5), nng(7)

NAME

nng_aio_set_input - set input parameter

SYNOPSIS

```
#include <nng/nng.h>

void nng_aio_set_input(nng_aio *aio, unsigned int index, void *param);
```

DESCRIPTION

The `nng_aio_set_input()` function sets the input parameter at *index* to *param* for the asynchronous operation associated with *aio*.

The type and semantics of input parameters are determined by specific operations; the caller must supply appropriate inputs for the operation to be performed.

The valid values of *index* range from zero (0) to three (3), as no operation currently defined can accept more than four parameters. (This limit could increase in the future.)

> **ℹ** If the *index* does not correspond to a defined input for the operation, then this function will have no effect.

> **⚠** It is an error to call this function while the *aio* is currently in use by an active asynchronous operation.

An input parameter set with this function may be retrieved later with the `nng_aio_get_input()` function.

RETURN VALUES

None.

ERRORS

None.

SEE ALSO

nng_aio_alloc(3), nng_aio_get_input(3), nng_aio_get_output(3), nng_aio_result(3), nng_aio(5), nng(7)

NAME

nng_aio_set_iov - set scatter/gather vector

SYNOPSIS

```
#include <nng/nng.h>

int nng_aio_set_iov(nng_aio *aio, unsigned int niov, nng_iov *iov);
```

DESCRIPTION

The nng_aio_set_iov() function sets a scatter/gather vector *iov* on the handle *aio*.

The *iov* is a pointer to an array of *niov* nng_iov structures, which have the following definition:

```
typedef struct nng_iov {
    void * iov_buf;
    size_t iov_len;
};
```

The *iov* is copied into storage in the *aio* itself, so that callers may use stack allocated nng_iov structures. The values pointed to by the iov_buf members are **not** copied by this function though.

Up to four nng_iov members may be supplied without causing any allocations, and thus this operation is guaranteed to succeed for values of *niov* less than four.

More than four (4) nng_iov members may be supplied, but this may require heap allocations, and so the operation may fail with NNG_ENOMEM. Additionally, not every operation can support longer vectors; the actual limit is determined by the system, but is generally at least sixteen (16). Furthermore, values for *niov* larger than sixty-four (64) will generally result in NNG_EINVAL.

RETURN VALUES

This function returns 0 on success, and non-zero otherwise.

ERRORS

NNG_ENOMEM	Insufficient free memory to perform operation.
NNG_EINVAL	Value of specified *niov* is too large.

SEE ALSO

nng_aio_alloc(3), nng_aio_cancel(3), nng_aio_count(3), nng_aio_result(3), nng_aio(5), nng_iov(5), nng(7)

NAME

nng_aio_set_msg - set message for asynchronous send

SYNOPSIS

```
#include <nng/nng.h>

void nng_aio_set_msg(nng_aio *aio, nng_msg *msg);
```

DESCRIPTION

The nng_aio_set_msg() function sets the message that will be used for an asynchronous send operation
(see nng_send_aio()).

⚠️   The nng_aio must not have an operation in progress.

RETURN VALUES

None.

ERRORS

None.

SEE ALSO

nng_aio_get_msg(3), nng_send_aio(3), nng_aio(5), nng_msg(5), nng(7)

NAME

nng_aio_set_output - set output result

SYNOPSIS

```
#include <nng/nng.h>

void nng_aio_set_output(nng_aio *aio, unsigned int index, void *result);
```

DESCRIPTION

The nng_aio_set_output() function sets the output result at *index* to *result* for the asynchronous operation associated with *aio*.

The type and semantics of output results are determined by specific operations; the operation must supply appropriate output results when the operation completes successfully.

The valid values of *index* range from zero (0) to three (3), as no operation currently defined can return more than four results. (This limit could increase in the future.)

> 🛈   Note that attempts to set results with an *index* greater than three (3) will be ignored.

An output result set with this function may be retrieved later with the nng_aio_get_output() function.

RETURN VALUES

None.

ERRORS

None.

SEE ALSO

nng_aio_alloc(3), nng_aio_finish(3), nng_aio_get_output(3), nng_aio_result(3), nng_aio(5), nng(7)

NAME

nng_aio_set_timeout - set asynchronous I/O timeout

SYNOPSIS

```
#include <nng/nng.h>

typedef int nng_duration;
void nng_aio_set_timeout(nng_aio *aio, nng_duration timeout);
```

DESCRIPTION

The nng_aio_set_timeout() function sets a *timeout* for the asynchronous operation associated with *aio*. This causes a timer to be started when the operation is actually started. If the timer expires before the operation is completed, then it is aborted with an error of NNG_ETIMEDOUT. The *timeout* is specified as a relative number of milliseconds.

If the timeout is NNG_DURATION_INFINITE, then no timeout is used. If the timeout is NNG_DURATION_DEFAULT, then a "default" or socket-specific timeout is used. (This is frequently the same as NNG_DURATION_INFINITE.)

> 💡 As most operations involve some context switching, it is usually a good idea to allow at least a few tens of milliseconds before timing them out — a too small timeout might not allow the operation to properly begin before giving up!

The value of *timeout* set for the *aio* is persistent, so that if the handle is reused for multiple operations, they will have the same relative timeout.

RETURN VALUES

None.

ERRORS

None.

SEE ALSO

nng_aio_alloc(3), nng_aio_cancel(3), nng_aio_result(3), nng_aio(5), nng_duration(5), nng(7)

NAME

nng_aio_stop - stop asynchronous I/O operation

SYNOPSIS

```
#include <nng/nng.h>

void nng_aio_stop(nng_aio *aio);
```

DESCRIPTION

The nng_aio_stop() function stops the asynchronous I/O operation associated with *aio* by aborting with NNG_ECANCELED, and then waits for it to complete or to be completely aborted.

If an operation is in progress when this function is called, that operation is canceled and the callback function is *not* allowed to run.

If the callback function is already running when this function is called, then it is allowed to complete before returning to the caller.

No new operations will be started on this *aio*.

> 🛈 Calling this function means that the operation may be aborted without completing its callback function.

> 💡 When multiple asynchronous I/O handles are in use and need to be shut down, it is safest to stop all of them, before deallocating any of this with nng_aio_free(), particularly if the callbacks might attempt to reschedule additional operations.

RETURN VALUES

None.

ERRORS

None.

SEE ALSO

nng_aio_cancel(3), nng_aio_free(3), nng_aio_wait(3), nng_aio_alloc(3), nng_aio(5), nng(7)

NAME

nng_aio_wait - wait for asynchronous I/O operation

SYNOPSIS

```
#include <nng/nng.h>

void nng_aio_wait(nng_aio *aio);
```

DESCRIPTION

The nng_aio_wait() function waits for an asynchronous I/O operation to complete. If the operation has not been started, or has already completed, then it returns immediately.

If the a callback was set with *aio* when it was allocated, then this function will not be called until the callback has completed.

RETURN VALUES

None.

ERRORS

None.

SEE ALSO

nng_aio_abort(3), nng_aio_alloc(3), nng_aio(5), nng(7)

NAME

nng_alloc - allocate memory

SYNOPSIS

```
#include <nng/nng.h>

void *nng_alloc(size_t size);
```

DESCRIPTION

The nng_alloc() function allocates a contiguous memory region of at least *size* bytes. The memory will be 64-bit aligned.

The returned memory can be used to hold message buffers, in which case it can be directly passed to nng_send() using the flag NNG_FLAG_ALLOC. Alternatively, it can be freed when no longer needed using nng_free().

⚠ Do not use the system free() function to release this memory. On some platforms this may work, but it is not guaranteed and may lead to a crash or other undesirable and unpredictable behavior.

RETURN VALUES

This function returns a pointer to the allocated memory on success, and NULL otherwise.

ERRORS

No errors are returned, but a NULL return value should be treated the same as NNG_ENOMEM.

SEE ALSO

nng_free(3), nng_send(3), nng_strerror(3), nng(7)

NAME

nng_bus_open - create bus socket

SYNOPSIS

```
#include <nng/nng.h>
#include <nng/protocol/bus0/bus.h>

int nng_bus0_open(nng_socket *s);

int nng_bus0_open_raw(nng_socket *s);
```

DESCRIPTION

The nng_bus0_open() function creates a *bus* version 0 socket and returns it at the location pointed to by *s*.

The nng_bus0_open_raw() function creates a *bus* version 0 socket in raw mode, and returns it at the location pointed to by *s*.

RETURN VALUES

These functions return 0 on success, and non-zero otherwise.

ERRORS

NNG_ENOMEM	Insufficient memory is available.
NNG_ENOTSUP	The protocol is not supported.

SEE ALSO

nng_socket(5), nng_bus(7), nng(7)

NAME

nng_close - close socket

SYNOPSIS

```
#include <nng/nng.h>

int nng_close(nng_socket s);
```

DESCRIPTION

The nng_close() function closes the supplied socket, *s*. Messages that have been submitted for sending may be flushed or delivered, depending upon the transport and the setting of the NNG_OPT_LINGER option.

Further attempts to use the socket after this call returns will result in NNG_ECLOSED. Threads waiting for operations on the socket when this call is executed may also return with an NNG_ECLOSED result.

> Closing the socket while data is in transmission will likely lead to loss of that data. There is no automatic linger or flush to ensure that the socket send buffers have completely transmitted. It is recommended to wait a brief period after calling nng_send() or similar functions, before calling this function.

RETURN VALUES

This function returns 0 on success, and non-zero otherwise.

ERRORS

NNG_ECLOSED   The socket *s* is already closed or was never opened.

SEE ALSO

nng_strerror(3), nng_options(5), nng_socket(5), nng(7)

NAME

nng_ctx_close - close context

SYNOPSIS

```
#include <nng/nng.h>

int nng_ctx_close(nng_ctx ctx);
```

DESCRIPTION

The nng_ctx_close() function closes the context *ctx*. Messages that have been submitted for sending may be flushed or delivered, depending upon the transport and the setting of the NNG_OPT_LINGER option.

Further attempts to use the context after this call returns will result in NNG_ECLOSED. Threads waiting for operations on the context when this call is executed may also return with an NNG_ECLOSED result.

ℹ️   Closing the socket associated with *ctx* (using nng_close()) also closes this context.

RETURN VALUES

This function returns 0 on success, and non-zero otherwise.

ERRORS

NNG_ECLOSED   The context *ctx* is already closed or was never opened.

SEE ALSO

nng_ctx_open(3), nng_strerror(3), nng_ctx(5), nng(7)

NAME

nng_ctx_getopt - get context option

SYNOPSIS

#include <nng/nng.h>

int nng_ctx_getopt(nng_ctx ctx, **const char** *opt, **void** *val, **size_t** *valszp);

int nng_ctx_getopt_bool(nng_ctx ctx, **const char** *opt, **bool** *bvalp);

int nng_ctx_getopt_int(nng_ctx ctx, **const char** *opt, **int** *ivalp);

int nng_ctx_getopt_ms(nng_ctx ctx, **const char** *opt, nng_duration *durp);

int nng_ctx_getopt_size(nng_ctx ctx, **const char** *opt, **size_t** *zp);

int nng_ctx_getopt_string(nng_ctx ctx, **const char** *opt, **char** **strp);

int nng_ctx_getopt_uint64(nng_ctx ctx, **const char** *opt, **uint64_t** *u64p);

DESCRIPTION

The nng_ctx_getopt() functions are used to retrieve option values for the context *ctx*. The actual options that may be retrieved in this way vary. A number of them are documented in nng_options(5).

> **ⓘ** Context options are protocol specific. The details will be documented with the protocol.

Forms

In all of these forms, the option *opt* is retrieved from the context *ctx*. The forms vary based on the type of the option they take.

The details of the type, size, and semantics of the option will depend on the actual option, and will be documented with the option itself.

nng_ctx_getopt()

This function is untyped and can be used to retrieve the value of any option. The caller must store a pointer to a buffer to receive the value in *val*, and the size of the buffer shall be stored at the location referenced by *valszp*.

When the function returns, the actual size of the data copied (or that would have been copied if sufficient space were present) is stored at the location referenced by *valszp*. If the caller's buffer is not large enough to hold the entire object, then the copy is truncated. Therefore the caller should check for truncation by verifying that the returned size in *valszp* does not exceed the original buffer size.

It is acceptable to pass NULL for *val* if the value in *valszp* is zero. This can be used to determine the size of the buffer needed to receive the object.

💡   It may be easier to use one of the typed forms of this function.

nng_ctx_getopt_bool()

     This function is for options which take a Boolean (`bool`). The value will be stored at *ivalp*.

nng_ctx_getopt_int()

     This function is for options which take an integer (`int`). The value will be stored at *ivalp*.

nng_ctx_getopt_ms()

     This function is used to retrieve time durations (such as timeouts), stored in *durp* as a number of milliseconds. (The special value `NNG_DUR_INFINITE` means an infinite amount of time, and the special value `NNG_DUR_DEFAULT` means a context-specific default.)

nng_ctx_getopt_size()

     This function is used to retrieve a size into the pointer *zp*, typically for buffer sizes, message maximum sizes, and similar options.

nng_ctx_getopt_string()

     This function is used to retrieve a string into *strp*. This string is created from the source using `nng_strdup()` and consequently must be freed by the caller using `nng_strfree()` when it is no longer needed.

nng_ctx_getopt_uint64()

     This function is used to retrieve a 64-bit unsigned value into the value referenced by *u64p*. This is typically used for options related to identifiers, network numbers, and similar.

RETURN VALUES

These functions return 0 on success, and non-zero otherwise.

ERRORS

NNG_EBADTYPE	Incorrect type for option.
NNG_ECLOSED	Parameter *s* does not refer to an open socket.
NNG_EINVAL	Size of destination *val* too small for object.
NNG_ENOMEM	Insufficient memory exists.
NNG_ENOTSUP	The option *opt* is not supported.
NNG_EWRITEONLY	The option *opt* is write-only.

SEE ALSO

nng_ctx_setopt(3), nng_strdup(3), nng_strerror(3), nng_strfree(3), nng_duration(5), nng_ctx(5), nng_options(5), nng(7)

NAME

nng_ctx_id - return numeric context identifier

SYNOPSIS

```
#include <nng/nng.h>

int nng_ctx_id(nng_ctx c);
```

DESCRIPTION

The nng_ctx_id() function returns a positive identifier for the context c, if it is valid. Otherwise it returns -1.

> **ⓘ** A context is considered valid if it was ever opened with nng_ctx_open() function. Contexts that are allocated on the stack or statically should be initialized with the macro NNG_CTX_INITIALIZER to ensure that they cannot be confused with a valid context before they are opened.

RETURN VALUES

This function returns the positive value for the context identifier, or -1 if the context is invalid.

ERRORS

None.

SEE ALSO

nng_ctx(5), nng(7)

NAME

nng_ctx_open - create context

SYNOPSIS

```
#include <nng/nng.h>

int nng_ctx_open(nng_ctx *ctxp, nng_socket s);
```

DESCRIPTION

The nng_ctx0_open() function creates a separate context to be used with the socket *s*, and returns it at the location pointed by *ctxp*.

ℹ️   Not every protocol supports creation of separate contexts.

Contexts allow the independent and concurrent use of stateful operations using the same socket. For example, two different contexts created on a *rep* socket can each receive requests, and send replies to them, without any regard to or interference with each other.

TIP: Using contexts is an excellent way to write simpler concurrent applications, while retaining the benefits of the protocol-specific advanced processing, avoiding the need to bypass that with raw mode sockets.

ℹ️   Use of contexts with raw mode sockets is nonsensical, and not supported.

RETURN VALUES

This function returns 0 on success, and non-zero otherwise.

ERRORS

NNG_ENOMEM	Insufficient memory is available.
NNG_ENOTSUP	The protocol does not support separate contexts, or the socket was opened in raw mode.

SEE ALSO

nng_ctx_close(3), nng_ctx_getopt(3), nng_ctx_recv(3), nng_ctx_send(3), nng_ctx_setopt(3), nng_strerror(3), nng_ctx(5), nng_socket(5), nng_rep(7), nng_req(7), nng(7)

NAME

nng_ctx_recv - receive message using context asynchronously

SYNOPSIS

```
#include <nng/nng.h>

void nng_ctx_recv(nng_ctx ctx, nng_aio *aio);
```

DESCRIPTION

The nng_ctx_recv() receives a message using the context *s* asynchronously.

When a message is successfully received by the context, it is stored in the *aio* by an internal call equivalent to nng_aio_set_msg(), then the completion callback on the *aio* is executed. In this case, nng_aio_result() will return zero. The callback function is responsible for retrieving the message and disposing of it appropriately.

> ⚠ Failing to accept and dispose of messages in this case can lead to memory leaks.

If for some reason the asynchronous receive cannot be completed successfully (including by being canceled or timing out), then the callback will still be executed, but nng_aio_result() will be non-zero.

> ℹ The semantics of what receiving a message means varies from protocol to protocol, so examination of the protocol documentation is encouraged.

RETURN VALUES

None. (The operation completes asynchronously.)

ERRORS

NNG_ECANCELED	The operation was aborted.
NNG_ECLOSED	The context *ctx* is not open.
NNG_ENOMEM	Insufficient memory is available.
NNG_ENOTSUP	The protocol for context *ctx* does not support receiving.
NNG_ESTATE	The context *ctx* cannot receive data in this state.
NNG_ETIMEDOUT	The receive timeout expired.

SEE ALSO

nng_aio_get_msg(3), nng_aio_set_msg(3), nng_msg_alloc(3), nng_strerror(3), nng_aio(5), nng_ctx(5), nng_msg(5), nng(7)

NAME

nng_ctx_send - send message using context asynchronously

SYNOPSIS

```
#include <nng/nng.h>

void nng_ctx_send(nng_ctx ctx, nng_aio *aio);
```

DESCRIPTION

The nng_ctx_send() sends a message using the context *ctx* asynchronously.

The message to send must have previously been set on the *aio* using the nng_aio_set_msg() function. The function assumes "ownership" of the message.

If the message was successfully queued for delivery to the socket, then the *aio* will be completed, and nng_aio_result() will return zero. In this case the socket will dispose of the message when it is finished with it.

> **ℹ** The operation will be "completed", and the callback associated with the *aio* executed, as soon as the socket accepts the message for sending. This does *not* indicate that the message was actually delivered, as it may still be buffered in the sending socket, buffered in the receiving socket, or in flight over physical media.

If the operation fails for any reason (including cancellation or timeout), then the *aio* callback will be executed and nng_aio_result() will return a non-zero error status. In this case, the callback has a responsibility to retrieve the message from the *aio* with nng_aio_get_msg() and dispose of it appropriately. (This may include retrying the send operation on the same or a different socket, or deallocating the message with nng_msg_free().)

> **ℹ** The semantics of what sending a message means varies from protocol to protocol, so examination of the protocol documentation is encouraged.

> **♀** Context send operations are asynchronous. If a synchronous operation is needed, one can be constructed by using a NULL callback on the *aio* and then waiting for the operation using nng_aio_wait().

RETURN VALUES

None. (The operation completes asynchronously.)

ERRORS

NNG_ECANCELED	The operation was aborted.
NNG_ECLOSED	The context *ctx* is not open.
NNG_EMSGSIZE	The message is too large.

NNG_ENOMEM	Insufficient memory is available.
NNG_ENOTSUP	The protocol for context *ctx* does not support sending.
NNG_ESTATE	The context *ctx* cannot send data in this state.
NNG_ETIMEDOUT	The send timeout expired.

SEE ALSO

nng_aio_get_msg(3), nng_aio_set_msg(3), nng_msg_alloc(3), nng_strerror(3), nng_aio(5), nng_ctx(5), nng_msg(5), nng(7)

NAME

nng_ctx_setopt - set context option

SYNOPSIS

```
#include <nng/nng.h>

int nng_ctx_setopt(nng_ctx ctx, const char *opt, const void *val, size_t valsz);

int nng_ctx_setopt_bool(nng_ctx ctx, const char *opt, int bval);

int nng_ctx_setopt_int(nng_ctx ctx, const char *opt, int ival);

int nng_ctx_setopt_ms(nng_ctx ctx, const char *opt, nng_duration dur);

int nng_ctx_setopt_size(nng_ctx ctx, const char *opt, size_t z);

int nng_ctx_setopt_string(nng_ctx ctx, const char *opt, const char *str);

int nng_ctx_setopt_uint64(nng_ctx ctx, const char *opt, uint64_t u64);
```

DESCRIPTION

The nng_ctx_setopt() functions are used to configure options for the context *ctx*. The actual options that may be configured in this way vary, and are specified by *opt*.

ⓘ   Context options are protocol specific. The details will be documented with the protocol.

Forms

The details of the type, size, and semantics of the option will depend on the actual option, and will be documented with the option itself.

nng_ctx_setopt()
: This function is untyped, and can be used to configure any arbitrary data. The *val* pointer addresses the data to copy, and *valsz* is the size of the objected located at *val*.

   💡   It may be easier to use one of the typed forms of this function.

nng_ctx_setopt_bool()
: This function is for options which take a Boolean (bool). The *bval* is passed to the option.

nng_ctx_setopt_int()
: This function is for options which take an integer (int). The *ival* is passed to the option.

nng_ctx_setopt_ms()
: This function is used to configure time durations (such as timeouts) using type nng_duration. The duration *dur* is an integer number of milliseconds.

`nng_ctx_setopt_size()`

This function is used to configure a size, *z*, typically for buffer sizes, message maximum sizes, and similar options.

`nng_ctx_setopt_string()`

This function is used to pass configure a string, *str*. Strings passed this way must be legal UTF-8 or ASCII strings, terminated with a NUL (\0) byte. (Other constraints may apply as well, see the documentation for each option for details.)

`nng_ctx_setopt_uint64()`

This function is used to configure a 64-bit unsigned value, *u64*. This is typically used for options related to identifiers, network numbers, and similar.

RETURN VALUES

These functions return 0 on success, and non-zero otherwise.

ERRORS

NNG_ECLOSED	Parameter *s* does not refer to an open socket.
NNG_EINVAL	The value being passed is invalid.
NNG_ENOTSUP	The option *opt* is not supported.
NNG_EREADONLY	The option *opt* is read-only.
NNG_ESTATE	The socket is in an inappropriate state for setting this option.

SEE ALSO

nng_ctx_getopt(3), nng_setopt(3), nng_strerror(3), nng_ctx(5), nng_options(5), nng_socket(5), nng(7)

NAME

nng_device - message forwarding device

SYNOPSIS

```
#include <nng/nng.h>

int nng_device(nng_socket s1, nng_socket s2);
```

DESCRIPTION

The nng_device() function forwards messages received from one socket *s1* to another socket *s2*, and vice versa.

This function is used to create forwarders, which can be used to create complex network topologies to provide for improved horizontal scalability, reliability, and isolation.

Only raw mode sockets may be used with this function. These can be created using _raw forms of the various socket constructors, such as nng_req0_open_raw().

The nng_device() function does not return until one of the sockets is closed.

Reflectors

One of the sockets passed may be an unopened socket initialized with the NNG_SOCKET_INITIALIZER special value. If this is the case, then the other socket must be valid, and must use a protocol that is bidirectional and can peer with itself (such as *pair* or *bus*.) In this case the device acts as a reflector or loop-back device, where messages received from the valid socket are merely returned back to the sender.

Forwarders

When both sockets are valid, then the result is a forwarder or proxy. In this case sockets *s1* and *s2* must be "compatible" with each other, which is to say that they should represent the opposite halves of a two protocol pattern, or both be the same protocol for a single protocol pattern. For example, if *s1* is a *pub* socket, then *s2* must be a *sub* socket. Or, if *s1* is a *bus* socket, then *s2* must also be a *bus* socket.

Operation

The nng_device() function moves messages between the provided sockets.

When a protocol has a backtrace style header, routing information is present in the header of received messages, and is copied to the header of the output bound message. The underlying raw mode protocols supply the necessary header adjustments to add or remove routing headers as needed. This allows replies to be returned to requesters, and responses to be routed back to surveyors.

Additionally, some protocols have a maximum time-to-live to protect against forwarding loops and especially amplification loops. In these cases, the default limit (usually 8), ensures that messages will self-terminate when they have passed through too many forwarders, protecting the network from unlimited message amplification that can arise through misconfiguration. This is controlled via the

NNG_OPT_MAXTTL option.

⚠ Not all protocols have support for guarding against forwarding loops, and even for those that do, forwarding loops can be extremely detrimental to network performance.

ℹ Devices (forwarders and reflectors) act in best effort delivery mode only. If a message is received from one socket that cannot be accepted by the other (due to backpressure or other issues), then the message is discarded.

💡 Use the request/reply pattern, which includes automatic retries by the requester, if reliable delivery is needed.

RETURN VALUES

This function continues running, and only returns an appropriate error when one occurs, or if one of the sockets is closed.

ERRORS

NNG_ECLOSED	At least one of the sockets is not open.
NNG_ENOMEM	Insufficient memory is available.
NNG_EINVAL	The sockets are not compatible, or are both invalid.

SEE ALSO

nng_options(5), nng_socket(5), nng(7)

NAME

nng_dial - create and start dialer

SYNOPSIS

```
#include <nng/nng.h>

int nng_dial(nng_socket s, const char *url, nng_dialer *dp, int flags);
```

DESCRIPTION

The nng_dial() function creates a newly initialized nng_dialer object, associated with socket *s*, and configured to listen at the address specified by *url*, and starts it. If the value of *dp* is not NULL, then the newly created dialer is stored at the address indicated by *dp*.

Dialers initiate a remote connection to a listener. Upon a successful connection being established, they create a pipe, add it to the socket, and then wait for that pipe to be closed. When the pipe is closed, the dialer attempts to re-establish the connection. Dialers will also periodically retry a connection automatically if an attempt to connect asynchronously fails.

> 💡 While it is convenient to think of dialers as "clients", the relationship between the listener or dialer is orthogonal to any server or client status that might be associated with a given protocol. For example, a *req* socket might have associated dialers, but might also have associated listeners. It may even have some of each at the same time!

Normally, the first attempt to connect to the address indicated by *url* is done synchronously, including any necessary name resolution. As a result, a failure, such as if the connection is refused, will be returned immediately, and no further action will be taken.

However, if the special value NNG_FLAG_NONBLOCK is supplied in *flags*, then the connection attempt is made asynchronously.

Furthermore, if the connection was closed for a synchronously dialed connection, the dialer will still attempt to redial asynchronously.

> 💡 While NNG_FLAG_NONBLOCK can help an application be more resilient, it also generally makes diagnosing failures somewhat more difficult.

Because the dialer is started immediately, it is generally not possible to apply extra configuration; if that is needed applications should consider using nng_dialer_create() and nng_dialer_start() instead.

RETURN VALUES

This function returns 0 on success, and non-zero otherwise.

ERRORS

NNG_EADDRINVAL   An invalid *url* was specified.

NNG_ECLOSED   The socket *s* is not open.

NNG_ECONNREFUSED   The remote peer refused the connection.

NNG_ECONNRESET   The remote peer reset the connection.

NNG_EINVAL   An invalid set of *flags* or an invalid *url* was specified.

NNG_ENOMEM   Insufficient memory is available.

NNG_EPEERAUTH   Authentication or authorization failure.

NNG_EPROTO   A protocol error occurred.

NNG_EUNREACHABLE   The remote address is not reachable.

SEE ALSO

nng_dialer_close(3), nng_dialer_create(3) nng_dialer_start(3), nng_listen(3), nng_strerror(3), nng_dialer(5), nng_pipe(5), nng(7)

NAME

nng_dialer_close - close dialer

SYNOPSIS

```
#include <nng/nng.h>

int nng_dialer_close(nng_dialer d);
```

DESCRIPTION

The nng_dialer_close() function closes the listener d. This also closes any nng_pipe objects that have been created by the dialer.

Once this function returns, the dialer d and any of its resources are deallocated. Therefore it is an error to attempt to access d after this function has returned. (Attempts to do so will result in NNG_ECLOSED errors.)

Dialers are implicitly closed when the socket they are associated with is closed.

RETURN VALUES

This function returns 0 on success, and non-zero otherwise.

ERRORS

NNG_ECLOSED   Parameter d does not refer to an open listener.

SEE ALSO

nng_close(3), nng_dial(3), nng_dialer_create(3) nng_strerror(3), nng_dialer(5), nng(7)

NAME

nng_dialer_create - create dialer

SYNOPSIS

```
#include <nng/nng.h>

int nng_dialer_create(nng_dialer *dialerp, nng_socket s, const char *url);
```

DESCRIPTION

The nng_dialer_create() function creates a newly initialized nng_dialer object, associated with socket *s*, and configured to connect to the address specified by *url*, and stores a pointer to at the location referenced by *dialerp*.

Dialers initiate a remote connection to a listener. Upon a successful connection being established, they create a pipe, add it to the socket, and then wait for that pipe to be closed. When the pipe is closed, they will re-initiate the connection. Dialers will also periodically retry a connection automatically if an attempt to connect asynchronously fails.

> 💡 While it is convenient to think of dialers as "clients", the relationship between the listener or dialer is orthogonal to any server or client status that might be associated with a given protocol. For example, a *req* socket might have associated dialers, but might also have associated listeners. It may even have some of each at the same time!

The dialer is not started, but may be further configured with the nng_dialer_setopt() family of functions.

Once it is fully configured, the dialer may be started using the nng_dialer_start() function.

> 💡 If no specific configuration is required, consider using the simpler nng_dial() function instead.

RETURN VALUES

This function returns 0 on success, and non-zero otherwise.

ERRORS

NNG_EADDRINVAL	An invalid *url* was specified.
NNG_ECLOSED	The socket *s* is not open.
NNG_ENOMEM	Insufficient memory is available.

SEE ALSO

nng_dial(3), nng_dialer_close(3), nng_dialer_getopt(3), nng_dialer_setopt(3), nng_dialer_start(3), nng_listener_create(3) nng_strerror(3), nng_dialer(5), nng(7)

NAME

nng_dialer_getopt - get dialer option

SYNOPSIS

```
#include <nng/nng.h>

int nng_dialer_getopt(nng_dialer d, const char *opt, void *val, size_t *valszp);

int nng_dialer_getopt_bool(nng_dialer d, const char *opt, bool *bvalp);

int nng_dialer_getopt_int(nng_dialer d, const char *opt, int *ivalp);

int nng_dialer_getopt_ms(nng_dialer d, const char *opt, nng_duration *durp);

int nng_dialer_getopt_ptr(nng_dialer d, const char *opt, void **ptr);

int nng_dialer_getopt_size(nng_dialer d, const char *opt, size_t *zp);

int nng_dialer_getopt_sockaddr(nng_dialer d, const char *opt, nng_sockaddr *sap);

int nng_dialer_getopt_string(nng_dialer d, const char *opt, char **strp);

int nng_dialer_getopt_uint64(nng_dialer d, const char *opt, uint64_t *u64p);
```

DESCRIPTION

The `nng_dialer_getopt()` functions are used to retrieve option values for the dialer *d*. The actual options that may be retrieved in this way vary, and many are documented in nng_options(5).

Additionally some transport-specific options and protocol-specific options are documented with the transports and protocols themselves.

Forms

In all of these forms, the option *opt* is retrieved from the dialer *d*. The forms vary based on the type of the option they take.

The details of the type, size, and semantics of the option will depend on the actual option, and will be documented with the option itself.

nng_dialer_getopt()

This function is untyped and can be used to retrieve the value of any option. The caller must store a pointer to a buffer to receive the value in *val*, and the size of the buffer shall be stored at the location referenced by *valszp*.

When the function returns, the actual size of the data copied (or that would have been copied if sufficient space were present) is stored at the location referenced by *valszp*. If the caller's buffer is not large enough to hold the entire object, then the copy is truncated. Therefore the caller should validate that the returned size in *valszp* does not exceed the original buffer size to check for truncation.

It is acceptable to pass `NULL` for *val* if the value in *valszp* is zero. This can be used to determine the size of the buffer needed to receive the object.

> 💡   It may be easier to use one of the typed forms of this function.

nng_dialer_getopt_bool()

This function is for options which take a Boolean (`bool`). The value will be stored at *bvalp*.

nng_dialer_getopt_int()

This function is for options which take an integer (`int`). The value will be stored at *ivalp*.

nng_dialer_getopt_ms()

This function is used to retrieve time durations (such as timeouts), stored in *durp* as a number of milliseconds. (The special value `NNG_DUR_INFINITE` means an infinite amount of time, and the special value `NNG_DUR_DEFAULT` means a context-specific default.)

nng_dialer_getopt_ptr()

This function is used to retrieve a pointer, *ptr*, to structured data. The data referenced by *ptr* is generally managed using other functions. Note that this form is somewhat special in that the object is generally not copied, but instead the **pointer** to the object is copied.

nng_dialer_getopt_size()

This function is used to retrieve a size into the pointer *zp*, typically for buffer sizes, message maximum sizes, and similar options.

nng_dialer_getopt_sockaddr()

This function is used to retrieve an `nng_sockaddr` into the value referenced by *sap*.

nng_dialer_getopt_string()

This function is used to retrieve a string into *strp*. This string is created from the source using `nng_strdup()` and consequently must be freed by the caller using `nng_strfree()` when it is no longer needed.

nng_dialer_getopt_uint64()

This function is used to retrieve a 64-bit unsigned value into the value referenced by *u64p*. This is typically used for options related to identifiers, network numbers, and similar.

RETURN VALUES

These functions returns 0 on success, and non-zero otherwise.

ERRORS

NNG_EBADTYPE	Incorrect type for option.
NNG_ECLOSED	Parameter *d* does not refer to an open dialer.
NNG_EINVAL	Size of destination *val* too small for object.
NNG_ENOMEM	Insufficient memory exists.
NNG_ENOTSUP	The option *opt* is not supported.

NNG_EWRITEONLY   The option *opt* is write-only.

SEE ALSO

nng_dialer_create(3) nng_dialer_setopt(3) nng_strdup(3), nng_strerror(3), nng_strfree(3), nng_dialer(5), nng_duration(5), nng_options(5), nng_sockaddr(5), nng(7)

NAME

nng_dialer_id - return numeric dialer identifier

SYNOPSIS

```
#include <nng/nng.h>

int nng_dialer_id(nng_dialer d);
```

DESCRIPTION

The nng_dialer_id() function returns a positive identifier for the dialer *d*, if it is valid. Otherwise it returns -1.

> ⓘ A dialer is considered valid if it was ever created with the nng_dialer_create() or nng_dial() functions. Dialers that are allocated on the stack or statically should be initialized with the macro NNG_DIALER_INITIALIZER to ensure that they cannot be confused with a valid dialer before they are created properly.

RETURN VALUES

This function returns the positive value for the dialer identifier, or -1 if the dialer is invalid.

ERRORS

None.

SEE ALSO

nng_dialer(5), nng(7)

NAME

nng_dialer_setopt - set dialer option

SYNOPSIS

```
#include <nng/nng.h>

int nng_dialer_setopt(nng_dialer d, const char *opt, const void *val,
    size_t valsz);

int nng_dialer_setopt_bool(nng_dialer d, const char *opt, bool bval);

int nng_dialer_setopt_int(nng_dialer d, const char *opt, int ival);

int nng_dialer_setopt_ms(nng_dialer d, const char *opt, nng_duration dur);

int nng_dialer_setopt_ptr(nng_dialer d, const char *opt, void *ptr);

int nng_dialer_setopt_size(nng_dialer d, const char *opt, size_t z);

int nng_dialer_setopt_string(nng_dialer d, const char *opt, const char *str);

int nng_dialer_setopt_uint64(nng_dialer d, const char *opt, uint64_t u64);
```

DESCRIPTION

The nng_dialer_setopt() functions are used to configure options for the dialer *d*. The actual options that may be configured in this way vary, and many are documented in nng_options(5).

Additionally some transport-specific options are documented with the transports themselves.

> ℹ️ Once a dialer has started, it is generally not possible to change its configuration.

Forms

In all of these forms, the option *opt* is configured on the dialer *d*.

The details of the type, size, and semantics of the option will depend on the actual option, and will be documented with the option itself.

nng_dialer_setopt()

This function is untyped, and can be used to configure any arbitrary data. The *val* pointer addresses the data to copy, and *valsz* is the size of the objected located at *val*.

> 💡 It may be easier to use one of the typed forms of this function.

nng_dialer_setopt_bool()

This function is for options which take a Boolean (bool). The *bval* is passed to the option.

nng_dialer_setopt_int()

This function is for options which take an integer (`int`). The *ival* is passed to the option.

nng_dialer_setopt_ms()

This function is used to configure time durations (such as timeouts) using type `nng_duration`. The duration *dur* is an integer number of milliseconds.

nng_dialer_setopt_ptr()

This function is used to pass a pointer, *ptr*, to structured data. The data referenced by *ptr* is generally managed by other functions. For example, TLS configuration objects created with (`nng_tls_config_alloc()`) can be passed this way.

> ⓘ   This form is somewhat special in that the object is generally not copied, but instead the **pointer** to the object is copied.

nng_dialer_setopt_size()

This function is used to configure a size, *z*, typically for buffer sizes, message maximum sizes, and similar options.

nng_dialer_setopt_string()

This function is used to pass configure a string, *str*. Strings passed this way must be legal UTF-8 or ASCII strings, terminated with a NUL (\0) byte. (Other constraints may apply as well, see the documentation for each option for details.)

nng_dialer_setopt_uint64()

This function is used to configure a 64-bit unsigned value, *u64*. This is typically used for options related to identifiers, network numbers, and such.

RETURN VALUES

These functions return 0 on success, and non-zero otherwise.

ERRORS

NNG_EBADTYPE	Incorrect type for option.
NNG_ECLOSED	Parameter *d* does not refer to an open dialer.
NNG_EINVAL	The value being passed is invalid.
NNG_ENOTSUP	The option *opt* is not supported.
NNG_EREADONLY	The option *opt* is read-only.
NNG_ESTATE	The dialer *d* is already started.

SEE ALSO

nng_dialer_create(3) nng_dialer_getopt(3) nng_strerror(3), nng_dialer(5), nng_duration(5), nng_options(5), nng(7)

NAME

nng_dialer_start - start dialer

SYNOPSIS

```
#include <nng/nng.h>

int nng_dialer_start(nng_dialer d, int flags);
```

DESCRIPTION

The nng_dialer_start() function starts the dialer *d*.

This causes the dialer to start connecting to the address with which it was created.

When a connection is established, it results in a pipe being created, which will be attached to the dialer's socket.

Normally, the first attempt to connect to the dialer's address is done synchronously, including any necessary name resolution. As a result, a failure, such as if the connection is refused, will be returned immediately, and no further action will be taken.

However, if the special value NNG_FLAG_NONBLOCK is supplied in *flags*, then the connection attempt is made asynchronously.

Furthermore, if the connection was closed for a synchronously dialed connection, the dialer will still attempt to redial asynchronously.

> 💡 While NNG_FLAG_NONBLOCK can help an application be more resilient, it also generally makes diagnosing failures somewhat more difficult.

Once a dialer has started, it is generally not possible to change its configuration.

RETURN VALUES

This function returns 0 on success, and non-zero otherwise.

ERRORS

NNG_EADDRINVAL	An invalid *url* was specified.
NNG_ECLOSED	The socket *s* is not open.
NNG_ECONNREFUSED	The remote peer refused the connection.
NNG_ECONNRESET	The remote peer reset the connection.
NNG_EINVAL	An invalid set of *flags* was specified.
NNG_ENOMEM	Insufficient memory is available.

NNG_EPEERAUTH	Authentication or authorization failure.
NNG_EPROTO	A protocol error occurred.
NNG_ESTATE	The dialer *d* is already started.
NNG_EUNREACHABLE	The remote address is not reachable.

SEE ALSO

nng_dial(3), nng_dialer_create(3) nng_strerror(3), nng_dialer(5), nng(7)

NAME

nng_free - free memory

SYNOPSIS

#include <nng/nng.h>

void nng_free(**void** *ptr, **size_t** size);

DESCRIPTION

The nng_free() function deallocates a memory region of size *size*, that was previously allocated by nng_alloc() or nng_recv() with the NNG_FLAG_ALLOC flag.

⚠ It is very important that *size* match the allocation size used to allocate the memory.

⚠ Do not attempt to use this function to deallocate memory obtained by a call to the system malloc() or calloc() functions, or the C++ new operator. Doing so may result in unpredictable behavior, including corruption of application memory.

RETURN VALUES

None.

ERRORS

None.

SEE ALSO

nng_alloc(3), nng_recv(3), nng(7)

NAME

nng_getopt - get socket option

SYNOPSIS

```
#include <nng/nng.h>

int nng_getopt(nng_socket s, const char *opt, void *val, size_t *valszp);

int nng_getopt_bool(nng_socket s, const char *opt, bool *bvalp);

int nng_getopt_int(nng_socket s, const char *opt, int *ivalp);

int nng_getopt_ms(nng_socket s, const char *opt, nng_duration *durp);

int nng_getopt_ptr(nng_socket s, const char *opt, void **ptr);

int nng_getopt_size(nng_socket s, const char *opt, size_t *zp);

int nng_getopt_string(nng_socket s, const char *opt, char **strp);

int nng_getopt_uint64(nng_socket s, const char *opt, uint64_t *u64p);
```

DESCRIPTION

The nng_getopt() functions are used to retrieve option values for the socket *s*. The actual options that may be retrieved in this way vary. A number of them are documented in nng_options(5).

Additionally transport-specific options and protocol-specific options are documented with the transports and protocols themselves.

Forms

In all of these forms, the option *opt* is retrieved from the socket *s*. The forms vary based on the type of the option they take.

The details of the type, size, and semantics of the option will depend on the actual option, and will be documented with the option itself.

nng_getopt()

This function is untyped and can be used to retrieve the value of any option. The caller must store a pointer to a buffer to receive the value in *val*, and the size of the buffer shall be stored at the location referenced by *valszp*.

When the function returns, the actual size of the data copied (or that would have been copied if sufficient space were present) is stored at the location referenced by *valszp*. If the caller's buffer is not large enough to hold the entire object, then the copy is truncated. Therefore the caller should check for truncation by verifying that the returned size in *valszp* does not exceed the original buffer size.

It is acceptable to pass NULL for *val* if the value in *valszp* is zero. This can be used to determine the size of the buffer needed to receive the object.

> 💡   It may be easier to use one of the typed forms of this function.

nng_getopt_bool()

This function is for options which take a Boolean (bool). The value will be stored at *ivalp*.

nng_getopt_int()

This function is for options which take an integer (int). The value will be stored at *ivalp*.

nng_getopt_ms()

This function is used to retrieve time durations (such as timeouts), stored in *durp* as a number of milliseconds. (The special value NNG_DUR_INFINITE means an infinite amount of time, and the special value NNG_DUR_DEFAULT means a context-specific default.)

nng_getopt_ptr()

This function is used to retrieve a pointer, *ptr*, to structured data. The data referenced by *ptr* is generally managed using other functions. Note that this form is somewhat special in that the object is generally not copied, but instead the **pointer** to the object is copied.

nng_getopt_size()

This function is used to retrieve a size into the pointer *zp*, typically for buffer sizes, message maximum sizes, and similar options.

nng_getopt_string()

This function is used to retrieve a string into *strp*. This string is created from the source using nng_strdup() and consequently must be freed by the caller using nng_strfree() when it is no longer needed.

nng_getopt_uint64()

This function is used to retrieve a 64-bit unsigned value into the value referenced by *u64p*. This is typically used for options related to identifiers, network numbers, and similar.

RETURN VALUES

These functions return 0 on success, and non-zero otherwise.

ERRORS

NNG_EBADTYPE	Incorrect type for option.
NNG_ECLOSED	Parameter *s* does not refer to an open socket.
NNG_EINVAL	Size of destination *val* too small for object.
NNG_ENOMEM	Insufficient memory exists.
NNG_ENOTSUP	The option *opt* is not supported.
NNG_EWRITEONLY	The option *opt* is write-only.

SEE ALSO

nng_dialer_getopt(3), nng_listener_getopt(3), nng_pipe_getopt(3), nng_setopt(3), nng_strdup(3), nng_strerror(3), nng_strfree(3), nng_duration(5), nng_options(5), nng_socket(5), nng(7)

NAME

nng_inproc_register - register inproc transport

SYNOPSIS

```
#include <nng/transport/inproc/inproc.h>

int nng_inproc_register(void);
```

DESCRIPTION

The nng_inproc_register() function registers the *inproc* transport for use.

RETURN VALUES

This function returns 0 on success, and non-zero otherwise.

ERRORS

NNG_ENOMEM	Insufficient memory is available.
NNG_ENOTSUP	The transport is not supported.

SEE ALSO

nng_inproc(5), nng(7)

NAME

nng_ipc_register - register ipc transport

SYNOPSIS

```
#include <nng/transport/ipc/ipc.h>

int nng_ipc_register(void);
```

DESCRIPTION

The nng_ipc_register() function registers the *ipc* transport for use.

RETURN VALUES

This function returns 0 on success, and non-zero otherwise.

ERRORS

NNG_ENOMEM	Insufficient memory is available.
NNG_ENOTSUP	The transport is not supported.

SEE ALSO

nng_ipc(5), nng(7)

NAME

nng_listen - create and start listener

SYNOPSIS

```
#include <nng/nng.h>

int nng_listen(nng_socket s, const char *url, nng_listener *lp, int flags);
```

DESCRIPTION

The nng_listen() function creates a newly initialized nng_listener object, associated with socket *s*, and configured to listen at the address specified by *url*, and starts it. If the value of *lp* is not NULL, then the newly created listener is stored at the address indicated by *lp*.

Listeners are used to accept connections initiated by remote dialers. An incoming connection generally results in and nng_pipe object being created and attached to the socket *s*. Unlike dialers, listeners generally can create many pipes, which may be open concurrently.

> While it is convenient to think of listeners as "servers", the relationship between the listener or dialer is orthogonal to any server or client status that might be associated with a given protocol. For example, a *req* socket might have associated dialers, but might also have associated listeners. It may even have some of each at the same time!

Normally, the act of "binding" to the address indicated by *url* is done synchronously, including any necessary name resolution. As a result, a failure, such as if the address is already in use, will be returned immediately. However, if the special value NNG_FLAG_NONBLOCK is supplied in *flags*, then this is done asynchronously; furthermore any failure to bind will be periodically reattempted in the background.

> While NNG_FLAG_NONBLOCK can help an application be more resilient, it also generally makes diagnosing failures somewhat more difficult.

Because the listener is started immediately, it is generally not possible to apply extra configuration; if that is needed applications should consider using nng_listener_create() and nng_listener_start() instead.

The created listener will continue to accept new connections, associating their pipes with the socket, until either it or the socket *s* is closed.

RETURN VALUES

This function returns 0 on success, and non-zero otherwise.

ERRORS

NNG_EADDRINUSE	The address specified by *url* is already in use.
NNG_EADDRINVAL	An invalid *url* was specified.

NNG_ECLOSED   The socket *s* is not open.

NNG_EINVAL   An invalid set of *flags* or an invalid *url* was specified.

NNG_ENOMEM   Insufficient memory is available.

SEE ALSO

nng_dial(3), nng_listener_close(3), nng_listener_create(3) nng_listener_start(3), nng_strerror(3), nng_listener(5), nng(7)

NAME

nng_listener_close - close listener

SYNOPSIS

```
#include <nng/nng.h>

int nng_listener_close(nng_listener l);
```

DESCRIPTION

The `nng_listener_close()` function closes the listener *l*. This also closes any pipes that have been created by the listener.

Once this function returns, the listener *l* and any of its resources are deallocated. Therefore it is an error to attempt to access *l* after this function has returned. (Attempts to do so will result in `NNG_ECLOSED` errors.)

Listeners are implicitly closed when the socket they are associated with is closed.

RETURN VALUES

This function returns 0 on success, and non-zero otherwise.

ERRORS

`NNG_ECLOSED`   Parameter *l* does not refer to an open listener.

SEE ALSO

nng_close(3), nng_listen(3), nng_listener_create(3) nng_strerror(3), nng_listener(5), nng(7)

NAME

nng_listener_create - create listener

SYNOPSIS

```
#include <nng/nng.h>

int nng_listener_create(nng_listener *listenerp, nng_socket s, const char *url);
```

DESCRIPTION

The nng_listener_create() function creates a newly initialized nng_listener object, associated with socket *s*, and configured to listen at the address specified by *url*, and stores a pointer to at the location referenced by *listenerp*.

Listeners are used to accept connections initiated by remote dialers. An incoming connection generally results in a pipe being created and attached to the socket *s*. Unlike dialers, listeners generally can create many pipes, which may be open concurrently.

> 💡 While it is convenient to think of listeners as "servers", the relationship between the listener or dialer is orthogonal to any server or client status that might be associated with a given protocol. For example, a *req* socket might have associated dialers, but might also have associated listeners. It may even have some of each at the same time!

The listener is not started, but may be further configured with the nng_listener_setopt() family of functions.

Once it is fully configured, the listener may be started using the nng_listener_start() function.

> 💡 If no specific configuration is required, consider using the simpler nng_listen() function instead.

RETURN VALUES

This function returns 0 on success, and non-zero otherwise.

ERRORS

NNG_EADDRINVAL	An invalid *url* was specified.
NNG_ECLOSED	The socket *s* is not open.
NNG_ENOMEM	Insufficient memory is available.

SEE ALSO

nng_dialer_create(3) nng_listen(3), nng_listener_close(3), nng_listener_getopt(3), nng_listener_setopt(3), nng_listener_start(3), nng_strerror(3), nng_listener(5), nng(7)

NAME

nng_listener_getopt - get listener option

SYNOPSIS

```
#include <nng/nng.h>

int nng_listener_getopt(nng_listener l, const char *opt, void *val, size_t *valszp);

int nng_listener_getopt_bool(nng_listener l, const char *opt, bool *bvalp);

int nng_listener_getopt_int(nng_listener l, const char *opt, int *ivalp);

int nng_listener_getopt_ms(nng_listener l, const char *opt, nng_duration *durp);

int nng_listener_getopt_ptr(nng_listener l, const char *opt, void **ptr);

int nng_listener_getopt_size(nng_listener l, const char *opt, size_t *zp);

int nng_listener_getopt_sockaddr(nng_listener l, const char *opt, nng_sockaddr *sap);

int nng_listener_getopt_string(nng_listener l, const char *opt, char **strp);

int nng_listener_getopt_uint64(nng_listener l, const char *opt, uint64_t *u64p);
```

DESCRIPTION

The nng_listener_getopt() functions are used to retrieve option values for the listener *l*. The actual options that may be retrieved in this way vary, and many are documented in nng_options(5).

Additionally some transport-specific options and protocol-specific options are documented with the transports and protocols themselves.

Forms

In all of these forms, the option *opt* is retrieved from the listener *l*. The forms vary based on the type of the option they take.

The details of the type, size, and semantics of the option will depend on the actual option, and will be documented with the option itself.

nng_listener_getopt()

This function is untyped and can be used to retrieve the value of any option. The caller must store a pointer to a buffer to receive the value in *val*, and the size of the buffer shall be stored at the location referenced by *valszp*.

When the function returns, the actual size of the data copied (or that would have been copied if sufficient space were present) is stored at the location referenced by *valszp*. If the caller's buffer is not large enough to hold the entire object, then the copy is truncated. Therefore the caller should validate that the returned size in *valszp* does not exceed the original buffer size to check for truncation.

It is acceptable to pass NULL for *val* if the value in *valszp* is zero. This can be used to determine the size of the buffer needed to receive the object.

> 💡   It may be easier to use one of the typed forms of this function.

nng_listener_getopt_bool()

This function is for options which take a Boolean (bool). The value will be stored at *bvalp*.

nng_listener_getopt_int()

This function is for options which take an integer (int). The value will be stored at *ivalp*.

nng_listener_getopt_ms()

This function is used to retrieve time durations (such as timeouts), stored in *durp* as a number of milliseconds.

nng_listener_getopt_ptr()

This function is used to retrieve a pointer, *ptr*, to structured data. The data referenced by *ptr* is generally managed using other functions. Note that this form is somewhat special in that the object is generally not copied, but instead the **pointer** to the object is copied.

nng_listener_getopt_size()

This function is used to retrieve a size into the pointer *zp*, typically for buffer sizes, message maximum sizes, and similar options.

nng_listener_getopt_sockaddr()

This function is used to retrieve an nng_sockaddr into the value referenced by *sap*.

nng_listener_getopt_string()

This function is used to retrieve a string into *strp*. This string is created from the source using nng_strdup() and consequently must be freed by the caller using nng_strfree() when it is no longer needed.

nng_listener_getopt_uint64()

This function is used to retrieve a 64-bit unsigned value into the value referenced by *u64p*. This is typically used for options related to identifiers, network numbers, and similar.

RETURN VALUES

These functions return 0 on success, and non-zero otherwise.

ERRORS

NNG_EBADTYPE	Incorrect type for option.
NNG_ECLOSED	Parameter *l* does not refer to an open listener.
NNG_EINVAL	Size of destination *val* too small for object.
NNG_ENOMEM	Insufficient memory exists.
NNG_ENOTSUP	The option *opt* is not supported.

NNG_EWRITEONLY   The option *opt* is write-only.

SEE ALSO

nng_listen(3), nng_listener_create(3) nng_listener_setopt(3) nng_getopt(3), nng_strdup(3),
nng_strerror(3), nng_strfree(3), nng_duration(5), nng_listener(5), nng_options(5), nng_sockaddr(5),
nng(7)

NAME

nng_listener_id - return numeric listener identifier

SYNOPSIS

```
#include <nng/nng.h>

int nng_listener_id(nng_listener l);
```

DESCRIPTION

The nng_listener_id() function returns a positive identifier for the listener *l*, if it is valid. Otherwise it returns -1.

> ℹ️ A listener is considered valid if it was ever created with the nng_listener_create() or nng_listen() functions. listeners that are allocated on the stack or statically should be initialized with the macro NNG_LISTENER_INITIALIZER to ensure that they cannot be confused with a valid listener before they are created properly.

RETURN VALUES

This function returns the positive value for the listener identifier, or -1 if the listener is invalid.

ERRORS

None.

SEE ALSO

nng_listener(5), nng(7)

NAME

nng_listener_setopt - set listener option

SYNOPSIS

```
#include <nng/nng.h>

int nng_listener_setopt(nng_listener l, const char *opt, const void *val,
    size_t valsz);

int nng_listener_setopt_int(nng_listener l, const char *opt, int ival);

int nng_listener_setopt_ms(nng_listener l, const char *opt, nng_duration dur);

int nng_listener_setopt_ptr(nng_listener l, const char *opt, void *ptr);

int nng_listener_setopt_size(nng_listener l, const char *opt, size_t z);

int nng_listener_setopt_string(nng_listener l, const char *opt, const char *str);

int nng_listener_setopt_uint64(nng_listener l, const char *opt, uint64_t u64);
```

DESCRIPTION

The nng_listener_setopt() functions are used to configure options for the listener *l*. The actual options that may be configured in this way vary, and many are documented in nng_options(5).

Additionally some transport-specific options and protocol-specific options are documented with the transports and protocols themselves.

ℹ️   Once a listener has started, it is generally not possible to change its configuration.

Forms

In all of these forms, the option *opt* is configured on the listener *l*.

The details of the type, size, and semantics of the option will depend on the actual option, and will be documented with the option itself.

💡   It may be easier to use one of the typed forms of this function.

nng_listener_setopt()
   This function is untyped, and can be used to configure any arbitrary data. The *val* pointer addresses the data to copy, and *valsz* is the size of the objected located at *val*.

nng_listener_setopt_bool()
   This function is for options which take a Boolean (bool). The *bval* is passed to the option.

nng_listener_setopt_int()

This function is for options which take an integer (int). The *ival* is passed to the option.

nng_listener_setopt_ms()

This function is used to configure time durations (such as timeouts) using type nng_duration. The duration *dur* is an integer number of milliseconds.

nng_listener_setopt_ptr()

This function is used to pass a pointer, *ptr*, to structured data. The data referenced by *ptr* is generally managed by other functions. For example, TLS configuration objects created with (nng_tls_config_alloc()) can be passed this way.

> **ℹ** This form is somewhat special in that the object is generally not copied, but instead the **pointer** to the object is copied.

nng_listener_setopt_size()

This function is used to configure a size, *z*, typically for buffer sizes, message maximum sizes, and similar options.

nng_listener_setopt_string()

This function is used to pass configure a string, *str*. Strings passed this way must be legal UTF-8 or ASCII strings, terminated with a NUL (\0) byte. (Other constraints may apply as well, see the documentation for each option for details.)

nng_listener_setopt_uint64()

This function is used to configure a 64-bit unsigned value, *u64*. This is typically used for options related to identifiers, network numbers, and similar.

RETURN VALUES

These functions return 0 on success, and non-zero otherwise.

ERRORS

NNG_EBADTYPE	Incorrect type for option.
NNG_ECLOSED	Parameter *l* does not refer to an open listener.
NNG_EINVAL	The value being passed is invalid.
NNG_ENOTSUP	The option *opt* is not supported.
NNG_EREADONLY	The option *opt* is read-only.
NNG_ESTATE	The listener *l* is already started.

SEE ALSO

nng_listen(3), nng_listener_create(3) nng_listener_getopt(3) nng_setopt(3), nng_strerror(3), nng_duration(5), nng_listener(5), nng_options(5), nng(7)

NAME

nng_listener_start - start listener

SYNOPSIS

```
#include <nng/nng.h>

int nng_listener_start(nng_listener l, int flags);
```

DESCRIPTION

The nng_listener_start() function starts the listener *l*.

This causes the listener to bind to the address it was created with, and to start accepting connections from remote dialers. Each new connection results in an nng_pipe object, which will be attached to the listener's socket.

Normally, the act of "binding" to its address is done synchronously, including any necessary name resolution. As a result, a failure, such as if the address is already in use, will be returned immediately. However, if the special value NNG_FLAG_NONBLOCK is supplied in *flags*, then this is done asynchronously; furthermore any failure to bind will be periodically reattempted in the background.

> 💡 While NNG_FLAG_NONBLOCK can help an application be more resilient, it also generally makes diagnosing failures somewhat more difficult.

Once a listener has started, it is generally not possible to change its configuration.

RETURN VALUES

This function returns 0 on success, and non-zero otherwise.

ERRORS

NNG_ECLOSED	Parameter *l* does not refer to an open listener.
NNG_ESTATE	The listener *l* is already started.

SEE ALSO

nng_listen(3), nng_listener_create(3) nng_listener(5), nng_strerror(3), nng(7)

NAME

nng_msg_alloc - allocate a message

SYNOPSIS

```
#include <nng/nng.h>

int nng_msg_alloc(nng_msg **msgp, size_t size);
```

DESCRIPTION

The nng_msg_alloc() function allocates a new message with body length *size* and stores the result in *msgp*. Messages allocated with this function contain a body and optionally a header. They are used with receive and transmit functions.

RETURN VALUES

This function returns 0 on success, and non-zero otherwise.

ERRORS

NNG_ENOMEM   Insufficient free memory exists to allocate a message.

SEE ALSO

nng_msg_free(3), nng_msg_body(3), nng_msg_dup(3), nng_msg_header(3), nng_msg_header_len(3), nng_msg_len(3), nng_msg_realloc(3), nng_strerror(3), nng_msg(5), nng(7)

NAME

nng_msg_append - append to message body

SYNOPSIS

```
#include <nng/nng.h>

int nng_msg_append(nng_msg *msg, const void *val, size_t size);
int nng_msg_append_u16(nng_msg *msg, uint16_t val16);
int nng_msg_append_u32(nng_msg *msg, uint32_t val32);
int nng_msg_append_u64(nng_msg *msg, uint64_t val64);
```

DESCRIPTION

The nng_msg_append() family of functions appends data to the end of the body of message *msg*, reallocating it if necessary. The first function appends *size* bytes, copying them from *val*. The remaining functions append the value specified (such as *val32*) in network-byte order (big-endian).

RETURN VALUES

These functions return 0 on success, and non-zero otherwise.

ERRORS

NNG_ENOMEM   Insufficient free memory exists.

SEE ALSO

nng_msg_alloc(3), nng_msg_body(3), nng_msg_chop(3), nng_msg_free(3), nng_msg_insert(3), nng_msg_len(3), nng_msg_realloc(3), nng_msg_trim(3), nng_strerror(3), nng_msg(5), nng(7)

NAME

nng_msg_body - return message body

SYNOPSIS

```
#include <nng/nng.h>

void *nng_msg_body(nng_msg *msg);
```

DESCRIPTION

The nng_msg_body() function returns a pointer to the start of the body content of the message *msg*.

ⓘ The value returned by this is invalidated by a call to any of the functions that modify the message itself. Such functions are nng_msg_free(), nng_msg_realloc(), any of the nng_msg_trim(), nng_msg_chop(), nng_msg_append(), or nng_msg_insert() variants.

RETURN VALUES

Pointer to start of message body.

ERRORS

None.

SEE ALSO

nng_msg_alloc(3), nng_msg_append(3), nng_msg_chop(3), nng_msg_free(3), nng_msg_insert(3), nng_msg_len(3), nng_msg_realloc(3), nng_msg_trim(3), nng_msg(5), nng(7)

NAME

nng_msg_chop - remove data from end of message body

SYNOPSIS

```
#include <nng/nng.h>

int nng_msg_chop(nng_msg *msg, size_t size);
int nng_msg_chop_u16(nng_msg *msg, uint16_t *val16);
int nng_msg_chop_u32(nng_msg *msg, uint32_t *val32);
int nng_msg_chop_u64(nng_msg *msg, uint64_t *val64);
```

DESCRIPTION

The nng_msg_chop() family of functions removes data from the end of the body of message *msg*. The first function removes *size* bytes. The remaining functions remove 2, 4, or 8 bytes, and stores them in the value (such as *val32*), after converting them from network-byte order (big-endian) to native byte order.

RETURN VALUES

These functions return 0 on success, and non-zero otherwise.

ERRORS

NNG_EINVAL   The message body is too short to remove the requested data.

SEE ALSO

nng_msg_alloc(3), nng_msg_append(3), nng_msg_body(3), nng_msg_free(3), nng_msg_insert(3), nng_msg_len(3), nng_msg_realloc(3), nng_msg_trim(3), nng_strerror(3), nng_msg(5), nng(7)

NAME

nng_msg_clear - clear message body content

SYNOPSIS

```
#include <nng/nng.h>

void nng_msg_clear(nng_msg *msg);
```

DESCRIPTION

The nng_msg_clear() function resets the body length of *msg* to zero.

RETURN VALUES

None.

ERRORS

None.

SEE ALSO

nng_msg(5), nng(7)

NAME

nng_msg_dup - duplicate a message

SYNOPSIS

```
#include <nng/nng.h>

int nng_msg_dup(nng_msg **dup, nng_msg_t *orig);
```

DESCRIPTION

The nng_msg_dup() makes a duplicate of the original message *orig*, and saves the result in the location pointed by *dup*. The actual message body and header content is copied, but the duplicate may contain a different amount of unused space than the original message.

RETURN VALUES

This function returns 0 on success, and non-zero otherwise.

ERRORS

NNG_ENOMEM   Insufficient free memory exists to duplicate a message.

SEE ALSO

nng_msg_alloc(3), nng_msg_free(3), nng_strerror(3), nng_msg(5), nng(7)

NAME

nng_msg_free - free a message

SYNOPSIS

```
#include <nng/nng.h>

void nng_msg_free(nng_msg *msg);
```

DESCRIPTION

The nng_msg_free() function deallocates the message *msg* entirely.

RETURN VALUES

None.

ERRORS

None.

SEE ALSO

nng_msg_alloc(3), nng_msg_realloc(3), nng_msg(5), nng(7)

NAME

nng_msg_get_pipe - get pipe for message

SYNOPSIS

```
#include <nng/nng.h>

nng_pipe nng_msg_get_pipe(nng_msg *msg);
```

DESCRIPTION

The nng_msg_get_pipe() returns the nng_pipe object associated with message *msg*. On receive, this is the pipe from which a message was received. On transmit, this would be the pipe that the message should be delivered to, if a specific peer is required.

> ℹ Not all protocols support overriding the destination pipe.

The most usual use case for this is to obtain information about the peer from which the message was received. This can be used to provide different behaviors for different peers, such as a higher level of authentication for peers located on an untrusted network. The nng_pipe_getopt() function is useful in this situation.

RETURN VALUES

This function returns the pipe associated with this message, which will be a positive value. If the pipe is non-positive, then that indicates that no specific pipe is associated with the message.

ERRORS

None.

SEE ALSO

nng_msg_alloc(3), nng_msg_set_pipe(3), nng_pipe_getopt(3), nng(7)

NAME

nng_msg_header - return message header

SYNOPSIS

```
#include <nng/nng.h>

void *nng_msg_header(nng_msg *msg);
```

DESCRIPTION

The nng_msg_header() function returns a pointer to the start of the header content of the message *msg*.

> ℹ The message header contains protocol-specific header content. Most applications should not need to access this content, but it is available for raw mode sockets (set with the NNG_OPT_RAW option.)

> ℹ The value returned by this is invalidated by a call to any of the functions that modify the message or the header content.

RETURN VALUES

Pointer to start of message header.

ERRORS

None.

SEE ALSO

nng_msg_alloc(3), nng_msg_body(3), nng_msg_free(3), nng_msg_header_append(3), nng_msg_header_chop(3), nng_msg_header_insert(3) nng_msg_header_len(3), nng_msg_header_trim(3), nng_msg(5), nng(7)

NAME

nng_msg_header_append - append to message header

SYNOPSIS

```
#include <nng/nng.h>

int nng_msg_header_append(nng_msg *msg, const void *val, size_t size);
int nng_msg_header_append_u16(nng_msg *msg, uint16_t val16);
int nng_msg_header_append_u32(nng_msg *msg, uint32_t val32);
int nng_msg_header_append_u64(nng_msg *msg, uint64_t val64);
```

DESCRIPTION

The nng_msg_header_append() family of functions appends data to the end of the headers of message *msg*, reallocating it if necessary. The first function appends *size* bytes, copying them from *val*.

The remaining functions append the value (such as *val32*) in network-byte order (big-endian).

RETURN VALUES

These functions return 0 on success, and non-zero otherwise.

ERRORS

NNG_ENOMEM   Insufficient free memory exists.

SEE ALSO

nng_msg_alloc(3), nng_msg_header(3), nng_msg_header_chop(3), nng_msg_header_insert(3), nng_msg_header_len(3), nng_msg_header_trim(3), nng_msg_free(3), nng_strerror(3), nng(7)

NAME

nng_msg_header_chop - remove data from end of message header

SYNOPSIS

```
#include <nng/nng.h>

int nng_msg_header_chop(nng_msg *msg, size_t size);
int nng_msg_header_chop_u16(nng_msg *msg, uint16_t *val16);
int nng_msg_header_chop_u32(nng_msg *msg, uint32_t *val32);
int nng_msg_header_chop_u64(nng_msg *msg, uint64_t *val64);
```

DESCRIPTION

The nng_msg_header_chop() family of functions removes data from the end of the header of message *msg*. The first function removes *size* bytes. The remaining functions remove 2, 4, or 8 bytes, and stores them in the value (such as *val32*), after converting them from network-byte order (big-endian) to native byte order.

RETURN VALUES

These function return 0 on success, and non-zero otherwise.

ERRORS

NNG_EINVAL   The message header is too short to remove the requested data.

SEE ALSO

nng_msg_alloc(3), nng_msg_header(3), nng_msg_header_append(3), nng_msg_header_insert(3), nng_msg_header_len(3), nng_msg_header_trim(3), nng_msg_free(3), nng_strerror(3), nng(7)

NAME

nng_msg_header_clear - clear message header

SYNOPSIS

```
#include <nng/nng.h>

void nng_msg_header_clear(nng_msg *msg);
```

DESCRIPTION

The nng_msg_clear() function resets the header length of *msg* to zero.

RETURN VALUES

None.

ERRORS

None.

SEE ALSO

nng_msg_alloc(3), nng_msg_free(3), nng(7)

NAME

nng_msg_header_insert - prepend to message header

SYNOPSIS

```
#include <nng/nng.h>

int nng_msg_header_insert(nng_msg *msg, const void *val, size_t size);
int nng_msg_header_insert_u16(nng_msg *msg, uint16_t val16);
int nng_msg_header_insert_u32(nng_msg *msg, uint32_t val32);
int nng_msg_header_insert_u64(nng_msg *msg, uint64_t val64);
```

DESCRIPTION

The nng_msg_header_insert() family of functions prepends data to the front of the headers of message *msg*, reallocating if necessary. The first function prepends *size* bytes, copying them from *val*. The remaining functions prepend the specified value (such as *val32*) in network-byte order (big-endian).

RETURN VALUES

These functions return 0 on success, and non-zero otherwise.

ERRORS

NNG_ENOMEM   Insufficient free memory exists.

SEE ALSO

nng_msg_alloc(3), nng_msg_header(3), nng_msg_header_append(3), nng_msg_header_chop(3), nng_msg_header_len(3), nng_msg_header_trim(3), nng_msg_free(3), nng_msg_realloc(3), nng_strerror(3), nng(7)

NAME

nng_msg_header_len - return message header length

SYNOPSIS

```
#include <nng/nng.h>

size_t nng_msg_header_len(nng_msg *msg);
```

DESCRIPTION

The nng_msg_header_len() returns the length of message header of *msg*.

RETURN VALUES

Length of message header.

ERRORS

None.

SEE ALSO

nng_msg_alloc(3), nng_msg_header(3), nng_msg(5), nng(7)

NAME

nng_msg_header_trim - remove data from start of message header

SYNOPSIS

```
#include <nng/nng.h>

int nng_msg_header_trim(nng_msg *msg, size_t size);
int nng_msg_header_trim_u16(nng_msg *msg, uint16_t *val16);
int nng_msg_header_trim_u32(nng_msg *msg, uint32_t *val32);
int nng_msg_header_trim_u64(nng_msg *msg, uint64_t *val64);
```

DESCRIPTION

The nng_msg_header_trim() family of functions remove data from the start of the header of message *msg*. The first function removes *size* bytes. The remaining functions removes 2, 4, or 8 bytes, and stores them in the value (such as *val32*), after converting them from network-byte order (big-endian) to native byte order.

RETURN VALUES

This function returns 0 on success, and non-zero otherwise.

ERRORS

NNG_EINVAL   The message header is too short to remove the requested data.

SEE ALSO

nng_msg_alloc(3), nng_msg_header(3), nng_msg_header_append(3), nng_msg_header_chop(3), nng_msg_header_insert(3), nng_msg_header_len(3), nng_msg_free(3), nng_strerror(3), nng_msg(5), nng(7)

NAME

nng_msg_insert - prepend to message body

SYNOPSIS

```
#include <nng/nng.h>

int nng_msg_insert(nng_msg *msg, const void *val, size_t size);
int nng_msg_insert(nng_msg *msg, uint16_t val16);
int nng_msg_insert(nng_msg *msg, uint32_t val32);
int nng_msg_insert(nng_msg *msg, uint64_t val64);
```

DESCRIPTION

The nng_msg_insert() family of functions prepends data to the front of the body of message *msg*, reallocating it if necessary. The first function prepends *size* bytes, copying them from *val*. The remaining functions prepend the specified value (such as *val32*) in network-byte order (big-endian).

> 💡 These functions make use of pre-allocated "headroom" in the message if available, so it can often avoid performing any reallocation. Applications should use this instead of reallocating and copying message content themselves, in order to benefit from this capability.

RETURN VALUES

These functions return 0 on success, and non-zero otherwise.

ERRORS

NNG_ENOMEM   Insufficient free memory exists.

SEE ALSO

nng_msg_alloc(3), nng_msg_append(3), nng_msg_body(3), nng_msg_chop(3), nng_msg_free(3), nng_msg_len(3), nng_msg_realloc(3), nng_msg_trim(3), nng_strerror(3), nng_msg(5), nng(7)

NAME

nng_msg_len - return message body length

SYNOPSIS

```
#include <nng/nng.h>

size_t nng_msg_len(nng_msg *msg);
```

DESCRIPTION

The nng_msg_len() returns the length of the body of message *msg*.

RETURN VALUES

Length of message body.

ERRORS

None.

SEE ALSO

nng_msg_alloc(3), nng_msg_body(3), nng_msg(5), nng(7)

NAME

nng_msg_realloc - reallocate a message

SYNOPSIS

```
#include <nng/nng.h>

int nng_msg_realloc(nng_msg *msg, size_t size);
```

DESCRIPTION

The nng_msg_realloc() function re-allocates a message so that it has a body of length *size*. This message attempts to avoid extra allocations, and will reuse the existing memory when possible.

> One way to further reduce message allocations is to allocate a message larger than needed, then use this function or nng_msg_chop() to reduce the message size to that actually needed. The extra space left over will still be present in the message, so that when the message size needs to grow due to this function or nng_msg_append() no actual memory allocations need to take place.

> Pointers to message body and header content obtained prior to this function must not be in use, as the underlying memory used for the message may have changed, particularly if the message size is increasing.

RETURN VALUES

This function returns 0 on success, and non-zero otherwise.

ERRORS

NNG_ENOMEM   Insufficient free memory exists to reallocate a message.

SEE ALSO

nng_msg_alloc(3), nng_msg_append(3), nng_msg_body(3), nng_msg_chop(3), nng_msg_free(3), nng_msg_insert(3), nng_msg_len(3), nng_msg_trim(3), nng_strerror(3), nng_msg(5), nng(7)

NAME

nng_msg_set_pipe - set pipe for message

SYNOPSIS

```
#include <nng/nng.h>

void nng_msg_set_pipe(nng_msg *msg, nng_pipe p);
```

DESCRIPTION

The nng_msg_set_pipe() sets the pipe associated with message *m* to *p*. This is most often useful when used with protocols that support directing a message to a specific peer. For example the *pair* version 1 protocol can do this when NNG_OPT_PAIR1_POLY mode is set.

🛈   Not all protocols support overriding the destination pipe.

RETURN VALUES

None.

ERRORS

None.

SEE ALSO

nng_msg_alloc(3), nng_msg_get_pipe(3), nng_pipe_getopt(3), nng_msg(5), nng(7)

NAME

nng_msg_trim - remove data from start of message body

SYNOPSIS

```
#include <nng/nng.h>

int nng_msg_trim(nng_msg *msg, size_t size);
int nng_msg_trim_u16(nng_msg *msg, uint16_t *val16);
int nng_msg_trim_u32(nng_msg *msg, uint32_t *val32);
int nng_msg_trim_u64(nng_msg *msg, uint64_t *val64);
```

DESCRIPTION

The nng_msg_trim() family of functions removes data from the start of the body of message *msg*. The first function removes *size* bytes. The remaining functions remove 2, 4, or 8 bytes, and stores them in the value (such as *val32*), after converting them from network-byte order (big-endian) to native byte order.

RETURN VALUES

These functions return 0 on success, and non-zero otherwise.

ERRORS

NNG_EINVAL   The message body is too short to remove the requested data.

SEE ALSO

nng_msg_alloc(3), nng_msg_append(3), nng_msg_body(3), nng_msg_chop(3), nng_msg_free(3), nng_msg_insert(3), nng_msg_len(3), nng_msg_realloc(3), nng_strerror(3), nng_msg(5), nng(7)

NAME

nng_pair_open - create pair socket

SYNOPSIS

Version 0

```
#include <nng/protocol/pair0/pair.h>

int nng_pair0_open(nng_socket *s);

int nng_pair0_open_raw(nng_socket *s);
```

Version 1

```
#include <nng/protocol/pair1/pair.h>

int nng_pair1_open(nng_socket *s);

int nng_pair1_open_raw(nng_socket *s);
```

DESCRIPTION

The nng_pair0_open() and nng_pair1_open() functions create a *pair* version 0 or version 1 socket and return it at the location pointed to by *s*.

The nng_pair0_open_raw() and nng_pair1_open_raw() functions create a *pair* version 0 or version 1 socket in raw mode and return it at the location pointed to by *s*.

RETURN VALUES

These functions returns 0 on success, and non-zero otherwise.

ERRORS

NNG_ENOMEM	Insufficient memory is available.
NNG_ENOTSUP	The protocol is not supported.

SEE ALSO

nng_socket(5), nng_pair(7), nng(7)

NAME

nng_pipe_close - close pipe

SYNOPSIS

```
#include <nng/nng.h>

int nng_pipe_close(nng_pipe p);
```

DESCRIPTION

The nng_pipe_close() function closes the supplied pipe, *p*. Messages that have been submitted for sending may be flushed or delivered, depending upon the transport and the setting of the NNG_OPT_LINGER option.

Further attempts to use the pipe after this call returns will result in NNG_ECLOSED.

> 💡 Pipes are automatically closed when their creator closes, or when the remote peer closes the underlying connection.

RETURN VALUES

This function returns 0 on success, and non-zero otherwise.

ERRORS

NNG_ECLOSED   The pipe *p* is already closed or was never opened.

SEE ALSO

nng_strerror(3), nng_options(5), nng_pipe(5), nng(7)

NAME

nng_pipe_dialer - return dialer that created pipe

SYNOPSIS

```
#include <nng/nng.h>

nng_dialer nng_pipe_dialer(nng_pipe p);
```

DESCRIPTION

The nng_pipe_dialer() function returns the nng_dialer that created the pipe *p*. If the pipe was not created by a dialer, then the returned value will have an identifier (nng_dialer_id()) of -1.

RETURN VALUES

This function returns the dialer that created the pipe, unless it was not created by a dialer, in which case a value initialized with NNG_DIALER_INITIALIZER will be returned.

ERRORS

None.

SEE ALSO

nng_pipe(5), nng_dialer(5), nng(7)

NAME

nng_pipe_getopt - get pipe option

SYNOPSIS

#include <nng/nng.h>

int nng_pipe_getopt(nng_pipe p, **const char** *opt, **void** *val, **size_t** *valszp);

int nng_pipe_getopt_bool(nng_pipe p, **const char** *opt, **int** *bvalp);

int nng_pipe_getopt_int(nng_pipe p, **const char** *opt, **int** *ivalp);

int nng_pipe_getopt_ms(nng_pipe p, **const char** *opt, nng_duration *durp);

int nng_dialer_getopt_ptr(nng_pipe p, **const char** *opt, **void** **ptr);

int nng_pipe_getopt_sockaddr(nng_pipe p, **const char** *opt, nng_sockaddr *sap);

int nng_pipe_getopt_string(nng_pipe p, **const char** *opt, **char** **strp);

int nng_pipe_getopt_size(nng_pipe p, **const char** *opt, **size_t** *zp);

int nng_pipe_getopt_uint64(nng_pipe p, **const char** *opt, **uint64_t** *u64p);

DESCRIPTION

The nng_pipe_getopt() functions are used to retrieve option values for the pipe *p*. The actual options that may be retrieved in this way vary, and many are documented in nng_options(5). Additionally some transport-specific options and protocol-specific options are documented with the transports and protocols themselves.

ⓘ   All "options" on a pipe are read-only values. Modification of options may be done before the pipe is
        created using nng_listener_setopt() or nng_dialer_setopt().

Any option that is set on a dialer or listener will normally be retrievable from pipes created by that dialer or listener.

Forms

In all of these forms, the option *opt* is retrieved from the pipe *p*.

The details of the type, size, and semantics of the option will depend on the actual option, and will be documented with the option itself.

nng_pipe_getopt()

This is untyped, and can be used to retrieve the value of any option. A pointer to a buffer to receive the value in *val*, and the size of the buffer shall be stored at the location referenced by *valszp*.

When the function returns, the actual size of the data copied (or that would have been copied if sufficient space were present) is stored at the location referenced by *valszp*. If the caller's buffer is not large enough to hold the entire object, then the copy is truncated. Therefore the caller should check for truncation by verifying that the size returned in *valszp* does not exceed the original buffer size.

It is acceptable to pass NULL for *val* if the value in *valszp* is zero. This can be used to determine the size of the buffer needed to receive the object.

> 💡 It may be easier to use one of the typed forms of this function.

nng_pipe_getopt_bool()

This function is for options which take a Boolean (bool). The value will be stored at *bvalp*.

nng_pipe_getopt_int()

This function is for options which take an integer (int). The value will be stored at *ivalp*.

nng_pipe_getopt_ms()

This function is used to retrieve time durations (nng_duration) in milliseconds, which are stored in *durp*.

nng_pipe_getopt_ptr()

This function is used to retrieve a pointer, *ptr*, to structured data. The data referenced by *ptr* is generally managed using other functions. Note that this form is somewhat special in that the object is generally not copied, but instead the **pointer** to the object is copied.

nng_pipe_getopt_size()

This function is used to retrieve a size into the pointer *zp*, typically for buffer sizes, message maximum sizes, and similar options.

nng_pipe_getopt_sockaddr()

This function is used to retrieve an nng_sockaddr into *sap*.

nng_pipe_getopt_string()

This function is used to retrieve a string into *strp*. This string is created from the source using nng_strdup() and consequently must be freed by the caller using nng_strfree() when it is no longer needed.

nng_pipe_getopt_uint64()

This function is used to retrieve a 64-bit unsigned value into the value referenced by *u64p*. This is typically used for options related to identifiers, network numbers, and similar.

RETURN VALUES

These functions return 0 on success, and non-zero otherwise.

ERRORS

NNG_EBADTYPE	Incorrect type for option.
NNG_ECLOSED	Parameter *p* does not refer to an open pipe.
NNG_ENOTSUP	The option *opt* is not supported.

NNG_ENOMEM	Insufficient memory exists.
NNG_EINVAL	Size of destination *val* too small for object.
NNG_EWRITEONLY	The option *opt* is write-only.

SEE ALSO

nng_dialer_setopt(3) nng_getopt(3), nng_listener_setopt(3) nng_msg_get_pipe(3) nng_strdup(3), nng_strerror(3), nng_strfree(3), nng_duration(5), nng_options(5), nng_pipe(5), nng_sockaddr(5), nng(7)

NAME

nng_pipe_id - return numeric pipe identifier

SYNOPSIS

```
#include <nng/nng.h>

int nng_pipe_id(nng_pipe p);
```

DESCRIPTION

The nng_pipe_id() function returns a positive identifier for the pipe *p*, if it is valid. Otherwise it returns -1.

> 🛈 A pipe is considered valid if it was ever created by the socket. Pipes that are allocated on the stack or statically should be initialized with the macro NNG_PIPE_INITIALIZER to ensure that they cannot be confused with a valid pipe.

RETURN VALUES

This function returns the positive value for the pipe identifier, or -1 if the pipe is invalid.

ERRORS

None.

SEE ALSO

nng_pipe(5), nng(7)

NAME

nng_pipe_listener - return listener that created pipe

SYNOPSIS

```
#include <nng/nng.h>

nng_listener nng_pipe_listener(nng_pipe p);
```

DESCRIPTION

The nng_pipe_listener() function returns the nng_listener that created the pipe *p*. If the pipe was not created by a listener, then the returned value will have an identifier (nng_listener_id()) of -1.

RETURN VALUES

This function returns the listener that created the pipe, unless it was not created by a listener, in which case a value initialized with NNG_LISTENER_INITIALIZER will be returned.

ERRORS

None.

SEE ALSO

nng_pipe(5), nng_listener(5), nng(7)

NAME

nng_pipe_notify - register pipe notification callback

SYNOPSIS

```
#include <nng/nng.h>

enum {
        NNG_PIPE_EV_ADD_PRE,
        NNG_PIPE_EV_ADD_POST,
        NNG_PIPE_EV_REM_POST,
};

typedef void (*nng_pipe_cb)(nng_pipe, int, void *);

int nng_pipe_notify(nng_socket s, int ev, nng_pipe_cb cb, void *arg);
```

DESCRIPTION

The nng_pipe_notify() function registers the callback function *cb* to be called whenever a pipe the pipe event specified by *ev* occurs on the socket *s*. The callback *cb* will be passed *arg* as its final argument.

A different callback may be supplied for each event. Each event may have at most one callback registered. Registering a callback implicitly unregisters any previously registered.

The following pipe events are supported:

NNG_PIPE_EV_ADD_PRE

   This event occurs after a connection and negotiation has completed, but before the pipe is added to the socket. If the pipe is closed (using nng_pipe_close()) at this point, the socket will never see the pipe, and no further events will occur for the given pipe.

NNG_PIPE_EV_ADD_POST

   This event occurs after the pipe is fully added to the socket. Prior to this time, it is not possible to communicate over the pipe with the socket.

NNG_PIPE_EV_REM_POST

   This event occurs after the pipe has been removed from the socket. The underlying transport may be closed at this point, and it is not possible communicate using this pipe.

> 💡 The callback *cb* may close a pipe for any reason by simply closing it using nng_pipe_close(). This might be done before the pipe is added to the socket (during NNG_PIPE_EV_ADD_PRE), for example, if the remote peer is not authorized.

> 💡 It is possible to register the same *cb* and *arg* for different events by calling this function separately for different values of *ev*.

> ℹ️ This function ignores invalid values for *ev*.

RETURN VALUES

This function returns 0 on success, and non-zero otherwise.

ERRORS

NNG_ECLOSED   The socket *s* does not refer to an open socket.

SEE ALSO

nng_pipe_close(3), nng_pipe_getopt(3), nng_pipe(5), nng_socket(5), nng(7)

NAME

nng_pipe_socket - return owning socket for pipe

SYNOPSIS

```
#include <nng/nng.h>

nng_socket nng_pipe_socket(nng_pipe p);
```

DESCRIPTION

The `nng_pipe_socket()` function returns the `nng_socket` that owns the pipe *p*.

> **ⓘ** The returned socket may be closed or in the process of closing, in which case it will not be usable with other functions.

RETURN VALUES

This function returns the socket that "owns" the pipe.

ERRORS

None.

SEE ALSO

nng_pipe(5), nng_socket(5), nng(7)

NAME

nng_pub_open - create pub socket

SYNOPSIS

```
#include <nng/nng.h>
#include <nng/protocol/pubsub0/pub.h>

int nng_pub0_open(nng_socket *s);

int nng_pub0_open_raw(nng_socket *s);
```

DESCRIPTION

The nng_pub0_open() function creates a *pub* version 0 socket and returns it at the location pointed to by *s*.

The nng_pub0_open_raw() function creates a *pub* version 0 socket in raw mode and returns it at the location pointed to by *s*.

RETURN VALUES

These functions return 0 on success, and non-zero otherwise.

ERRORS

NNG_ENOMEM	Insufficient memory is available.
NNG_ENOTSUP	The protocol is not supported.

SEE ALSO

nng_socket(5), nng_pub(7), nng_sub(7), nng(7)

NAME

nng_pull_open - create pull socket

SYNOPSIS

```
#include <nng/nng.h>
#include <nng/protocol/pipeline0/pull.h>

int nng_pull0_open(nng_socket *s);

int nng_pull0_open_raw(nng_socket *s);
```

DESCRIPTION

The nng_pull0_open() function creates a *pull* version 0 socket and returns it at the location pointed to by *s*.

The nng_pull0_open_raw() function creates a *pull* version 0 socket in raw mode and returns it at the location pointed to by *s*.

RETURN VALUES

These functions return 0 on success, and non-zero otherwise.

ERRORS

NNG_ENOMEM	Insufficient memory is available.
NNG_ENOTSUP	The protocol is not supported.

SEE ALSO

nng_socket(5), nng_pull(7), nng_push(7), nng(7)

NAME

nng_push_open - create push socket

SYNOPSIS

```
#include <nng/nng.h>
#include <nng/protocol/pipeline0/push.h>

int nng_push0_open(nng_socket *s);

int nng_push0_open_raw(nng_socket *s);
```

DESCRIPTION

The nng_push0_open() function creates a *push* version 0 socket and returns it at the location pointed to by *s*.

The nng_push0_open_raw() function creates a *push* version 0 socket in raw mode and returns it at the location pointed to by *s*.

RETURN VALUES

These functions return 0 on success, and non-zero otherwise.

ERRORS

NNG_ENOMEM	Insufficient memory is available.
NNG_ENOTSUP	The protocol is not supported.

SEE ALSO

nng_socket(5), nng_pull(7), nng_push(7), nng(7)

NAME

nng_recv - recv data

SYNOPSIS

```
#include <nng/nng.h>

int nng_recv(nng_socket s, void *data, size_t *sizep int flags);
```

DESCRIPTION

The nng_recv() receives a message.

The *flags* is a bit mask that may contain any of the following values:

NNG_FLAG_NONBLOCK

The function returns immediately, even if no message is available. Without this flag, the function will wait until a message is received by the socket *s*, or any configured timer expires.

NNG_FLAG_ALLOC

If this flag is present, then a "zero-copy" mode is used. In this case the caller must set the value of *data* to the location of another pointer (of type void *), and the *sizep* pointer must be set to a location to receive the size of the message body. The function will then allocate a message buffer (as if by nng_alloc()), fill it with the message body, and store it at the address referenced by *data*, and update the size referenced by *sizep*. The caller is responsible for disposing of the received buffer either by the nng_free() function or passing the message (also with the NNG_FLAG_ALLOC flag) in a call to nng_send().

If the special flag NNG_FLAG_ALLOC (see above) is not specified, then the caller must set *data* to a buffer to receive the message body content, and must store the size of that buffer at the location pointed to by *sizep*. When the function returns, if it is successful, the size at *sizep* will be updated with the actual message body length copied into *data*.

> ⓘ   The semantics of what receiving a message means vary from protocol to protocol, so examination of the protocol documentation is encouraged. (For example, with a *req* socket a message may only be received after a request has been sent, and a *sub* socket may only receive messages corresponding to topics to which it has subscribed.) Furthermore, some protocols may not support receiving data at all, such as *pub*.

> ♀   The NNG_FLAG_ALLOC flag can be used to reduce data copies, thereby increasing performance, particularly if the buffer is reused to send a response using the same flag.

RETURN VALUES

This function returns 0 on success, and non-zero otherwise.

ERRORS

NNG_EAGAIN	The operation would block, but NNG_FLAG_NONBLOCK was specified.
NNG_ECLOSED	The socket *s* is not open.
NNG_EINVAL	An invalid set of *flags* was specified.
NNG_EMSGSIZE	The received message did not fit in the size provided.
NNG_ENOMEM	Insufficient memory is available.
NNG_ENOTSUP	The protocol for socket *s* does not support receiving.
NNG_ESTATE	The socket *s* cannot receive data in this state.
NNG_ETIMEDOUT	The operation timed out.

SEE ALSO

nng_alloc(3), nng_free(3), nng_recvmsg(3), nng_send(3), nng_strerror(3), nng(7)

NAME

nng_recv_aio - receive message asynchronously

SYNOPSIS

```
#include <nng/nng.h>

void nng_recv_aio(nng_socket s, nng_aio *aio);
```

DESCRIPTION

The nng_recv_aio() receives a message using the socket *s* asynchronously.

When a message is successfully received by the socket, it is stored in the *aio* by an internal call equivalent to nng_aio_set_msg(), then the completion callback on the *aio* is executed. In this case, nng_aio_result() will return zero. The callback function is responsible for retrieving the message and disposing of it appropriately.

⚠️   Failing to accept and dispose of messages in this case can lead to memory leaks.

If for some reason the asynchronous receive cannot be completed successfully (including by being canceled or timing out), then the callback will still be executed, but nng_aio_result() will be non-zero.

ℹ️   The semantics of what receiving a message means varies from protocol to protocol, so examination of the protocol documentation is encouraged. (For example, with a *pub* socket the data is broadcast, so that any peers who have a suitable subscription will be able to receive it using nng_recv() or a similar function.) Furthermore, some protocols may not support receiving (such as *pub*) or may require other conditions. (For example, *req* sockets cannot normally receive data, which are replies to requests, until they have first sent a request.)

RETURN VALUES

None. (The operation completes asynchronously.)

ERRORS

NNG_ECANCELED	The operation was aborted.
NNG_ECLOSED	The socket *s* is not open.
NNG_ENOMEM	Insufficient memory is available.
NNG_ENOTSUP	The protocol for socket *s* does not support receiving.
NNG_ESTATE	The socket *s* cannot receive data in this state.
NNG_ETIMEDOUT	The receive timeout expired.

SEE ALSO

nng_aio_get_msg(3), nng_aio_set_msg(3), nng_msg_alloc(3), nng_strerror(3), nng_aio(5), nng_msg(5), nng_socket(5), nng(7)

NAME

nng_recvmsg - recv message

SYNOPSIS

```
#include <nng/nng.h>

int nng_recvmsg(nng_socket s, nng_msg **msgp, int flags);
```

DESCRIPTION

The nng_recvmsg() receives a message on socket *s*, storing the received message at the location pointed to by *msgp*.

> Using this function gives access to the message structure, and thus may offer more functionality than the simpler nng_recv() function.

The *flags* may contain the following value:

NNG_FLAG_NONBLOCK
    The function returns immediately, even if no message is available. Without this flag, the function will wait until a message is received by the socket *s*, or any configured timer expires.

> The semantics of what receiving a message means vary from protocol to protocol, so examination of the protocol documentation is encouraged. (For example, with an *req* socket a message may only be received after a request has been sent, and an *sub* socket may only receive messages corresponding to topics to which it has subscribed.) Furthermore, some protocols may not support receiving data at all, such as *pub*.

RETURN VALUES

This function returns 0 on success, and non-zero otherwise.

ERRORS

NNG_EAGAIN	The operation would block, but NNG_FLAG_NONBLOCK was specified.
NNG_ECLOSED	The socket *s* is not open.
NNG_EINVAL	An invalid set of *flags* was specified.
NNG_ENOMEM	Insufficient memory is available.
NNG_ENOTSUP	The protocol for socket *s* does not support receiving.
NNG_ESTATE	The socket *s* cannot receive data in this state.
NNG_ETIMEDOUT	The operation timed out.

SEE ALSO

nng_msg_free(3), nng_recv(3), nng_sendmsg(3), nng_strerror(3), nng(7)

NAME

nng_rep_open - create rep socket

SYNOPSIS

```
#include <nng/nng.h>
#include <nng/protocol/reqrep0/rep.h>

int nng_rep0_open(nng_socket *s);
```

DESCRIPTION

The nng_rep0_open() function creates a *rep* version 0 socket and returns it at the location pointed to by
s.

The nng_rep0_open_raw() function creates a *rep* version 0 socket in raw mode and returns it at the
location pointed to by *s*.

RETURN VALUES

These functions return 0 on success, and non-zero otherwise.

ERRORS

NNG_ENOMEM	Insufficient memory is available.
NNG_ENOTSUP	The protocol is not supported.

SEE ALSO

nng_socket(5), nng_rep(7), nng_req(7), nng(7)

NAME

nng_req_open - create req socket

SYNOPSIS

```
#include <nng/nng.h>
#include <nng/protocol/reqrep0/req.h>

int nng_req0_open(nng_socket *s);

int nng_req0_open_raw(nng_socket *s);
```

DESCRIPTION

The nng_req0_open() function creates a *req* version 0 socket and returns it at the location pointed to by *s*.

The nng_req0_open_raw() function creates a *req* version 0 socket in raw mode and returns it at the location pointed to by *s*.

RETURN VALUES

These functions return 0 on success, and non-zero otherwise.

ERRORS

NNG_ENOMEM	Insufficient memory is available.
NNG_ENOTSUP	The protocol is not supported.

SEE ALSO

nng_options(5), nng_socket(5), nng_rep(7), nng_req(7), nng(7)

NAME

nng_respondent_open - create respondent socket

SYNOPSIS

```
#include <nng/nng.h>
#include <nng/protocol/survey0/respond.h>

int nng_respondent0_open(nng_socket *s);

int nng_respondent0_open_raw(nng_socket *s);
```

DESCRIPTION

The nng_respondent0_open() function creates a *respondent* version 0 socket and returns it at the location pointed to by *s*.

The nng_respondent0_open_raw() function creates a *respondent* version 0 socket in raw mode and returns it at the location pointed to by *s*.

RETURN VALUES

These functions return 0 on success, and non-zero otherwise.

ERRORS

NNG_ENOMEM	Insufficient memory is available.
NNG_ENOTSUP	The protocol is not supported.

SEE ALSO

nng_socket(5), nng_respondent(7), nng_surveyor(7), nng(7)

NAME

nng_send - send data

SYNOPSIS

```
#include <nng/nng.h>

int nng_send(nng_socket s, void *data, size_t size, int flags);
```

DESCRIPTION

The nng_send() function sends a message containing the *data* of length *size* using the socket *s*.

> The semantics of what sending a message means vary from protocol to protocol, so examination of the protocol documentation is encouraged. (For example, with an *nng* socket the data is broadcast, so that any peers who have a suitable subscription will be able to receive it using nng_recv() or a similar function.) Furthermore, some protocols may not support sending data (such as *sub*) or may require other conditions. (For example, *rep* sockets cannot normally send data, which are responses to requests, until they have first received a request.)

The *flags* may contain either of (or neither of) the following values:

NNG_FLAG_NONBLOCK
The function returns immediately, regardless of whether the socket is able to accept the data or not. If the socket is unable to accept the data (such as if backpressure exists because the peers are consuming messages too slowly, or no peer is present), then the function will return with NNG_EAGAIN. If this flag is not specified, then the function will block if such a condition exists.

NNG_FLAG_ALLOC
The *data* was allocated using nng_alloc(), or was obtained from a call to nng_recv() with the NNG_FLAG_ALLOC flag. If this function returns success, then the *data* is "owned" by the function, and it will assume responsibility for calling nng_free() when it is no longer needed. In the absence of this flag, the *data* is copied by the implementation before the function returns to the caller.

> The NNG_FLAG_ALLOC flag can be used to reduce data copies, thereby increasing performance.

> Regardless of the presence or absence of NNG_FLAG_NONBLOCK, there may be queues between the sender and the receiver. Furthermore, there is no guarantee that the message has actually been delivered. Finally, with some protocols, the semantic is implicitly NNG_FLAG_NONBLOCK, such as with *pub* sockets, which are best-effort delivery only.

> When using NNG_FLAG_ALLOC, it is important that the value of *size* match the actual allocated size of the data. Using an incorrect size results in unspecified behavior, which may include heap corruption, program crashes, or trans-dimensional mutation of the program's author.

RETURN VALUES

This function returns 0 on success, and non-zero otherwise.

ERRORS

NNG_EAGAIN	The operation would block, but NNG_FLAG_NONBLOCK was specified.
NNG_ECLOSED	The socket *s* is not open.
NNG_EINVAL	An invalid set of *flags* was specified.
NNG_EMSGSIZE	The value of *size* is too large.
NNG_ENOMEM	Insufficient memory is available.
NNG_ENOTSUP	The protocol for socket *s* does not support sending.
NNG_ESTATE	The socket *s* cannot send data in this state.
NNG_ETIMEDOUT	The operation timed out.

SEE ALSO

nng_alloc(3), nng_free(3), nng_recv(3), nng_sendmsg(3), nng_strerror(3), nng_socket(5), nng(7)

NAME

nng_send_aio - send message asynchronously

SYNOPSIS

```
#include <nng/nng.h>

void nng_send_aio(nng_socket s, nng_aio *aio);
```

DESCRIPTION

The nng_send_aio() sends a message using the socket *s* asynchronously.

The message to send must have previously been set on the *aio* using the nng_aio_set_msg() function. The function assumes "ownership" of the message.

If the message was successfully queued for delivery to the socket, then the *aio* will be completed, and nng_aio_result() will return zero. In this case the socket will dispose of the message when it is finished with it.

> **ℹ** The operation will be "completed", and the callback associated with the *aio* executed, as soon as the socket accepts the message for sending. This does *not* indicate that the message was actually delivered, as it may still be buffered in the sending socket, buffered in the receiving socket, or in flight over physical media.

If the operation fails for any reason (including cancellation or timeout), then the *aio* callback will be executed and nng_aio_result() will return a non-zero error status. In this case, the callback has a responsibility to retrieve the message from the *aio* with nng_aio_get_msg() and dispose of it appropriately. (This may include retrying the send operation on the same or a different socket, or deallocating the message with nng_msg_free().)

> **ℹ** The semantics of what sending a message means varies from protocol to protocol, so examination of the protocol documentation is encouraged. (For example, with a *pub* socket the data is broadcast, so that any peers who have a suitable subscription will be able to receive it using nng_recv() or a similar function.) Furthermore, some protocols may not support sending (such as *sub*) or may require other conditions. (For example, *rep* sockets cannot normally send data, which are responses to requests, until they have first received a request.)

RETURN VALUES

None. (The operation completes asynchronously.)

ERRORS

NNG_ECANCELED	The operation was aborted.
NNG_ECLOSED	The socket *s* is not open.
NNG_EMSGSIZE	The message is too large.

NNG_ENOMEM	Insufficient memory is available.
NNG_ENOTSUP	The protocol for socket *s* does not support sending.
NNG_ESTATE	The socket *s* cannot send data in this state.
NNG_ETIMEDOUT	The send timeout expired.

SEE ALSO

nng_aio_get_msg(3), nng_aio_set_msg(3), nng_msg_alloc(3), nng_strerror(3), nng_aio(5), nng_msg(5), nng_socket(5), nng(7)

NAME

nng_sendmsg - send message

SYNOPSIS

```
#include <nng/nng.h>

int nng_sendmsg(nng_socket s, nng_msg *msg, int flags);
```

DESCRIPTION

The nng_sendmsg() sends message *msg* using the socket *s*.

If the function returns zero, indicating it has accepted the message for delivery, then the *msg* is "owned" by the socket *s*, and the caller must not make any further use of it. The socket will free the message when it is finished.

If the function returns non-zero, then it is the caller's responsibility to dispose of the *msg*, which may include freeing it, sending it to another socket, or simply trying again later.

> Using this function gives access to the message structure, and may offer more functionality than the simpler nng_send() function.

> The semantics of what sending a message means vary from protocol to protocol, so examination of the protocol documentation is encouraged. (For example, with a *pub* socket the data is broadcast, so that any peers who have a suitable subscription will be able to receive it using nng_recv() or a similar function.) Furthermore, some protocols may not support sending (such as *sub*) or may require other conditions. (For example, *rep* sockets cannot normally send data, which are responses to requests, until they have first received a request.)

The *flags* may contain the following value:

NNG_FLAG_NONBLOCK
The function returns immediately, regardless of whether the socket is able to accept the data or not. If the socket is unable to accept the data (such as if backpressure exists because the peers are consuming messages too slowly, or no peer is present), then the function will return with NNG_EAGAIN. If this flag is not specified, then the function will block if such a condition exists.

> Regardless of the presence or absence of NNG_FLAG_NONBLOCK, there may be queues between the sender and the receiver. Furthermore, there is no guarantee that the message has actually been delivered. Finally, with some protocols, the semantic is implicitly NNG_FLAG_NONBLOCK, such as with *pub* sockets, which are best-effort delivery only.

RETURN VALUES

This function returns 0 on success, and non-zero otherwise.

ERRORS

NNG_EAGAIN	The operation would block, but NNG_FLAG_NONBLOCK was specified.
NNG_ECLOSED	The socket *s* is not open.
NNG_EINVAL	An invalid set of *flags* was specified.
NNG_EMSGSIZE	The value of *size* is too large.
NNG_ENOMEM	Insufficient memory is available.
NNG_ENOTSUP	The protocol for socket *s* does not support sending.
NNG_ESTATE	The socket *s* cannot send data in this state.
NNG_ETIMEDOUT	The operation timed out.

SEE ALSO

nng_msg_alloc(3), nng_recvmsg(3), nng_send(3), nng_strerror(3), nng_msg(5), nng_socket(5), nng(7)

NAME

nng_setopt - set socket option

SYNOPSIS

```
#include <nng/nng.h>

int nng_setopt(nng_socket s, const char *opt, const void *val, size_t valsz);

int nng_setopt_bool(nng_socket s, const char *opt, int bval);

int nng_setopt_int(nng_socket s, const char *opt, int ival);

int nng_setopt_ms(nng_socket s, const char *opt, nng_duration dur);

int nng_setopt_ptr(nng_socket s, const char *opt, void *ptr);

int nng_setopt_size(nng_socket s, const char *opt, size_t z);

int nng_setopt_string(nng_socket s, const char *opt, const char *str);

int nng_setopt_uint64(nng_socket s, const char *opt, uint64_t u64);
```

DESCRIPTION

The nng_setopt() functions are used to configure options for the socket *s*. The actual options that may be configured in this way vary, and are specified by *opt*. A number of them are documented in nng_options(5).

Additionally some transport-specific and protocol-specific options are documented with the transports and protocols themselves.

Forms

The details of the type, size, and semantics of the option will depend on the actual option, and will be documented with the option itself.

nng_setopt()
   This function is untyped, and can be used to configure any arbitrary data. The *val* pointer addresses the data to copy, and *valsz* is the size of the objected located at *val*.

   💡   It may be easier to use one of the typed forms of this function.

nng_setopt_bool()
   This function is for options which take a Boolean (bool). The *bval* is passed to the option.

nng_setopt_int()
   This function is for options which take an integer (int). The *ival* is passed to the option.

`nng_setopt_ms()`

This function is used to configure time durations (such as timeouts) using type `nng_duration`. The duration *dur* is an integer number of milliseconds.

`nng_setopt_ptr()`

This function is used to pass a pointer, *ptr*, to structured data. The data referenced by *ptr* is generally managed by other functions. For example, TLS configuration objects created with (`nng_tls_config_alloc()`) can be passed this way.

> ℹ This form is somewhat special in that the object is generally not copied, but instead the **pointer** to the object is copied.

`nng_setopt_size()`

This function is used to configure a size, *z*, typically for buffer sizes, message maximum sizes, and similar options.

`nng_setopt_string()`

This function is used to pass configure a string, *str*. Strings passed this way must be legal UTF-8 or ASCII strings, terminated with a NUL (\0) byte. (Other constraints may apply as well, see the documentation for each option for details.)

`nng_setopt_uint64()`

This function is used to configure a 64-bit unsigned value, *u64*. This is typically used for options related to identifiers, network numbers, and similar.

RETURN VALUES

These functions return 0 on success, and non-zero otherwise.

ERRORS

NNG_ECLOSED	Parameter *s* does not refer to an open socket.
NNG_EINVAL	The value being passed is invalid.
NNG_ENOTSUP	The option *opt* is not supported.
NNG_EREADONLY	The option *opt* is read-only.
NNG_ESTATE	The socket is in an inappropriate state for setting this option.

SEE ALSO

nng_getopt(3), nng_dialer_setopt(3), nng_listener_setopt(3), nng_strerror(3), nng_options(5), nng_socket(5), nng(7)

NAME

nng_sleep_aio - sleep asynchronously

SYNOPSIS

```
#include <nng/nng.h>

void nng_sleep_aio(nng_duration msec, nng_aio *aio);
```

DESCRIPTION

The `nng_sleep_aio()` function performs an asynchronous "sleep", causing the callback for *aio* to be executed after *msec* milliseconds. If the sleep finishes completely, the result will always be zero.

> **ⓘ** If a timeout is set on *aio* using `nng_aio_set_timeout()`, and it is shorter than *msec*, then the sleep will wake up early, with a result code of `NNG_ETIMEDOUT`.

RETURN VALUES

None.

ERRORS

None.

SEE ALSO

nng_aio_abort(3), nng_aio_alloc(3), nng_aio_set_timeout(3), nng_strerror(3), nng_aio(5), nng_duration(5), nng(7)

NAME

nng_socket_id - return numeric socket identifier

SYNOPSIS

```
#include <nng/nng.h>

int nng_socket_id(nng_socket s);
```

DESCRIPTION

The nng_socket_id() function returns a positive identifier for the socket *s*, if it is valid. Otherwise it returns -1.

> **ⓘ** A socket is considered valid if it was ever opened with a protocol constructor, such as the nng_req0_open() function. Sockets that are allocated on the stack or statically should be initialized with the macro NNG_SOCKET_INITIALIZER to ensure that they cannot be confused with a valid socket before they are opened.

RETURN VALUES

This function returns the positive value for the socket identifier, or -1 if the socket is invalid.

ERRORS

None.

SEE ALSO

nng_socket(5), nng(7)

NAME

nng_stat_child - get child statistic

SYNOPSIS

```
#include <nng/nng.h>

typedef struct nng_stat nng_stat;

nng_stat *nng_stat_child(nng_stat *parent);
```

DESCRIPTION

The nng_stat_child() function returns the first child statistic of the statistic *parent*. If no children are present, then NULL is returned.

> 💡 Only statistics with type (see nng_stat_type()) of NNG_STAT_SCOPE will have children.

RETURN VALUES

The first child statistic of *parent*, or NULL if *parent* has no children.

ERRORS

None.

SEE ALSO

libnng(3), nng_stat_next(3), nng_stats_get(3), nng_stat(5), nng(7)

NAME

nng_stat_desc - get statistic description

SYNOPSIS

```
#include <nng/nng.h>

typedef struct nng_stat nng_stat;

const char *nng_stat_desc(nng_stat *stat);
```

DESCRIPTION

The nng_stat_desc() function returns a brief, human-readable description for the statistic *stat*.

💡   This description can be used for a tool-tip in user interfaces displaying these statistic values.

ℹ   At this time, only English descriptions are provided.

RETURN VALUES

The description of statistic *stat*.

ERRORS

None.

SEE ALSO

libnng(3), nng_stats_name(3), nng_stats_get(3), nng_stat(5), nng(7)

NAME

nng_stat_name - get statistic name

SYNOPSIS

```
#include <nng/nng.h>

typedef struct nng_stat nng_stat;

const char *nng_stat_name(nng_stat *stat);
```

DESCRIPTION

The nng_stat_name() function returns the name for the statistic *stat*.

ℹ   The global root statistic will have the empty string ("") as it's name.

RETURN VALUES

The name of statistic *stat*.

ERRORS

None.

SEE ALSO

libnng(3), nng_stats_get(3), nng_stat(5), nng(7)

NAME

nng_stat_next - get next statistic

SYNOPSIS

```
#include <nng/nng.h>

typedef struct nng_stat nng_stat;

nng_stat *nng_stat_next(nng_stat *stat);
```

DESCRIPTION

The nng_stat_next() function returns the next sibling statistic of the statistic *stat*. If no more siblings are present, then NULL is returned.

RETURN VALUES

The next sibling statistic of *stat*, or NULL if *stat* is the last sibling.

ERRORS

None.

SEE ALSO

libnng(3), nng_stat_child(3), nng_stats_get(3), nng_stat(5), nng(7)

NAME

nng_stat_string - get statistic string value

SYNOPSIS

```
#include <nng/nng.h>

typedef struct nng_stat nng_stat;

const char *nng_stat_string(nng_stat *stat);
```

DESCRIPTION

The nng_stat_string() function returns a string value for the statistic *stat*, which must be of type NNG_STAT_STRING (see nng_stat_type(3)).

If the statistic is not of type NNG_STAT_STRING, then NULL will be returned.

RETURN VALUES

The string value associated with *stat*, or NULL if the statistic is not a string type.

ERRORS

None.

SEE ALSO

libnng(3), nng_stats_get(3), nng_stats_type(3), nng_stats_value(3), nng_stat(5), nng(7)

NAME

nng_stat_timestamp - get statistic timestamp

SYNOPSIS

```
#include <nng/nng.h>

typedef struct nng_stat nng_stat;

uint64_t nng_stat_timestamp(nng_stat *stat);
```

DESCRIPTION

The `nng_stat_timestamp()` function returns the a timestamp, which is measured as a number of milliseconds since some arbitrary value in the past.

Even within the same snapshot, statistics might have different timestamp values, as the timestamp represents the time when that particular statistic was captured.

> 💡 These values are intended to facilitate calculation of rates, by comparing values from one snapshot with a subsequent one.

> 💡 The values used here have the same offset as the `nng_clock()` supplementation function. This can be useful when converting these values to local clock time.

RETURN VALUES

The timestamp when *stat* was captured, measured as a number of milliseconds since some time in the past.

ERRORS

None.

SEE ALSO

libnng(3), nng_stats_get(3), nng_stat_value(3), nng_clock(3supp), nng_stat(5), nng(7)

NAME

nng_stat_value - get statistic value

SYNOPSIS

```
#include <nng/nng.h>

typedef struct nng_stat nng_stat;

enum {
        NNG_STAT_SCOPE,
        NNG_STAT_LEVEL,
        NNG_STAT_COUNTER,
        NNG_STAT_STRING,
        NNG_STAT_BOOLEAN,
        NNG_STAT_ID
};

int nng_stat_type(nng_stat *stat);
```

DESCRIPTION

The nng_stat_type() function returns the type of the statistic *stat*.

The returned type will be one of the following values:

NNG_STAT_SCOPE
  This is a placeholder providing scope, and carries no value on its own. Instead it is a parent node with child statistics (see nng_stat_child().)

NNG_STAT_LEVEL
  This is a numeric statistic, but its value is a level, so rate calculations based on changes in this value should not be considered significant.

NNG_STAT_COUNTER
  This is a numeric statistic that represents an increasing count, typically of events, messages, or bytes. Frequently, it is interesting to consider changes in this statistic divided by time to obtain a rate. (For example, throughput might be calculated as changes in a byte counter divided by the interval over which the change occurred.)

NNG_STAT_STRING
  This is a string, and carries no numeric value. Instead the nng_stat_string(3) function should be used to obtain the value.

NNG_STAT_BOOLEAN
  This is a boolean value. The nng_stat_value() function will return zero to represent a false value, and one to represent a true value.

NNG_STAT_ID: The statistic is a numeric ID. These are generally immutable values that represent an identity that might be used with another interface.

For `NNG_STAT_COUNTER` and `NNG_STAT_LEVEL` statistics, the `nng_stat_unit()` function will provide more detail about the units measured by the static.

RETURN VALUES

The statistic type for *stat*.

ERRORS

None.

SEE ALSO

libnng(3), nng_stats_get(3), nng_stat_string(3), nng_stat_unit(3), nng_stat_value(3), nng_stat(5), nng(7)

NAME

nng_stat_value - get statistic value

SYNOPSIS

```
#include <nng/nng.h>

typedef struct nng_stat nng_stat;

enum {
        NNG_UNIT_NONE,
        NNG_UNIT_BYTES,
        NNG_UNIT_MESSAGES,
        NNG_UNIT_MILLIS,
        NNG_UNIT_EVENTS
};

int nng_stat_unit(nng_stat *stat);
```

DESCRIPTION

The nng_stat_unit() function returns the unit of quantity measured by the statistic *stat*.

The returned value will be one of the following values:

NNG_UNIT_NONE
There are no particular units measured. In some cases there may be units, but the type of the unit will be obvious from the name (see nng_stat_name()) of the statistic.

NNG_UNIT_BYTES
The statistic is a count of bytes.

NNG_UNIT_MESSAGES
The statistic is a count of messages. Typically, one message corresponds to a single nng_msg structure.

NNG_UNIT_MILLIS
The statistic is a count of milliseconds.

NNG_STAT_EVENTS
The statistic is a count of some other type of event.

For statistics that are neither NNG_STAT_COUNTER nor NNG_STAT_LEVEL type (see nng_stat_type()), the unit will generally be NNG_UNIT_NONE.

Normally rates can be calculated for NNG_STAT_COUNTER values for any of these units, but for NNG_UNIT_MILLIS rate calculations are generally meaningless.

RETURN VALUES

The units measured by *stat*.

ERRORS

None.

SEE ALSO

libnng(3), nng_stats_get(3), nng_stat_name(3), nng_stat_type(3), nng_stat_value(3), nng_msg(5), nng_stat(5), nng(7)

NAME

nng_stat_value - get statistic value

SYNOPSIS

```
#include <nng/nng.h>

typedef struct nng_stat nng_stat;

uint64_t nng_stat_string(nng_stat *stat);
```

DESCRIPTION

The nng_stat_value() function returns a numeric value for the statistic *stat*. If the statistic has a boolean value, then zero is returned for false, and one is returned for true. Otherwise, if the string is not of numeric type, then zero is returned. See nng_stat_type(3) for a description of statistic types.

RETURN VALUES

The numeric or boolean value associated with *stat*.

ERRORS

None.

SEE ALSO

libnng(3), nng_stats_get(3), nng_stat_type(3), nng_stat_unit(3), nng_stat(5), nng(7)

NAME

nng_stats_free - free statistics snapshot

SYNOPSIS

```
#include <nng/nng.h>

typedef nng_stat nng_stat;

void nng_stats_free(nng_stat *);
```

DESCRIPTION

The nng_stats_free() function deallocates a statistics snapshot previously collected with nng_stats_get(). After calling this, all values associated with the snapshot are invalidated.

⚠️   Only the top of the collected statistics tree can be freed using this function.

RETURN VALUES

None.

ERRORS

None.

SEE ALSO

nng_stats_get(3), nng_stat(5), nng(7)

NAME

nng_stats_get - get statistics snapshot

SYNOPSIS

```
#include <nng/nng.h>

typedef struct nng_stat nng_stat;

int nng_stats_get(nng_stat *statsp)
```

DESCRIPTION

The nng_stat_get() function attempts to obtain a snapshot of all the various diagnostic statistics that are present in the system.

> The process of collecting statistics is designed to have minimal impact on the system, but there is still some impact.

The statistics are organized as a tree, rooted with a parent statistic of type NNG_STAT_SCOPE that carries no value, and which has an empty name. This parent statistic is returned through the *statsp* pointer.

The nng_stat_child() and nng_stat_next() function can be used to iterate over the the tree.

When no longer needed, the statistics can be freed with the nng_stats_free() function, but that function must be called only with the root statistic that is returned through the *statsp* pointer.

> The values of individual statistics are guaranteed to be atomic, but due the way statistics are collected there can be discrepancies between them at certain times. For example, statistics counting bytes and messages received may not reflect the same number of messages, depending on when the snapshot is taken. This potential inconsistency arises as a result of optimizations to minimize the impact of statistics on actual operations.

> The names, values, and semantics of statistics provided may change from release to release. These are provided for informational and debugging use only, and applications should not rely on the presence, names, or meanings of any individual statistics.

RETURN VALUES

This function returns a pointer to the allocated memory on success, and NULL otherwise.

ERRORS

NNG_ENOMEM	Insufficient free memory to collect statistics.
NNG_ENOTSUP	Statistics are not supported (compile time option).

SEE ALSO

nng_stats_free(3), nng_stat_child(3), nng_stat_desc(3), nng_stat_name(3), nng_stat_next(3), nng_stat_string(3), nng_stat_type(3), nng_stat_timestamp(3), nng_stat_unit(3), nng_stat_value(3), nng_stat(5), nng(7)

NAME

nng_strdup - duplicate string

SYNOPSIS

```
#include <nng/nng.h>

char *nng_strdup(const char *src);
```

DESCRIPTION

The nng_strdup() duplicates the string *src* and returns it.

This is logically equivalent to using nng_alloc() to allocate a region of memory of strlen(s) + 1 bytes, and then using strcpy() to copy the string into the destination before returning it.

The returned string should be deallocated with nng_strfree(), or may be deallocated using the nng_free() using the length of the returned string plus one (for the NUL terminating byte).

> ⚠ Do not use the system free() or similar functions to deallocate the string, since those may use a different memory arena!

RETURN VALUES

This function returns the new string on success, and NULL on failure.

ERRORS

No errors are returned, but a NULL return value should be treated the same as NNG_ENOMEM.

SEE ALSO

nng_alloc(3), nng_free(3), nng(7)

NAME

nng_strerror - return an error description

SYNOPSIS

```
#include <nng/nng.h>

const char * nng_strerror(int err);
```

DESCRIPTION

The nng_strerror() returns the human-readable description of the given *nng* error in err.

🛈   The returned error message is provided in US English, but in the future locale-specific strings may
     be presented instead.

🛈   The specific strings associated with specific error messages are subject to change. Therefore
     applications must not depend on the message, but may use them verbatim when supplying
     information to end-users, such as in diagnostic messages or log entries.

RETURN VALUES

This function returns the human-readable error message, terminated by a NUL byte.

SEE ALSO

libnng(3), nng(7)

NAME

nng_free - free memory

SYNOPSIS

```
#include <nng/nng.h>

void nng_strfree(char *str);
```

DESCRIPTION

The nng_strfree() function deallocates the string *str*. This is equivalent to using nng_free() with the length of *str* plus one (for the NUL terminating byte) as the size.

> ⚠ This should only be used with strings that were allocated by nng_strdup() or nng_alloc(). In all cases, the allocation size of the string must be the same as strlen(*str*) + 1.

> ⚠ Consequently, if the a string created with nng_strdup() is modified to be shorter, then it is incorrect to call this function. (The nng_free() function can be used instead in that case, using the length of the original string plus one for the size.)

RETURN VALUES

None.

ERRORS

None.

SEE ALSO

nng_alloc(3), nng_free(3), nng_strdup(3), nng(7)

NAME

nng_sub_open - create sub socket

SYNOPSIS

```
#include <nng/nng.h>
#include <nng/protocol/pubsub0/sub.h>

int nng_sub0_open(nng_socket *s);

int nng_sub0_open_raw(nng_socket *s);
```

DESCRIPTION

The nng_sub0_open() function creates a *sub* version 0 socket and returns it at the location pointed to by *s*.

The nng_sub0_open() function creates a *sub* version 0 socket in raw mode and returns it at the location pointed to by *s*.

RETURN VALUES

These functions return 0 on success, and non-zero otherwise.

ERRORS

NNG_ENOMEM	Insufficient memory is available.
NNG_ENOTSUP	The protocol is not supported.

SEE ALSO

nng_socket(5), nng_pub(7), nng_sub(7), nng(7)

NAME

nng_surveyor_open - create surveyor socket

SYNOPSIS

```
#include <nng/nng.h>
#include <nng/protocol/survey0/survey.h>

int nng_surveyor0_open(nng_socket *s);

int nng_surveyor0_open_raw(nng_socket *s);
```

DESCRIPTION

The nng_surveyor0_open() function creates a *surveyor* version 0 socket and returns it at the location pointed to by *s*.

The nng_surveyor0_open_raw() function creates a *surveyor* version 0 socket in raw mode and returns it at the location pointed to by *s*.

RETURN VALUES

These functions return 0 on success, and non-zero otherwise.

ERRORS

NNG_ENOMEM	Insufficient memory is available.
NNG_ENOTSUP	The protocol is not supported.

SEE ALSO

nng_socket(5), nng_respondent(7), nng_surveyor(7), nng(7)

NAME

nng_tcp_register - register tcp transport

SYNOPSIS

```
#include <nng/transport/tcp/tcp.h>

int nng_tcp_register(void);
```

DESCRIPTION

The nng_tcp_register() function registers the *tcp* transport for use.

RETURN VALUES

This function returns 0 on success, and non-zero otherwise.

ERRORS

NNG_ENOMEM	Insufficient memory is available.
NNG_ENOTSUP	The transport is not supported.

SEE ALSO

nng_tcp(7), nng(7)

NAME

nng_tls_register - register tls transport

SYNOPSIS

```
#include <nng/transport/tls/tls.h>

int nng_tls_register(void);
```

DESCRIPTION

The nng_tls_register() function registers the *tls* transport for use.

RETURN VALUES

This function returns 0 on success, and non-zero otherwise.

ERRORS

NNG_ENOMEM	Insufficient memory is available.
NNG_ENOTSUP	The transport is not supported.

SEE ALSO

nng_tls(5), nng(7)

NAME

nng_url_clone - clone URL structure

SYNOPSIS

```
#include <nng/nng.h>

int nng_url_clone(nng_url **dup, nng_url *orig);
```

DESCRIPTION

The nng_url_clone() makes a clone of the original URL structure *orig*, and saves the result in the location pointed by *dup*. This clone includes fully duplicating each of the member fields.

RETURN VALUES

This function returns 0 on success, and non-zero otherwise.

ERRORS

NNG_ENOMEM   Insufficient free memory exists to duplicate a message.

SEE ALSO

nng_url_free(3), nng_url_parse(3), nng_strerror(3), nng(7)

NAME

nng_url_free - free a URL structure

SYNOPSIS

```
#include <nng/nng.h>

void nng_url_free(nng_url *url);
```

DESCRIPTION

The nng_url_free() function deallocates the *url* entirely, including any of its members.

RETURN VALUES

None.

ERRORS

None.

SEE ALSO

nng_url_clone(3), nng_url_parse(3), nng(7)

NAME

nng_url_parse - create URL structure from a string

SYNOPSIS

```
#include <nng/nng.h>

int nng_url_parse(nng_url **urlp, const char *str);
```

DESCRIPTION

The nng_url_parse() function parses the string *str* containing an RFC 3986 [https://tools.ietf.org/html/rfc3986] compliant URL, and creates a structure containing the results. A pointer to the resulting structure is stored in *urlp*.

The nng_url structure has at least the following members:

```
struct nng_url {
    char *u_scheme;    // Scheme, such as "http"; always lower case.
    char *u_rawurl;    // Unparsed URL, with minimal canonicalization.
    char *u_userinfo;  // Userinfo component, or NULL.
    char *u_host;      // Full host, including port if present.
    char *u_hostname;  // Hostname only (or address), or empty string.
    char *u_port;      // Port number, may be default or empty string.
    char *u_path;      // Path if present, empty string otherwise.
    char *u_query;     // Query info if present, NULL otherwise.
    char *u_fragment;  // Fragment if present, NULL otherwise.
    char *u_requri;    // Request-URI (path[?query][#fragment])
};
```

URL Canonicalization

The nng_url_parse() function also canonicalizes the results, as follows:

1. The URL is parsed into the various components.

2. The u_scheme, u_hostname, u_host, and u_port members are converted to lower case.

3. Percent-encoded values for unreserved characters [https://tools.ietf.org/html/rfc3986#section-2.3] converted to their unencoded forms.

4. Additionally URL percent-encoded values for characters in the path and with numeric values larger than 127 (i.e. not ASCII) are decoded.

5. The resulting u_path is checked for invalid UTF-8 sequences, consisting of surrogate pairs, illegal byte sequences, or overlong encodings. If this check fails, then the entire URL is considered invalid, and the function returns NNG_EINVAL.

6. Path segments consisting of . and .. are resolved as per RFC 3986 6.2.2.3 [https://tools.ietf.org/html/rfc3986#section-6.2.2.3].

7. Further, empty path segments are removed, meaning that duplicate slash (/) separators are

removed from the path.

8. If a port was not specified, but the scheme defines a default port, then u_port will be filled in with the value of the default port.

> Only the u_userinfo, u_query, and u_fragment members will ever be NULL. The other members will be filled in with either default values or the empty string if they cannot be determined from *str*.

RETURN VALUES

This function returns 0 on success, and non-zero otherwise.

ERRORS

NNG_ENOMEM	Insufficient free memory exists to allocate a message.
NNG_EINVAL	An invalid URL was supplied.

SEE ALSO

nng_url_clone(3), nng_url_free(3), nng_strerror(3), nng(7)

NAME

nng_version - report library version

SYNOPSIS

```
#include <nng/nng.h>

const char * nng_version(void);
```

DESCRIPTION

The nng_version() function returns a human readable version number for the *nng* library. This is intended for output in programs, and so forth.

Additionally, compile time version information is available via some predefined macros:

NNG_MAJOR_VERSION
    Major version number.

NNG_MINOR_VERSION
    Minor version number.

NNG_PATCH_VERSION
    Patch version number.

The *nng* library is developed and released using Semantic Versioning 2.0 [http://www.semver.org], and the version numbers reported refer to both the API and the library itself. (The ABI — application binary interface — between the library and the application is controlled in a similar, but different manner depending upon the link options and how the library is built.)

RETURN VALUES

C string (NUL-terminated) containing the library version number.

ERRORS

None.

SEE ALSO

libnng(3), nng(7)

NAME

nng_ws_register - register WebSocket transport

SYNOPSIS

```
#include <nng/transport/websocket/ws.h>

int nng_ws_register(void);
```

DESCRIPTION

The nng_ws_register() function registers the *ws* transport for use.

RETURN VALUES

This function returns 0 on success, and non-zero otherwise.

ERRORS

NNG_ENOMEM	Insufficient memory is available.
NNG_ENOTSUP	The transport is not supported.

SEE ALSO

nng_ws(7), nng(7)

NAME

nng_ws_register - register WebSocket secure transport

SYNOPSIS

```
#include <nng/transport/websocket/ws.h>

int nng_wss_register(void);
```

DESCRIPTION

The nng_wss_register() function registers the *wss* transport for use.

RETURN VALUES

This function returns 0 on success, and non-zero otherwise.

ERRORS

NNG_ENOMEM	Insufficient memory is available.
NNG_ENOTSUP	The transport is not supported.

SEE ALSO

nng_ws(7), nng(7)

NAME

nng_zt_register - register ZeroTier transport

SYNOPSIS

```
#include <nng/transport/zerotier/zerotier.h>

int nng_zt_register(void);
```

DESCRIPTION

The nng_zt_register() function registers the *zt* transport for use.

RETURN VALUES

This function returns 0 on success, and non-zero otherwise.

ERRORS

NNG_ENOMEM	Insufficient memory is available.
NNG_ENOTSUP	The transport is not supported.

SEE ALSO

nng_zerotier(7), nng(7)

Section 3compat

Compatible Library Functions

NAME

nn_allocmsg - allocate message (compatible API)

SYNOPSIS

```
#include <nanomsg/nn.h>

void *nn_allocmsg(size_t size, int type);
```

DESCRIPTION

The nn_allocmsg() allocates a message structure of size *size*, and is primarily used to support zero-copy send operations, making use of the NNG_MSG special size indicator. The value returned is a pointer to the start of the message payload buffer.

The value of *size* must be positive, and small enough to hold reasonable message data plus book-keeping information.

> ℹ️ This function is provided for API compatibility with legacy *libnanomsg*. Consider using the relevant modern API instead.

The value of *type* **must** be zero. (This argument was reserved to support different kinds of memory spaces for RDMA devices, but this was never developed in the legacy API.)

The returned message must be disposed of by either nn_freemsg() or nn_send() when the caller is finished with it.

RETURN VALUES

This function returns a pointer to message buffer space, or NULL on failure.

ERRORS

ENOMEM	Insufficient memory is available.
EINVAL	An invalid *size* or *type* was specified.
ETERM	The library is shutting down.

SEE ALSO

nn_errno(3compat), nn_freemsg(3compat), nn_reallocmsg(3compat), nn_send(3compat), nng_compat(3compat), nng(7)

NAME

nn_bind - accept connections from remote peers (compatible API)

SYNOPSIS

```
#include <nanomsg/nn.h>

int nn_bind(int sock, const char *url)
```

DESCRIPTION

The nn_bind() function arranges for the socket *sock* to accept connections at the address specified by *url*. An "endpoint identifier" for this socket's association with the *url* is returned to the caller on success. This ID can be used with nn_shutdown() to "unbind" the socket from the address at *url*.

> ℹ️ This function is provided for API compatibility with legacy *libnanomsg*. Consider using the relevant modern API instead.

> ℹ️ The bind operation is performed asynchronously, and may not have completed before this function returns control to the caller.

> ⚠️ Only transports supported by legacy *libnanomsg* may be used with this function. In particular, only the schemes tcp://, ipc://, inproc://, and ws:// are supported with this function. (Use the modern API to use other schemes.)

RETURN VALUES

This function returns a positive identifier on success, and -1 on error.

ERRORS

EADDRINUSE	The address specified by *url* is already in use.
EADDRNOTAVAIL	The address specified by *url* is not available.
EBADF	The socket *sock* is not open.
EINVAL	An invalid *url* was supplied.

SEE ALSO

nn_connect(3compat), nn_errno(3compat), nn_shutdown(3compat), nn_socket(3compat), nn_compat(3compat), nng(7)

NAME

nn_close - close socket (compatible API)

SYNOPSIS

```
#include <nanomsg/nn.h>

int nn_close(int sock);
```

DESCRIPTION

The nn_close() function closes the socket *sock*. Any operations that are currently in progress will be terminated, and will fail with error EBADF.

> ℹ️ This function is provided for API compatibility with legacy *libnanomsg*. Consider using the relevant modern API instead.

RETURN VALUES

This function returns zero on success, and -1 on failure.

ERRORS

EBADF	The socket is not open.
ETERM	The library is shutting down.

SEE ALSO

nn_errno(3compat), nn_socket(3compat), nng_compat(3compat), nng(7)

NAME

nn_cmsg - message control data (compatible API)

SYNOPSIS

#include <nanomsg/nn.h>

```
struct nn_cmsghdr {
    size_t cmsg_len;
    int    cmsg_level;
    int    cmsg_type;
};
```

DESCRIPTION

The nn_cmsghdr structure describes a block of control data that is associated with a message either sent by nn_sendmsg() or received by nn_recvmsg().

ℹ   This structure and supporting macros are provided for API compatibility with legacy *libnanomsg*. Consider using the relevant modern API instead.

Each header is followed by cmsg_len bytes of data, plus any padding required to align the structure.

The only defined ancillary data at this time is the protocol headers used by the protocols. This uses cmsg_level set to PROTO_SP and the cmsg_type set to SP_HDR. The actual data for this will vary from depending on the protocol used.

Convenience macros are provided to make working with these fields easier.

struct nn_cmsghdr *NN_CMSG_FIRSTHDR(struct nn_msghdr *hdr)
This macro returns the first struct nn_cmsghdr header in *hdr*.

struct nn_cmsghdr *NN_CMSG_NXTHDR(struct nn_msghdr *hdr, struct nn_cmsghdr *ch)
This macro returns a pointer to the next struct nn_cmsghdr in *hdr* after *ch*.

void *NN_CMSG_DATA(struct nn_cmsghdr *ch)
This macro returns a pointer to the header-specific data for *ch*.

size_t NN_CMSG_ALIGN(size_t len)
This macro returns the length specified by *len*, plus any padding required to provide the necessary alignment for another structure.

size_t NN_CMSG_SPACE(size_t len)
This macro returns the amount of space required for a header, with *len* bytes of following data, and any necessary padding.

size_t NN_CMSG_LEN(size_t len)
This macro evaluates to the length of the header (including alignment), and the associated data of length *len*, but without any trailing padding to align for another header.

SEE ALSO

nn_recvmsg(3compat), nn_sendmsg(3compat), nng_compat(3compat), nng(7)

NAME

nn_connect - connect to remote peer (compatible API)

SYNOPSIS

```
#include <nanomsg/nn.h>

int nn_connect(int sock, const char *url)
```

DESCRIPTION

The nn_connect() function arranges for the socket *sock* to initiate connection to a peer at the address specified by *url*. An "endpoint identifier" for this socket's association with the *url* is returned to the caller on success. This ID can be used with nn_shutdown() to "unbind" the socket from the address at *url*.

> This function is provided for API compatibility with legacy *libnanomsg*. Consider using the relevant modern API instead.

> The connect operation is performed asynchronously, and may not have completed before this function returns control to the caller.

> Only transports supported by legacy *libnanomsg* may be used with this function. In particular, only the schemes tcp://, ipc://, inproc://, and ws:// are supported with this function. (Use the modern API to use other schemes.)

RETURN VALUES

This function returns a positive identifier success, and -1 on error.

ERRORS

ECONNREFUSED   The connection attempt was refused.

EBADF   The socket *sock* is not open.

EINVAL   An invalid *url* was supplied.

SEE ALSO

nn_bind(3compat), nn_errno(3compat), nn_shutdown(3compat), nn_socket(3compat), nn_compat(3compat), nng(7)

NAME

nn_device - create forwarding device (compatible API)

SYNOPSIS

```
#include <nanomsg/nn.h>

int nn_device(int sock1, int sock2);
```

DESCRIPTION

The nn_device() function is used to create a forwarder, where messages received on one of the two sockets *sock1* and *sock2* are forwarded to the other.

ⓘ   This function is provided for API compatibility with legacy *libnanomsg*. Consider using the relevant modern API instead.

The two sockets must be compatible, and must be raw mode sockets. More detail about devices and how they can be used is available in the new style nng_device() documentation.

RETURN VALUES

This function blocks forever, and will return -1 only when one of the sockets is closed or an error occurs.

ERRORS

EBADF	One of the two sockets is invalid or not open, or has
EINVAL	The sockets are not compatible with each other, or not both raw.
ENOMEM	Insufficient memory is available.

SEE ALSO

nn_errno(3compat), nn_socket(3compat), nng_compat(3compat), nng(7)

NAME

nn_errno - return most recent error (compatible API)

SYNOPSIS

```
#include <nanomsg/nn.h>

int nn_errno(void);
```

DESCRIPTION

The nn_errno() function returns the error number corresponding to the most recent failed operation by the calling thread.

> ℹ️ This function is provided for API compatibility with legacy *libnanomsg*. Consider using the relevant modern API instead.

> ⚠️ The error numbers returned from this function may include errors caused by system functions, which overlap the usual errno variable, and this function simply returns the value of errno. However, the values returned may include numeric values that are not defined by the system, but are unique to *libnanomsg*, such as EFSM.

This library implements the following error numbers, in addition to any others that might be set for errno by the underlying system:

RETURN VALUES

This function returns the value of errno. If no operation has failed, then this will be zero.

ERRORS

EINTR	Operation interrupted.
ENOMEM	Insufficient memory.
EINVAL	Invalid argument.
EBUSY	Resource is busy.
ETIMEDOUT	Operation timed out.
ECONNREFUSED	Connection refused by peer.
EBADF	Invalid or closed socket.
EAGAIN	Operation would block.
ENOTSUP	Protocol or option not supported.
EADDRINUSE	Requested address is already in use.
EFSM	Protocol state incorrect.

EPROTO	Protocol error.
EHOSTUNREACH	Remote peer is unreachable.
EADDRNOTAVAIL	Requested address is not available.
EACCES	Permission denied.
EMSGSIZE	Message is too large.
ECONNABORTED	Connection attempt aborted.
ECONNRESET	Connection reset by peer.
EEXIST	Resource already exists.
EMFILE	Too many open files.
ENOSPC	Insufficient persistent storage.

SEE ALSO

nn_strerror(3compat), nng_compat(3compat), nng(7)

NAME

nn_freemsg - free message (compatible API)

SYNOPSIS

```
#include <nanomsg/nn.h>

int nn_freemsg(void *msg);
```

DESCRIPTION

The nn_freemsg() deallocates a message previously allocated with nn_allocmsg() or similar functions.

ℹ️   This function is provided for API compatibility with legacy *libnanomsg*. Consider using the relevant
      modern API instead.

RETURN VALUES

This function always returns 0.

ERRORS

None.

SEE ALSO

nn_allocmsg(3compat), nn_freemsg(3compat), nn_errno(3compat), nng_compat(3compat), nng(7)

NAME

nn_get_statistic - get statistic (stub)

SYNOPSIS

```
#include <nanomsg/nn.h>

uint64_t nn_get_statistic(int sock, int stat);
```

DESCRIPTION

The nn_get_statistic() function exists only as a stub, and always returns zero.

> ℹ️ This function is provided for API compatibility with legacy *libnanomsg*. Consider using the relevant modern API instead.

RETURN VALUES

Zero.

ERRORS

None.

SEE ALSO

nng_compat(3compat), nng(7)

NAME

nn_getsockopt - get socket option (compatible API)

SYNOPSIS

```
#include <nanomsg/nn.h>

int nn_getsockopt(int sock, int level, int option, void *val, size_t *szp);
```

DESCRIPTION

The nn_getsockopt() function gets a socket option on socket *sock*. The option retrieved is determined by the *level* and *option*.

ⓘ This function is provided for API compatibility with legacy *libnanomsg*. Consider using the relevant modern API instead.

The value pointed to by *szp* must be initialized to the size of the buffer pointed to by *val*. No more than this many bytes of the option will be copied into the destination buffer on success. On success, the value pointed to by *szp* will be updated with the actual size of the option.

♀ To determine the size to receive an option, first call this function with *val* set to NULL and the value addressed by *szp* initialized to zero.

The *level* determines whether the option is a generic socket option, or is transport-specific. The values possible for level are as follows:

NN_SOL_SOCKET	Generic socket option
NN_IPC	Transport specific option for IPC.
NN_TCP	Transport specific option for TCP.
NN_WS	Transport specific option for WebSocket.

The following generic socket options are possible (all are of type int and thus size 4, unless otherwise indicated.)

NN_SNDBUF
Send buffer size in bytes.

ⓘ In *nng* buffers are sized as a count of messages rather than bytes; accordingly this value is the *nng* queue depth multiplied by 1024 (representing an estimate that the average message size is 1kB). Applications that have unusual message sizes may wish to adjust the value used here accordingly.

NN_RCVBUF
Receive buffer size in bytes.

ⓘ The same caveats for NN_SNDBUF apply here as well.

NN_SNDTIMEO

Send time-out in milliseconds. Send operations will fail with ETIMEDOUT if no message can be received after this many milliseconds have transpired since the operation was started. A value of -1 means that no timeout is applied.

NN_RCVTIMEO

Receive time-out in milliseconds. Receive operations will fail with ETIMEDOUT if no message can be received after this many milliseconds have transpired since the operation was started. A value of -1 means that no timeout is applied.

NN_RCVMAXSIZE

Maximum receive size in bytes. The socket will discard messages larger than this on receive. The default, 1MB, is intended to prevent denial-of-service attacks. The value -1 removes any limit.

NN_RECONNECT_IVL

Reconnect interval in milliseconds. After an outgoing connection is closed or fails, the socket will automatically attempt to reconnect after this many milliseconds. This is the starting value for the time, and is used in the first reconnection attempt after a successful connection is made. The default is 100.

NN_RECONNECT_IVL_MAX

Maximum reconnect interval in milliseconds. Subsequent reconnection attempts after a failed attempt are made at exponentially increasing intervals (back-off), but the interval is capped by this value. If this value is smaller than NN_RECONNECT_IVL, then no exponential back-off is performed, and each reconnect interval will be determined solely by NN_RECONNECT_IVL. The default is zero.

NN_LINGER

This option is always zero and exists only for compatibility.

> **ⓘ** This option was unreliable in early releases of *libnanomsg*, and is unsupported in *nng* and recent *libnanomsg* releases. Applications needing assurance of message delivery should either include an explicit notification (automatic with the NN_REQ protocol) or allow sufficient time for the socket to drain before closing the socket or exiting.

NN_SNDPRIO

This option is not implemented at this time.

NN_RCVPRIO

This option is not implemented at this time.

NN_IPV4ONLY

This option is not implemented at this time.

NN_SOCKET_NAME

This option is a string, and represents the socket name. It can be changed to help with identifying different sockets with their different application-specific purposes.

NN_MAXTTL

Maximum "hops" through proxies and devices a message may go through. This value, if positive, provides some protection against forwarding loops in device chains.

> **ⓘ** Not all protocols offer this protection, so care should still be used in configuring device forwarding.

NN_DOMAIN

This option of type int represents either the value AF_SP or AF_SP_RAW, corresponding to the value that the socket was created with.

NN_PROTOCOL

This option option of type int contains the numeric protocol number that the socket is used with.

NN_RCVFD

This option returns a file descriptor suitable for use in with poll() or select() (or other system-specific polling functions). This descriptor will be readable when a message is available for receiving at the socket. This option is of type int on all systems except Windows, where it is of type SOCKET.

> ⓘ The file descriptor should not be read or written by the application, and is not the same as any underlying descriptor used for network sockets.

NN_SNDFD

This option returns a file descriptor suitable for use in with poll() or select() (or other system-specific polling functions). This descriptor will be readable when the socket is able to accept a message for sending. This option is of type int on all systems except Windows, where it is of type SOCKET.

> ⓘ The file descriptor should not be read or written by the application, and is not the same as any underlying descriptor used for network sockets. Furthermore, the file descriptor should only be polled for *readability*.

The following option is available for NN_REQ sockets using the NN_REQ level:

NN_REQ_RESEND_IVL

Request retry interval in milliseconds. If an NN_REQ socket does not receive a reply to a request within this period of time, the socket will automatically resend the request. The default value is 60000 (one minute).

The following option is available for NN_SURVEYOR sockets using the NN_SURVEYOR level:

NN_SURVEYOR_DEADLINE

Survey deadline in milliseconds for NN_SURVEYOR sockets. After sending a survey message, the socket will only accept responses from respondents for this long. Any responses arriving after this expires are silently discarded.

In addition, the following transport specific options are offered:

NN_IPC_SEC_ATTR

This NN_IPC option is not supported at this time.

NN_IPC_OUTBUFSZ

This NN_IPC option is not supported at this time.

NN_IPC_INBUFSZE

This NN_IPC option is not supported at this time.

NN_TCP_NODELAY

This NN_TCP option is not supported at this time.

NN_WS_MSG_TYPE
> This NN_WS option is not supported, as *nng* only supports binary messages in this implementation.

RETURN VALUES

This function returns zero on success, and -1 on failure.

ERRORS

EBADF	The socket *sock* is not an open socket.
ENOMEM	Insufficient memory is available.
ENOPROTOOPT	The level and/or option is invalid.
EINVAL	The option, or the value passed, is invalid.
ETERM	The library is shutting down.
EACCES	The option cannot be changed.

SEE ALSO

nng_socket(5), nn_close(3compat), nn_errno(3compat), nn_getsockopt(3compat), nng_compat(3compat), nng(7)

NAME

nn_poll - poll sockets (compatible API)

SYNOPSIS

```
#include <nanomsg/nn.h>

#define NN_POLLIN  1
#define NN_POLLOUT 2

struct nn_pollfd {
    int      fd;
    uint16_t events;
    uint16_t revents;
};

int nn_poll(struct nn_pollfd *pfds, int npfd, int timeout);
```

DESCRIPTION

The nn_poll() function polls a group of sockets for readiness to send or receive.

ℹ️   This function is provided for API compatibility with legacy *libnanomsg*. Consider using the relevant modern API instead.

The array of *nfds* sockets to poll for are passed into *pfds*. Each member of this array is initialized with the fd field set to the socket, and the events field set to a mask that can contain either or both of the flags NN_POLLIN and NN_POLLOUT.

The flag NN_POLLIN indicates that a socket is ready for receiving without blocking (a message is available on the socket), and the flag NN_POLLOUT indicates that a socket is ready for sending without blocking.

Upon success, the function returns the number of updates the revents field of each member of the *pfds* array, setting it to indicate whether the requested status is true or not.

ℹ️   The revents field will only have a flag set if the corresponding flag was also set in the events field.

If the *timeout* field is positive, then this function will wait for up the that many milliseconds. If none of the requested events occurs before that timeout occurs, then the function will return -1 and set the error to ETIMEDOUT.

If the *timeout* is zero, then this function will return immediately, after updating the current status of the sockets.

If the *timeout* is -1, then the function waits forever, or until one of the requested events occurs.

⚠️   This function is only suitable for use with sockets obtained with the nn_socket() function, and is not compatible with file descriptors obtained via any other means. This includes file descriptors obtained using the NN_SNDFD or NN_RCVFD options with nn_getsockopt()

This function is significantly less efficient than other polling or asynchronous I/O mechanisms, and is provided for API compatibility only. It's use is discouraged.

This function is **not** supported on systems other than POSIX derived platforms and Windows.

RETURN VALUES

This function returns the number of sockets with events on success, or -1 on error.

ERRORS

ENOMEM	Insufficient memory available.
EBADF	One of the sockets is not open.
ETIMEDOUT	Operation timed out.
ENOTSUP	This function is not supported on this platform.

SEE ALSO

nn_errno(3compat), nn_recv(3compat), nn_send(3compat), nn_socket(3compat), nn_compat(3compat), nng(7)

NAME

nn_reallocmsg - reallocate message (compatible API)

SYNOPSIS

```
#include <nanomsg/nn.h>

void *nn_reallocmsg(void *old, size_t size);
```

DESCRIPTION

The nn_reallocmsg() reallocates the message *old*, making it of size *size*.

> **ⓘ** This function is provided for API compatibility with legacy *libnanomsg*. Consider using the relevant modern API instead.

On success, the contents of *old* are copied into the new message (truncating if appropriate), then *old* is deallocated, and a pointer to the new message payload is returned.

On failure, the *old* message is unchanged, and the value NULL is returned to the caller.

RETURN VALUES

This function returns a pointer to message buffer space, or NULL on failure.

ERRORS

ENOMEM	Insufficient memory is available.
EINVAL	An invalid *size* was specified.
ETERM	The library is shutting down.

SEE ALSO

nn_allocmsg(3compat), nn_freemsg(3compat), nn_errno(3compat), nng_compat(3compat), nng(7)

NAME

nn_send - receive data (compatible API)

SYNOPSIS

```
#include <nanomsg/nn.h>

int nn_recv(int sock, void *data, size_t size, int flags)
```

DESCRIPTION

The nn_recv() function receives a message from the socket *sock*. The message body must fit within *size* bytes, and will be stored at the location specified by *data*, unless *size* is the special value NN_MSG, indicating a zero-copy operation.

> ℹ This function is provided for API compatibility with legacy *libnanomsg*. Consider using the relevant modern API instead.

If *size* has the special value NN_MSG, then a zero-copy operation is performed. In this case, instead of copying the message data into the address specified by *data*, a new message large enough to hold the message data will be allocated (as if by the function nn_allocmsg()), and the message payload will be stored accordingly. In this case, the value stored at *data* will not be message data, but a pointer to the message itself. In this case, on success, the caller shall take responsibility for the final disposition of the message (such as by sending it to another peer using nn_send()) or nn_freemsg().

The *flags* field may contain the special flag NN_DONTWAIT. In this case, if the no message is available for immediate receipt, the operation shall not block, but instead will fail with the error EAGAIN.

RETURN VALUES

This function returns the number of bytes sent on success, and -1 on error.

ERRORS

EAGAIN	The operation would block.
EBADF	The socket *sock* is not open.
EFSM	The socket cannot receive in this state.
ENOTSUP	This protocol cannot receive.
ETIMEDOUT	Operation timed out.

SEE ALSO

nn_errno(3compat), nn_recvmsg(3compat), nn_send(3compat), nn_socket(3compat), nn_compat(3compat), nng(7)

NAME

nn_recvmsg - receive message (compatible API)

SYNOPSIS

```
#include <nanomsg/nn.h>

int nn_recvmsg(int sock, struct nn_msghdr *hdr, int flags);
```

DESCRIPTION

The nn_recvmsg() function receives a message into the header described by *hdr* using the socket *sock*.

ℹ This function is provided for API compatibility with legacy *libnanomsg*. Consider using the relevant modern API instead.

The *flags* field may contain the special flag NN_DONTWAIT. In this case, if no message is ready for receiving on *sock*, the operation shall not block, but instead will fail with the error EAGAIN.

The *hdr* points to a structure of type struct nn_msghdr, which has the following definition:

```
struct nn_iovec {
    void * iov_base;
    size_t iov_len;
};

struct nn_msghdr {
    struct nn_iovec *msg_iov;
    int             msg_iovlen;
    void *          msg_control;
    size_t          msg_controllen;
};
```

The msg_iov is an array of scatter items, permitting the message to be spread into different memory blocks. There are msg_iovlen elements in this array, each of which has the base address (iov_base) and length (iov_len) indicated.

The last member of this array may have the iov_len field set to NN_MSG, in which case the function shall allocate a message buffer, and store the pointer to it at the address indicated by iov_base. This can help save an extra copy operation. The buffer should be deallocated by nn_freemsg() or similar when it is no longer needed.

The values of msg_control and msg_controllen describe a buffer of ancillary data associated with the message. This is currently only useful to obtain the message headers used with raw mode sockets. In all other circumstances these fields should be zero. Details about this structure are covered in nn_cmsg(3compat).

RETURN VALUES

This function returns the number of bytes received on success, and -1 on error.

ERRORS

EAGAIN	The operation would block.
EBADF	The socket *sock* is not open.
EFSM	The socket cannot receive in this state.
EINVAL	The *hdr* is invalid.
ENOTSUP	This protocol cannot receive.
ETIMEDOUT	Operation timed out.

SEE ALSO

nn_cmsg(3compat), nn_errno(3compat), nn_recv(3compat), nn_send(3compat), nn_socket(3compat), nn_compat(3compat), nng(7)

NAME

nn_send - send data (compatible API)

SYNOPSIS

```
#include <nanomsg/nn.h>

int nn_send(int sock, const void *data, size_t size, int flags)
```

DESCRIPTION

The nn_send() function creates a message containing *data* (of size *size*), and sends using the socket *sock*.

ⓘ   This function is provided for API compatibility with legacy *libnanomsg*. Consider using the relevant modern API instead.

If *size* has the special value NN_MSG, then a zero-copy operation is performed. In this case, *data* points not to the message content itself, but instead is a pointer to the pointer, an extra level of pointer indirection. The message must have been previously allocated by nn_allocmsg() or nn_recvmsg(), using the same NN_MSG size. In this case, the "ownership" of the message shall remain with the caller, unless the function returns 0, indicating that the function has taken responsibility for delivering or disposing of the message.

The *flags* field may contain the special flag NN_DONTWAIT. In this case, if the socket is unable to accept more data for sending, the operation shall not block, but instead will fail with the error EAGAIN.

ⓘ   The send operation is performed asynchronously, and may not have completed before this function returns control to the caller.

RETURN VALUES

This function returns the number of bytes sent on success, and -1 on error.

ERRORS

EAGAIN	The operation would block.
EBADF	The socket *sock* is not open.
EFSM	The socket cannot send in this state.
ENOTSUP	This protocol cannot send.
ETIMEDOUT	Operation timed out.

SEE ALSO

nn_errno(3compat), nn_recv(3compat), nn_sendmsg(3compat), nn_socket(3compat), nn_compat(3compat), nng(7)

NAME

nn_sendmsg - send message (compatible API)

SYNOPSIS

```
#include <nanomsg/nn.h>

int nn_sendmsg(int sock, const struct nn_msghdr *hdr, int flags);
```

DESCRIPTION

The nn_sendmsg() function sends the message described by *hdr* using the socket *sock*.

ⓘ   This function is provided for API compatibility with legacy *libnanomsg*. Consider using the relevant modern API instead.

The *flags* field may contain the special flag NN_DONTWAIT. In this case, if the socket is unable to accept more data for sending, the operation shall not block, but instead will fail with the error EAGAIN.

The *hdr* points to a structure of type struct nn_msghdr, which has the following definition:

```
struct nn_iovec {
    void * iov_base;
    size_t iov_len;
};

struct nn_msghdr {
    struct nn_iovec *msg_iov;
    int             msg_iovlen;
    void *          msg_control;
    size_t          msg_controllen;
};
```

The msg_iov is an array of gather items, permitting the message to be spread into different memory blocks. There are msg_iovlen elements in this array, each of which has the base address (iov_base) and length (iov_len) indicated.

For buffers allocated for zero copy (such as by nn_allocmsg()), the value of iov_base should be the address of the pointer to the buffer, rather than the address of the buffer itself. In this case, the value of iov_len should be NN_MSG, as the length is inferred from the allocated message. If the msg_iovlen field is NN_MSG, then this function will free the associated buffer after it is done with it, if it returns successfully. (If the function returns with an error, then the caller retains ownership of the associated buffer and may retry the operation or free the buffer at its choice.)

The values of msg_control and msg_controllen describe a buffer of ancillary data to send the message. This is currently only useful to provide the message headers used with raw mode sockets. In all other circumstances these fields should be zero. Details about this structure are covered in nn_cmsg(3compat).

ℹ The send operation is performed asynchronously, and may not have completed before this function returns control to the caller.

RETURN VALUES

This function returns the number of bytes sent on success, and -1 on error.

ERRORS

EAGAIN	The operation would block.
EBADF	The socket *sock* is not open.
EFSM	The socket cannot send in this state.
EINVAL	The *hdr* is invalid.
ENOTSUP	This protocol cannot send.
ETIMEDOUT	Operation timed out.

SEE ALSO

nn_cmsg(3compat), nn_errno(3compat), nn_recv(3compat), nn_send(3compat), nn_socket(3compat), nn_compat(3compat), nng(7)

NAME

nn_setsockopt - set socket option (compatible API)

SYNOPSIS

```
#include <nanomsg/nn.h>

int nn_setsockopt(int sock, int level, int option, const void *val, size_t sz);
```

DESCRIPTION

The nn_setsockopt() function sets a socket option on socket *sock*, affecting the behavior of the socket. The option set is determined by the *level* and *option*. The value of the option is set by *val*, and *sz*, which are pointers to the actual value and the size of the value, respectively.

> ℹ This function is provided for API compatibility with legacy *libnanomsg*. Consider using the relevant modern API instead.

The *level* determines whether the option is a generic socket option, or is transport-specific. The values possible for level are as follows:

NN_SOL_SOCKET	Generic socket option
NN_IPC	Transport specific option for IPC.
NN_TCP	Transport specific option for TCP.
NN_WS	Transport specific option for WebSocket.

The following generic socket options are possible (all are of type int and thus size 4, unless otherwise indicated.)

NN_SNDBUF
   Send buffer size in bytes.

> ℹ In *nng* buffers are sized as a count of messages rather than bytes, and so an attempt to estimate a conversion based upon a predetermined message size of 1kB is made. The value supplied is rounded up to the nearest value divisible by 1024, and then divided by 1024 to convert to a message count. Applications that have unusual message sizes may wish to adjust the value used here accordingly.

NN_RCVBUF
   Receive buffer size in bytes.

> ℹ The same caveats for NN_SNDBUF apply here as well.

NN_SNDTIMEO
   Send time-out in milliseconds. Send operations will fail with ETIMEDOUT if no message can be received after this many milliseconds have transpired since the operation was started. A value of -1 means that no timeout is applied.

NN_RCVTIMEO

Receive time-out in milliseconds. Receive operations will fail with ETIMEDOUT if no message can be received after this many milliseconds have transpired since the operation was started. A value of -1 means that no timeout is applied.

NN_RCVMAXSIZE

Maximum receive size in bytes. The socket will discard messages larger than this on receive. The default, 1MB, is intended to prevent denial-of-service attacks. The value -1 removes any limit.

NN_RECONNECT_IVL

Reconnect interval in milliseconds. After an outgoing connection is closed or fails, the socket will automatically attempt to reconnect after this many milliseconds. This is the starting value for the time, and is used in the first reconnection attempt after a successful connection is made. The default is 100.

NN_RECONNECT_IVL_MAX

Maximum reconnect interval in milliseconds. Subsequent reconnection attempts after a failed attempt are made at exponentially increasing intervals (back-off), but the interval is capped by this value. If this value is smaller than NN_RECONNECT_IVL, then no exponential back-off is performed, and each reconnect interval will be determined solely by NN_RECONNECT_IVL. The default is zero.

NN_LINGER

This option is ignored, and exists only for compatibility.

> This option was unreliable in early releases of *libnanomsg*, and is unsupported in *nng* and recent *libnanomsg* releases. Applications needing assurance of message delivery should either include an explicit notification (automatic with the NN_REQ protocol) or allow sufficient time for the socket to drain before closing the socket or exiting.

NN_SNDPRIO

This option is not implemented at this time.

NN_RCVPRIO

This option is not implemented at this time.

NN_IPV4ONLY

This option is not implemented at this time.

NN_SOCKET_NAME

This option is a string, and represents the socket name. It can be changed to help with identifying different sockets with their different application-specific purposes.

NN_MAXTTL

Maximum "hops" through proxies and devices a message may go through. This value, if positive, provides some protection against forwarding loops in device chains.

> Not all protocols offer this protection, so care should still be used in configuring device forwarding.

The following option is available for NN_REQ sockets using the NN_REQ level:

NN_REQ_RESEND_IVL

Request retry interval in milliseconds. If an NN_REQ socket does not receive a reply to a request within this period of time, the socket will automatically resend the request. The default value is 60000 (one minute).

The following options are available for NN_SUB sockets using the NN_SUB level:

NN_SUB_SUBSCRIBE
Subscription topic, for NN_SUB sockets. This sets a subscription topic. When a message from a publisher arrives, it is compared against all subscriptions. If the first *sz* bytes of the message are not identical to *val*, then the message is silently discarded.

💡   To receive all messages, subscribe to an empty topic (*sz* equal to zero).

NN_SUB_UNSUBSCRIBE
Removes a subscription topic that was earlier established.

The following option is available for NN_SURVEYOR sockets using the NN_SURVEYOR level:

NN_SURVEYOR_DEADLINE
Survey deadline in milliseconds for NN_SURVEYOR sockets. After sending a survey message, the socket will only accept responses from respondents for this long. Any responses arriving after this expires are silently discarded.

In addition, the following transport specific options are offered:

NN_IPC_SEC_ATTR
This NN_IPC option is not supported at this time.

NN_IPC_OUTBUFSZ
This NN_IPC option is not supported at this time.

NN_IPC_INBUFSZE
This NN_IPC option is not supported at this time.

NN_TCP_NODELAY
This NN_TCP option is not supported at this time.

NN_WS_MSG_TYPE
This NN_WS option is not supported, as *nng* only supports binary messages in this implementation.

RETURN VALUES

This function returns zero on success, and -1 on failure.

ERRORS

EBADF	The socket *sock* is not an open socket.
ENOMEM	Insufficient memory is available.
ENOPROTOOPT	The level and/or option is invalid.
EINVAL	The option, or the value passed, is invalid.
ETERM	The library is shutting down.

EACCES   The option cannot be changed.

SEE ALSO

nng_socket(5), nn_close(3compat), nn_errno(3compat), nn_getsockopt(3compat),
nng_compat(3compat), nng(7)

NAME

nn_shutdown - shut down endpoint (compatible API)

SYNOPSIS

```
#include <nanomsg/nn.h>

int nn_shutdown(int sock, int ep)
```

DESCRIPTION

The nn_shutdown() shuts down the "endpoint" *ep* on the socket *sock*. This will stop the socket from either accepting new connections, or establishing old ones. Additionally, any established connections associated with *ep* will be closed.

ⓘ   This function is provided for API compatibility with legacy *libnanomsg*. Consider using the relevant modern API instead.

RETURN VALUES

This function returns zero on success, and -1 on error.

ERRORS

EBADF	The socket *sock* is not open.
EINVAL	An invalid *ep* was supplied.

SEE ALSO

nn_bind(3compat), nn_connect(3compat), nn_errno(3compat), nn_socket(3compat), nn_compat(3compat), nng(7)

NAME

nn_socket - create socket (compatible API)

SYNOPSIS

```
#include <nanomsg/nn.h>

int nn_socket(int af, int proto);
```

DESCRIPTION

The nn_socket() function creates socket using the address family *af* and protocol *proto* and returns it.

> **ℹ** This function is provided for API compatibility with legacy *libnanomsg*. Consider using the relevant modern API instead.

> **⚠** Mixing the compatibility API and the modern API is not supported on a given socket.

> **ℹ** Some protocols, transports, and features are only available in the modern API.

The address family *af* can be one of two values:

AF_SP	Normal socket.
AF_SP_RAW	"Raw mode" socket.

The protocol indicates the protocol to be used when creating the socket. The following protocols are defined:

NN_PAIR	Pair protocol.
NN_PUB	Publisher protocol.
NN_SUB	Subscriber protocol.
NN_REQ	Requestor protocol.
NN_REP	Replier protocol.
NN_PUSH	Push protocol.
NN_PULL	Pull protocol.
NN_SURVEYOR	Surveyor protocol.
NN_RESPONDENT	Respondent protocol.
NN_BUS	Bus protocol.

RETURN VALUES

This function returns a valid socket number on success, and -1 on failure.

ERRORS

ENOMEM	Insufficient memory is available.
ENOTSUP	The protocol is not supported.
ETERM	The library is shutting down.

SEE ALSO

nng_socket(5), nn_close(3compat), nn_errno(3compat), nng_compat(3compat), nng(7)

NAME

nn_strerror - return message for error (compatible API)

SYNOPSIS

```
#include <nanomsg/nn.h>

const char *nn_strerror(int err);
```

DESCRIPTION

The nn_strerror() function returns a human readable message corresponding to the given error number *err*.

> ℹ️ This function is provided for API compatibility with legacy *libnanomsg*. Consider using the relevant modern API instead.

RETURN VALUES

This function returns the message corresponding to *err*.

ERRORS

None.

SEE ALSO

nn_errno(3compat), nng_compat(3compat), nng(7)

NAME

nn_term - terminate library (compatible API)

SYNOPSIS

```
#include <nanomsg/nn.h>

void nn_term(void);
```

DESCRIPTION

The nn_term() function closes any open sockets, and frees all resources allocated by the library. Any operations that are currently in progress will be terminated, and will fail with error EBADF or ETERM.

> ℹ️ This function is provided for API compatibility with legacy *libnanomsg*. Consider using the relevant modern API instead.

> ⚠️ This function is not thread-safe, and is not suitable for use in library calls. The intended purpose of this is to clean up at application termination; for example by registering this function with atexit(). This can help prevent false leak reports caused when memory checkers notice global resources allocated by the library. Libraries should never use this function, but should explicitly close their own sockets directly.

RETURN VALUES

None.

ERRORS

None.

SEE ALSO

nn_errno(3compat), nn_socket(3compat), nng_compat(3compat), nng(7)

NAME

nng_compat - compatibility with nanomsg 1.0

SYNOPSIS

```
#include <nanomsg/nn.h>

#include <nanomsg/bus.h>
#include <nanomsg/pair.h>
#include <nanomsg/pipeline.h>
#include <nanomsg/pubsub.h>
#include <nanomsg/reqrep.h>
#include <nanomsg/survey.h>

#include <nanomsg/inproc.h>
#include <nanomsg/ipc.h>
#include <nanomsg/tcp.h>
#include <nanomsg/ws.h>
```

DESCRIPTION

The *nng* library provides source-level compatibility for most *nanomsg* 1.0 applications.

> ⚠ This is intended to facilitate converting legacy applications to use the *nng* library. New applications should use the newer *nng* API instead.

Applications making use of this must take care to link with *libnng* instead of *libnn*.

> 💡 While not recommended for long term use, the value returned by nng_socket_id() can be used with these functions just like a value returned by nn_socket(). This can be way to facilitate incremental transition to the new API.

> ℹ Some capabilities, protocols, and transports, will not be accessible using this API, as the compatible API has no provision for expression of certain concepts introduced in the newer *nng* API.

> ℹ While reasonable efforts have been made to provide for compatibility, some things may behave differently, and some less common parts of the *nanomsg* 1.0 API are not supported at this time, including certain options and the statistics API. See the Caveats section below.

Compiling

When compiling legacy *nanomsg* applications, it will generally be necessary to change the include search path to add the "compat" subdirectory of the directory where headers were installed. For example, if *nng* is installed in $prefix, then header files will normally be located in $prefix/include/nng. In this case, to build legacy *nanomsg* apps against *nng* you would add $prefix/include/nng/compat to your compiler's search path.

Alternatively, you can change your source code so that #include statements referring to <nanomsg> instead refer to <nng/compat/nanomsg>. For example, instead of:

```
#include <nanomsg/nn.h>
#include <nanomsg/reqrep.h>
```

you would have this:

```
#include <nng/compat/nanomsg/nn.h>
#include <nng/compat/nanomsg/reqrep.h>
```

Legacy applications built using these methods should be linked against *libnng* instead of *libnn*, just like any other *nng* application.

Functions

The following functions are provided:

Caveats

The following caveats apply when using the legacy API with *nng*.

- Socket numbers can be quite large. The legacy *libnanomsg* attempted to reuse socket numbers, like file descriptors in UNIX systems. The *nng* library avoids this to prevent accidental reuse or collision after a descriptor is closed. Consequently, socket numbers can become quite large, and should probably not be used for array indices.

- The following options (nn_getsockopt) are unsupported: NN_SNDPRIO, NN_RCVPRIO, NN_IPV4ONLY. The priority options may be supported in the future, when the underlying capability is present in *nng*.

- Access to statistics using this legacy API (nn_get_statistic()) is unsupported.

- Some transports can support longer URLs than legacy *libnanomsg* can. It is a good idea to use short pathnames in URLs if interoperability is a concern.

- Only absolute paths are supported in ipc:// URLs. For example, ipc:///tmp/mysocket is acceptable, but ipc://mysocket is not.

- The WebSocket transport in this implementation (ws:// URLs) only supports BINARY frames.

- Some newer transports are unusable from this mode. In particular, this legacy API offers no way to configure TLS or ZeroTier parameters that may be required for use.

- ABI versioning of the compatibility layer is not supported, and the NN_VERSION_ macros are not present.

- Runtime symbol information is not implemented. Specifically, there is no nn_symbol() function yet. (This may be addressed later if there is a need.)

- The TCP transport (tcp:// URLs) does not support specifying the local address or interface when binding. (This could be fixed in the future, but most likely this will be available only using the new API.)

- The values of NN_RCVMAXSIZE are constrained. Specifically, values set larger than 2GB using the new API will be reported as unlimited (-1) in the new API, and the value 0 will disable any enforcement, just like -1. (There is no practical reason to ever want to limit the receive size to zero.)

- This implementation counts buffers in terms of messages rather than bytes. As a result, the buffer sizes accessed with NN_SNDBUF and NN_RCVBUF are rounded up to a whole number of kilobytes, then divided by 1024, in order to approximate buffering assuming 1 KB messages. Few applications should need to adjust the default values.

SEE ALSO

libnng(3), nng(7)

Supplemental HTTP Functions

NAME

nng_http_client_alloc - allocate HTTP client

SYNOPSIS

```
#include <nng/nng.h>
#include <nng/supplemental/http/http.h>

int nng_http_client_alloc(nng_http_client *clientp, const nng_url *url);
```

DESCRIPTION

The nng_http_client_alloc() allocates an HTTP client suitable for connecting to the server identified by *url* and stores a pointer to it in the location referenced by *clientp*.

RETURN VALUES

This function returns 0 on success, and non-zero otherwise.

ERRORS

NNG_ENOMEM	Insufficient free memory exists.
NNG_ENOTSUP	HTTP not supported.

SEE ALSO

nng_http_client_connect(3http), nng_http_client_free(3http), nng_strerror(3), nng_url_parse(3), nng(7)

NAME

nng_http_client_connect - establish HTTP client connection

SYNOPSIS

```
#include <nng/nng.h>
#include <nng/supplemental/http/http.h>

void nng_http_client_connect(nng_http_client *client, nng_aio *aio);
```

DESCRIPTION

The nng_http_client_connect() starts the process of establishing an HTTP connection from *client* to the server that was indicated in the URL that *client* was configured with.

The result of the operation will be stored in the *aio* when the operation is complete, and will be obtainable via nng_aio_result().

On success, a pointer to the underlying HTTP client (type nng_http_conn *) will be stored in the first output result of the *aio*, and can be obtained by nng_aio_get_output() with an *index* of zero (0).

RETURN VALUES

None.

ERRORS

NNG_EADDRINVAL	The server is configured with an invalid address.
NNG_ECANCELED	The operation was aborted.
NNG_ECONNREFUSED	The TCP connection was refused by the server.
NNG_ECONNRESET	The TCP connection was reset by the server.
NNG_ENOMEM	Insufficient free memory exists.

EXAMPLE

```
        nng_aio *aio;
        nng_url *url;
        nng_http_client *client;
        nng_http_conn *conn;
        int rv;

        // Error checks elided for clarity.
        nng_url_parse(&url, "http://www.google.com");
        nng_aio_alloc(&aio, NULL, NULL);
        nng_http_client_alloc(&client, url);

        nng_http_client_connect(client, aio);

        // Wait for connection to establish (or attempt to fail).
        nng_aio_wait(aio);

        if ((rv = nng_aio_result(aio)) != 0) {
                printf("Connection failed: %s\n", nng_strerror(rv));
        } else {
                // Connection established, get it.
                conn = nng_aio_get_output(aio, 0);

                // ... do something with it here

                // Close the connection when done to avoid leaking it.
                nng_http_conn_close(conn);
        }
```

SEE ALSO

nng_aio_get_output(3), nng_aio_result(3), nng_aio_wait(3), nng_strerror(3),
nng_http_client_alloc(3http), nng_http_conn_close(3http), nng_http_conn_read(3http),
nng_http_conn_write(3http), nng(7)

NAME

nng_http_client_free - free HTTP client

SYNOPSIS

```
#include <nng/nng.h>
#include <nng/supplemental/http/http.h>

void nng_http_client_free(nng_http_client *client);
```

DESCRIPTION

The nng_http_client_free() frees the HTTP client and any associated resources referenced by *client*.

i Any connections created by nng_http_client_connect() are unaffected, and so the caller must close those explicitly if desired.

RETURN VALUES

None.

ERRORS

None.

SEE ALSO

nng_http_client_alloc(3), nng_http_client_connect(3), nng(7)

NAME

nng_http_client_get_tls - get HTTP client TLS configuration

SYNOPSIS

```
#include <nng/nng.h>
#include <nng/supplemental/http/http.h>

int nng_http_client_get_tls(nng_http_client *client, nng_tls_config **cfgp);
```

DESCRIPTION

The nng_http_client_get_tls() obtains the TLS configuration of *client* and saves a pointer to it in the address referenced by *cfgp*.

The object will be returned with an extra hold (see nng_tls_config_hold()) placed on it on behalf of the caller. The caller should free this hold by calling nng_tls_config_free() with it is done with the TLS configuration.

RETURN VALUES

This function returns 0 on success, and non-zero otherwise.

ERRORS

NNG_EINVAL	TLS not configured on client.
NNG_ENOMEM	Insufficient free memory exists.
NNG_ENOTSUP	Either HTTP or TLS not supported.

SEE ALSO

nng_http_client_alloc(3http), nng_http_client_connect(3http), nng_http_client_set_tls(3http), nng_tls_config_alloc(3tls), nng_tls_config_free(3tls), nng_tls_config_hold(3tls), nng_strerror(3), nng(7)

NAME

nng_http_client_set_tls - set HTTP client TLS configuration

SYNOPSIS

```
#include <nng/nng.h>
#include <nng/supplemental/http/http.h>

int nng_http_client_set_tls(nng_http_client *client, nng_tls_config *cfg);
```

DESCRIPTION

The nng_http_client_set_tls() sets the TLS configuration of *client* to *cfg*.

This change overwrites any previous TLS configuration.

⚠ This also invalidates any previously obtained values from nng_http_client_get_tls().

ℹ Any connections established with nng_http_client_connect() will continue to use any TLS configuration that they were started with.

RETURN VALUES

This function returns 0 on success, and non-zero otherwise.

ERRORS

NNG_ENOMEM	Insufficient free memory exists.
NNG_ENOTSUP	Either HTTP or TLS not supported.

SEE ALSO

nng_http_client_alloc(3http), nng_http_client_connect(3http), nng_http_client_get_tls(3http), nng_tls_config_alloc(3tls), nng_strerror(3), nng(7)

NAME

nng_http_client_transact - perform one HTTP transaction

SYNOPSIS

```
#include <nng/nng.h>
#include <nng/supplemental/http/http.h>

void nng_http_client_transact(nng_http_client *client, nng_http_req *req,
    nng_http_res *res, nng_aio *aio);
```

DESCRIPTION

The nng_http_client_transact() function is used to perform a complete HTTP exchange. It creates a new connection using *client*, performs the transaction by sending the request *req* (and attached body data) to the remote server, then reading the response *res*, and finally closes the connection that it created. The entire response is read, including any associated body, which can subsequently be obtained using nng_http_res_get_data().

This function is intended to make creation of client applications easier, by performing multiple asynchronous operations required to complete an entire HTTP transaction.

A similar function, nng_http_conn_transact(), exists. That function behaves similarily, but uses an existing connection, which can be reused.

> **ⓘ** This function does not support reading data sent using chunked transfer encoding, and if the server attempts to do so, the underlying connection will be closed and an NNG_ENOTSUP error will be returned. This limitation is considered a bug, and a fix is planned for the future.

> **⚠** If the remote server tries to send an extremely large buffer, then a corresponding allocation will be made, which can lead to denial of service attacks. Client applications should take care to use this only with reasonably trust-worthy servers.

This function returns immediately, with no return value. Completion of the operation is signaled via the *aio*, and the final result may be obtained via nng_aio_result(). That result will either be zero or an error code.

RETURN VALUES

None.

ERRORS

NNG_ECANCELED	The operation was canceled.
NNG_ECLOSED	The connection was closed.
NNG_ECONNRESET	The peer closed the connection.
NNG_ENOMEM	Insufficient free memory to perform the operation.

NNG_ENOTSUP	HTTP operations are not supported, or peer sent chunked encoding.
NNG_EPROTO	An HTTP protocol error occurred.
NNG_ETIMEDOUT	Timeout waiting for data from the connection.

SEE ALSO

nng_aio_alloc(3), nng_aio_result(3), nng_strerror(3), nng_http_client_connect(3http), nng_http_conn_transact(3http), nng_http_res_get_data(3http), nng(7)

NAME

nng_http_conn_close - close HTTP connection

SYNOPSIS

```
#include <nng/nng.h>
#include <nng/supplemental/http/http.h>

void nng_http_conn_close(nng_http_conn *conn);
```

DESCRIPTION

The nng_http_conn_close() function closes the supplied HTTP connection *conn*, including any disposing of any underlying file descriptors or related resources.

Once this function, no further access to the *conn* structure may be made.

RETURN VALUES

None.

ERRORS

None.

SEE ALSO

nng_http_client_connect(3http), nng_http_handler_alloc(3http), nng_strerror(3), nng(7)

NAME

nng_http_conn_read - read from HTTP connection

SYNOPSIS

```
#include <nng/nng.h>
#include <nng/supplemental/http/http.h>

void nng_http_conn_read(nng_http_conn *conn, nng_aio *aio);
```

DESCRIPTION

The nng_http_conn_read() function starts an asynchronous read from the HTTP connection *conn*, into the scatter/gather vector located in the asynchronous I/O structure *aio*.

ℹ The nng_aio_set_iov() function must have been called first, to set the scatter/gather vector for *aio*.

This function returns immediately, with no return value. Completion of the operation is signaled via the *aio*, and the final result may be obtained via nng_aio_result(). That result will either be zero or an error code.

The I/O operation completes as soon as at least one byte has been read, or an error has occurred. Therefore, the number of bytes read may be less than requested. The actual number of bytes read can be determined with nng_aio_count().

♀ This function is intended to facilitate uses cases that involve changing the protocol from HTTP, such as WebSocket. Most applications will never need to use this function.

RETURN VALUES

None.

ERRORS

NNG_ECANCELED	The operation was canceled.
NNG_ECLOSED	The connection was closed.
NNG_ECONNRESET	The peer closed the connection.
NNG_EINVAL	The *aio* does not contain a valid scatter/gather vector.
NNG_ENOMEM	Insufficient free memory to perform the operation.
NNG_ENOTSUP	HTTP operations are not supported.
NNG_ETIMEDOUT	Timeout waiting for data from the connection.

SEE ALSO

nng_aio_alloc(3), nng_aio_count(3), nng_aio_result(3), nng_aio_set_iov(3),
nng_http_handler_alloc(3http), nng_http_client_connect(3http), nng_http_conn_read_all(3http),
nng_strerror(3), nng(7)

NAME

nng_http_conn_read_all - read all from HTTP connection

SYNOPSIS

```
#include <nng/nng.h>
#include <nng/supplemental/http/http.h>

void nng_http_conn_read_all(nng_http_conn *conn, nng_aio *aio);
```

DESCRIPTION

The nng_http_conn_read_all() function starts an asynchronous read from the HTTP connection *conn*, into the scatter/gather vector located in the asynchronous I/O structure *aio*.

> ℹ️ The nng_aio_set_iov() function must have been called first, to set the scatter/gather vector for *aio*.

This function returns immediately, with no return value. Completion of the operation is signaled via the *aio*, and the final result may be obtained via nng_aio_result(). That result will either be zero or an error code.

The I/O operation completes only when the entire amount of data requested has been read, or an error has occurred. If the operation completes successfully, then the entire requested data has been read.

It is still possible for a partial read to complete in the event of an error. The actual number of bytes read can be determined with nng_aio_count().

> 💡 The main purpose for this function is to facilitate reading HTTP body content, after first determining the length of the body content from the relevant HTTP headers (typically Content-Length).

RETURN VALUES

None.

ERRORS

NNG_ECANCELED	The operation was canceled.
NNG_ECLOSED	The connection was closed.
NNG_ECONNRESET	The peer closed the connection.
NNG_EINVAL	The *aio* does not contain a valid scatter/gather vector.
NNG_ENOMEM	Insufficient free memory to perform the operation.
NNG_ENOTSUP	HTTP operations are not supported.
NNG_ETIMEDOUT	Timeout waiting for data from the connection.

SEE ALSO

nng_aio_alloc(3), nng_aio_count(3), nng_aio_result(3), nng_aio_set_iov(3), nng_strerror(3), nng_http_client_connect(3), nng_http_conn_read(3), nng(7)

NAME

nng_http_conn_read_req - read HTTP request

SYNOPSIS

```
#include <nng/nng.h>
#include <nng/supplemental/http/http.h>

void nng_http_conn_read_req(nng_http_conn *conn, nng_http_req *req,
    nng_aio *aio);
```

DESCRIPTION

The nng_http_conn_read_req() function starts an asynchronous read from the HTTP connection *conn*, reading an HTTP request into the *req*, including all of the related headers.

ⓘ   Any HTTP entity/body data associated with the request is **not** read automatically. The caller should use nng_http_conn_read_all() to read the entity data, based on the details of the request itself.

This function returns immediately, with no return value. Completion of the operation is signaled via the *aio*, and the final result may be obtained via nng_aio_result(). That result will either be zero or an error code.

RETURN VALUES

None.

ERRORS

NNG_ECANCELED	The operation was canceled.
NNG_ECLOSED	The connection was closed.
NNG_ECONNRESET	The peer closed the connection.
NNG_ENOMEM	Insufficient free memory to perform the operation.
NNG_ENOTSUP	HTTP operations are not supported.
NNG_ETIMEDOUT	Timeout waiting for data from the connection.

SEE ALSO

nng_aio_alloc(3), nng_aio_result(3), nng_strerror(3), nng_http_client_connect(3http), nng_http_conn_read_all(3http), nng(7)

NAME

nng_http_conn_read_res - read HTTP response

SYNOPSIS

```
#include <nng/nng.h>
#include <nng/supplemental/http/http.h>

void nng_http_conn_read_res(nng_http_conn *conn, nng_http_res *res,
    nng_aio *aio);
```

DESCRIPTION

The nng_http_conn_read_res() function starts an asynchronous read from the HTTP connection *conn*, reading an HTTP response into the *res*, including all of the related headers.

> 🛈 Any HTTP entity/body data associated with the response is **not** read automatically. The caller should use nng_http_conn_read_all to read the entity data, based on the details of the response itself.

This function returns immediately, with no return value. Completion of the operation is signaled via the *aio*, and the final result may be obtained via nng_aio_result(). That result will either be zero or an error code.

> 🛈 Consider using the nng_http_client_transact() or nng_http_conn_transact() functions, which provide a simpler interface for performing a complete HTTP client transaction.

RETURN VALUES

None.

ERRORS

NNG_ECANCELED	The operation was canceled.
NNG_ECLOSED	The connection was closed.
NNG_ECONNRESET	The peer closed the connection.
NNG_ENOMEM	Insufficient free memory to perform the operation.
NNG_ENOTSUP	HTTP operations are not supported.
NNG_ETIMEDOUT	Timeout waiting for data from the connection.

SEE ALSO

nng_aio_alloc(3), nng_aio_result(3), nng_strerror(3), nng_http_client_connect(3http), nng_http_client_transact(3http), nng_http_conn_transact(3http), nng_http_conn_read_all(3http), nng(7)

NAME

nng_http_conn_transact - perform one HTTP transaction on connection

SYNOPSIS

```
#include <nng/nng.h>
#include <nng/supplemental/http/http.h>

void nng_http_conn_transact(nng_http_conn *conn, nng_http_req *req,
    nng_http_res *res, nng_aio *aio);
```

DESCRIPTION

The nng_http_conn_transact() function is used to perform a complete HTTP exchange over the connection *conn*, sending the request *req* (and attached body data) to the remote server, and reading the response *res*. The entire response is read, including any associated body, which can subsequently be obtained using nng_http_res_get_data().

This function is intended to make creation of client applications easier, by performing multiple asynchronous operations required to complete an entire HTTP transaction.

If an error occurs, the caller should close *conn* with nng_http_conn_close(), as it may not necessarily be usable with other transactions.

A similar function, nng_http_client_transact(), exists. That function behaves similarily, but creates a connection on demand for the transaction, and disposes of it when finished.

⚠   If the remote server tries to send an extremely large buffer, then a corresponding allocation will be made, which can lead to denial of service attacks. Client applications should take care to use this only with reasonably trust-worthy servers.

⚠   A given connection *conn* should be used with only one operation or transaction at a time as HTTP/1.1 has no support for request interleaving.

This function returns immediately, with no return value. Completion of the operation is signaled via the *aio*, and the final result may be obtained via nng_aio_result(). That result will either be zero or an error code.

RETURN VALUES

None.

ERRORS

NNG_ECANCELED	The operation was canceled.
NNG_ECLOSED	The connection was closed.
NNG_ECONNRESET	The peer closed the connection.

NNG_ENOMEM	Insufficient free memory to perform the operation.
NNG_ENOTSUP	HTTP operations are not supported.
NNG_EPROTO	An HTTP protocol error occurred.
NNG_ETIMEDOUT	Timeout waiting for data from the connection.

SEE ALSO

nng_aio_alloc(3), nng_aio_result(3), nng_strerror(3), nng_http_client_connect(3http),
nng_http_client_transact(3http), nng_http_conn_read_res(3http), nng_http_conn_read_all(3http),
nng_http_conn_write_req(3http), nng_http_res_get_data(3http), nng(7)

NAME

nng_http_conn_write - write to HTTP connection

SYNOPSIS

```
#include <nng/nng.h>
#include <nng/supplemental/http/http.h>

void nng_http_conn_write(nng_http_conn *conn, nng_aio *aio);
```

DESCRIPTION

The nng_http_conn_write() function starts an asynchronous write to the HTTP connection *conn* from the scatter/gather vector located in the asynchronous I/O structure *aio*.

> ℹ The nng_aio_set_iov() function must have been called first, to set the scatter/gather vector for *aio*.

This function returns immediately, with no return value. Completion of the operation is signaled via the *aio*, and the final result may be obtained via nng_aio_result(). That result will either be zero or an error code.

The I/O operation completes as soon as at least one byte has been written, or an error has occurred. Therefore, the number of bytes written may be less than requested. The actual number of bytes written can be determined with nng_aio_count().

> 💡 This function is intended to facilitate uses cases that involve changing the protocol from HTTP, such as WebSocket. Most applications will never need to use this function.

RETURN VALUES

None.

ERRORS

NNG_ECANCELED	The operation was canceled.
NNG_ECLOSED	The connection was closed.
NNG_ECONNRESET	The peer closed the connection.
NNG_EINVAL	The *aio* does not contain a valid scatter/gather vector.
NNG_ENOMEM	Insufficient free memory to perform the operation.
NNG_ENOTSUP	HTTP operations are not supported.
NNG_ETIMEDOUT	Timeout waiting for data from the connection.

SEE ALSO

nng_aio_alloc(3), nng_aio_count(3), nng_aio_result(3), nng_aio_set_iov(3),
nng_http_client_connect(3http), nng_http_conn_write_all(3http), nng_http_handler_alloc(3http),
nng_strerror(3), nng(7)

NAME

nng_http_conn_write_all - write all to HTTP connection

SYNOPSIS

```
#include <nng/nng.h>
#include <nng/supplemental/http/http.h>

void nng_http_conn_write_all(nng_http_conn *conn, nng_aio *aio);
```

DESCRIPTION

The nng_http_conn_write_all() function starts an asynchronous write to the HTTP connection *conn*, into the scatter/gather vector located in the asynchronous I/O structure *aio*.

> ℹ️ The nng_aio_set_iov() function must have been called first, to set the scatter/gather vector for *aio*.

This function returns immediately, with no return value. Completion of the operation is signaled via the *aio*, and the final result may be obtained via nng_aio_result(). That result will either be zero or an error code.

The I/O operation completes only when the entire amount of data requested has been written, or an error has occurred. If the operation completes successfully, then the entire requested data has been written.

It is still possible for a partial write to complete in the event of an error. The actual number of bytes written can be determined with nng_aio_count().

> 💡 The main purpose for this function is to facilitate writing HTTP body content.

> 💡 Usually an HTTP request or response will have been written immediately prior to this with http_conn_write_req() or http_conn_write_res(). In that case the request or response should have also contained an Content-Length header, and possibly a Content-Type header.

> 💡 An easier solution to sending HTTP content data, is to include the content with the request or reply using a function like nng_http_req_copy_data(). In that case, the body data will be written automatically by the http_conn_write_req() or http_conn_write_res() function.

RETURN VALUES

None.

ERRORS

NNG_ECANCELED	The operation was canceled.
NNG_ECLOSED	The connection was closed.

NNG_ECONNRESET	The peer closed the connection.
NNG_EINVAL	The *aio* does not contain a valid scatter/gather vector.
NNG_ENOMEM	Insufficient free memory to perform the operation.
NNG_ENOTSUP	HTTP operations are not supported.
NNG_ETIMEDOUT	Timeout waiting for data from the connection.

SEE ALSO

nng_aio_alloc(3), nng_aio_count(3), nng_aio_result(3), nng_aio_set_iov(3), nng_http_client_connect(3http), nng_http_conn_write(3http), http_conn_write_req(3http), http_conn_write_res(3http), nng_http_req_copy_data(3http), nng_http_req_set_data(3http), nng_http_res_copy_data(3http), nng_http_res_set_data(3http), nng_strerror(3), nng(7)

NAME

nng_http_conn_write_req - write HTTP request

SYNOPSIS

```
#include <nng/nng.h>
#include <nng/supplemental/http/http.h>

void nng_http_conn_write_req(nng_http_conn *conn, nng_http_req *req,
    nng_aio *aio);
```

DESCRIPTION

The nng_http_conn_write_req() function starts an asynchronous write of the HTTP request *req* to the connection *conn*. The entire request is sent, including headers, and if present, the request body data. (The request body can be set with nng_http_req_set_data() or nng_http_req_copy_data().)

This function returns immediately, with no return value. Completion of the operation is signaled via the *aio*, and the final result may be obtained via nng_aio_result(). That result will either be zero or an error code.

> ℹ Consider using the nng_http_client_transact() or nng_http_conn_transact() functions, which provide a simpler interface for performing a complete HTTP client transaction.

RETURN VALUES

None.

ERRORS

NNG_ECANCELED	The operation was canceled.
NNG_ECLOSED	The connection was closed.
NNG_ECONNRESET	The peer closed the connection.
NNG_ENOMEM	Insufficient free memory to perform the operation.
NNG_ENOTSUP	HTTP operations are not supported.
NNG_ETIMEDOUT	Timeout waiting for data from the connection.

SEE ALSO

nng_aio_alloc(3), nng_aio_result(3), nng_http_client_connect(3http), nng_http_client_transact(3http), nng_http_conn_read_all(3http), nng_http_conn_transact(3http), nng_strerror(3), nng(7)

NAME

nng_http_conn_write_res - write HTTP response

SYNOPSIS

```
#include <nng/nng.h>
#include <nng/supplemental/http/http.h>

void nng_http_conn_write_res(nng_http_conn *conn, nng_http_res *res,
    nng_aio *aio);
```

DESCRIPTION

The nng_http_conn_write_res() function starts an asynchronous write of the HTTP response *res* to the connection *conn*. The entire response is sent, including headers, and if present, the response body data. (The response body can be set with nng_http_res_set_data() or nng_http_res_copy_data().)

This function returns immediately, with no return value. Completion of the operation is signaled via the *aio*, and the final result may be obtained via nng_aio_result(). That result will either be zero or an error code.

Persistent Connections

By default, for HTTP/1.1 connections, the connection is kept open, and will be reused to receive new requests.

If however the *res* contains a header of Connection: with a value of Close (case-insensitive) or the response corresponds to HTTP/1.0, then the connection is immediately after sending the response.

> ℹ️ Consider using the nng_http_client_transact() or nng_http_conn_transact() functions, which provide a simpler interface for performing a complete HTTP client transaction.

RETURN VALUES

None.

ERRORS

NNG_ECANCELED	The operation was canceled.
NNG_ECLOSED	The connection was closed.
NNG_ECONNRESET	The peer closed the connection.
NNG_ENOMEM	Insufficient free memory to perform the operation.
NNG_ENOTSUP	HTTP operations are not supported.
NNG_ETIMEDOUT	Timeout waiting for data from the connection.

SEE ALSO

nng_aio_alloc(3), nng_aio_result(3), nng_http_client_connect(3http), nng_http_client_transact(3http), nng_http_conn_read_all(3http), nng_http_conn_transact(3http), nng_strerror(3), nng(7)

NAME

nng_http_handler_alloc - allocate HTTP server handler

SYNOPSIS

```
#include <nng/nng.h>
#include <nng/supplemental/http/http.h>

typedef struct nng_http_handler nng_http_handler;

int nng_http_handler_alloc(nng_http_handler **hp, const char *path,
    void (*func)(nng_aio *);

int nng_http_handler_alloc_directory(nng_http_handler **hp, const char *path,
    const char *dirname);

int nng_http_handler_alloc_file(nng_http_handler **hp, const char *path,
    const char *filename);

int nng_http_handler_alloc_redirect(nng_http_handler **hp, const char *path,
    uint16_t status, const char *location);

int nng_http_handler_alloc_static(nng_http_handler **hp, const char *path,
    const void *data, size_t size, const char *content_type);
```

DESCRIPTION

The nng_http_handler_alloc() family of functions allocate a handler which will be used to process requests coming into an HTTP server. On success, a pointer to the handler is stored at the located pointed to by *hp*.

Every handler has a Request-URI to which it refers, which is determined by the *path* argument. Only the path component of the Request URI is considered when determining whether the handler should be called.

Additionally each handler has a method it is registered to handle (the default is GET, see nng_http_handler_set_method()), and optionally a 'Host' header it can be matched against (see nng_http_handler_set_host()).

In some cases, a handler may reference a logical tree rather (directory) rather than just a single element. (See nng_http_handler_set_tree()).

Custom Handler

The generic (first) form of this creates a handler that uses a user-supplied function to process HTTP requests. This function uses the asynchronous I/O framework. The function takes a pointer to an nng_aio structure.

The *aio* will be passed with the following input values (retrieved with nng_aio_get_input()):

0: `nng_http_req` * *request*
> The client's HTTP request.

1: `nng_http_handler` * *handler*
> Pointer to the handler object.

2: `nng_http_conn` * *conn*
> The underlying HTTP connection.

The handler should create an `nng_http_res` * response (such as via `nng_http_res_alloc()` or `nng_http_res_alloc_error()`) and store that in as the first output (index 0) with `nng_aio_set_output()`.

Alternatively, the handler may send the HTTP response (and any associated body data) itself using the connection. In that case the output at index 0 of the *aio* should be NULL.

Finally, using the `nng_aio_finish()` function, the *aio* should be completed successfully. If any non-zero status is returned back to the caller instead, then a generic 500 response will be created and sent, if possible, and the connection will be closed.

The *aio* may be scheduled for deferred completion using the `nng_aio_defer()` function.

> ℹ The callback function should **NOT** call `nng_aio_begin()`, as that will already have been done by the server framework.

Directory Handler

The second member of this family, `nng_http_handler_alloc_directory()`, creates a handler configured to serve a directory tree. The *uri* is taken as the root, and files are served from the directory tree rooted at *path*.

When the client Request-URI resolves to a directory in the file system, the handler looks first for a file named `index.html` or `index.htm`. If one is found, then that file is returned back to the client. If no such index file exists, then an `NNG_HTTP_STATUS_NOT_FOUND` (404) error is sent back to the client.

The `Content-Type` will be set automatically based upon the extension of the requested file name. If a content type cannot be determined from the extension, then `application/octet-stream` is used.

File Handler

The third member of this family, `nng_http_handler_alloc_file()`, creates a handler to serve up a single file; it does not traverse directories or search for `index.html` or `index.htm` files.

The `Content-Type` will be set automatically based upon the extension of the requested file name. If a content type cannot be determined from the extension, then `application/octet-stream` is used.

Redirect Handler

The fourth member is used to arrange for a server redirect from one URL to another. The reply will be with status code *status*, which should be a 3XX code such as 301, and a `Location:` header will contain the URL referenced by *location*, with any residual suffix from the request URI appended.

> 💡 Use `nng_http_handler_set_tree()` to redirect an entire tree. For example, it is possible to redirect an entire HTTP site to another HTTPS site by specifying / as the path and then using the base of the new site, such as `https://newsite.example.com` as the new location.

> 💡 Be sure to use the appropriate value for *status*. Permanent redirection should use 301 and temporary redirections should use 307. In REST APIs, using a redirection to supply the new location of an object created with POST should use 303.

Static Handler

The fifth member of this family, `nng_http_handler_alloc_static()`, creates a handler to serve up fixed content located in program data. The client is sent the *data*, with Content-Length of *size* bytes, and Content-Type of *content_type*.

RETURN VALUES

These functions return 0 on success, and non-zero otherwise.

ERRORS

NNG_EINVAL	An invalid *path* was specified.
NNG_ENOMEM	Insufficient free memory exists to allocate a message.
NNG_ENOTSUP	No support for HTTP in the library.

SEE ALSO

nng_aio_defer(3), nng_aio_finish(3), nng_aio_get_input(3), nng_aio_set_output(3),
nng_http_handler_collect_body(3http), nng_http_handler_free(3http),
nng_http_handler_set_host(3http), nng_http_handler_set_method(3http),
nng_http_handler_set_tree(3http), nng_http_res_alloc(3http), nng_http_res_alloc_error(3http),
nng_http_server_add_handler(3http), nng_strerror(3), nng_aio(5), nng(7)

NAME

nng_http_handler_collect_body - set HTTP handler to collect request body

SYNOPSIS

```
#include <nng/nng.h>
#include <nng/supplemental/http/http.h>

int nng_http_handler_collect_body(nng_http_handler *handler, bool want, size_t maxsz);
```

DESCRIPTION

The nng_http_handler_collect_data() function causes the *handler* to collect any request body that was submitted with the request, and attach it to the nng_http_req before the handler is called.

Subsequently the data can be retrieved by the handler from the request with the nng_http_req_get_data() function.

The collection is enabled if *want* is true. Furthermore, the data that the client may sent is limited by the value of *maxsz*. If the client attempts to send more data than *maxsz*, then the request will be terminated with a 400 "Bad Request" status.

> 💡 Limiting the size of incoming request data can provide protection against denial of service attacks, as a buffer of the client-supplied size must be allocated to receive the data.

In order to provide an unlimited size, use (size_t)-1 for *maxsz*. The value 0 for *maxsz* can be used to prevent any data from being passed by the client.

The built-in handlers for files, directories, and static data limit the *maxsz* to zero by default. Otherwise the default setting is to enable this capability with a default value of *maxsz* of 1 megabyte.

> ℹ️ The handler looks for data indicated by the Content-Length: HTTP header. If this header is absent, the request is assumed not to contain any data.

> ℹ️ This specifically does not support the Chunked transfer-encoding. This is considered a bug, and is a deficiency for full HTTP/1.1 compliance. However, few clients send data in this format, so in practice this should create few limitations.

RETURN VALUES

This function returns 0 on success, and non-zero otherwise.

ERRORS

NNG_ENOTSUP   No support for HTTP in the library.

SEE ALSO

nng_http_handler_alloc(3http), nng_http_server_add_handler(3http), nng_http_req_get_data(3http), nng(7)

NAME

nng_http_handler_free - free HTTP server handler

SYNOPSIS

```
#include <nng/nng.h>
#include <nng/supplemental/http/http.h>

void nng_http_handler_free(nng_http_handler *h);
```

DESCRIPTION

The nng_http_handler_free() function frees an allocated HTTP server handler.

> ⚠ It is an error to free a handler that is registered with a server. Any handlers that are registered with servers are automatically freed when the server itself is deallocated.

RETURN VALUES

None.

ERRORS

None.

SEE ALSO

nng_http_handler_alloc(3http), nng_http_server_add_handler(3http), nng(7)

NAME

nng_http_handler_get_data - return extra data for HTTP handler

SYNOPSIS

```
#include <nng/nng.h>
#include <nng/supplemental/http/http.h>

void *nng_http_handler_get_data(nng_http_handler *handler);
```

DESCRIPTION

The nng_http_handler_get_data() function returns the data previously stored on *handler* using the function nng_http_handler_set_data().

RETURN VALUES

None.

ERRORS

None.

SEE ALSO

nng_http_handler_alloc(3http), nng_http_server_set_data(3http),
nng_http_server_add_handler(3http), nng(7)

NAME

nng_http_handler_set_data - set extra data for HTTP handler

SYNOPSIS

```
#include <nng/nng.h>
#include <nng/supplemental/http/http.h>

int nng_http_handler_set_data(nng_http_handler *handler, void *data,
    void (*dtor)(void *));
```

DESCRIPTION

The nng_http_handler_set_data() function is used to set an additional *data* for the *handler*. The stored *data* can be retrieved later in the handler function using nng_http_handler_get_data().

Additionally, when the handler is deallocated, if *dtor* is not NULL, then it will be called with *data* as its argument. The intended use of this function is deallocate any resources associated with *data*.

RETURN VALUES

This function returns 0 on success, and non-zero otherwise.

ERRORS

NNG_ENOMEM   Insufficient free memory to perform the operation.

NNG_ENOTSUP   No support for HTTP in the library.

SEE ALSO

nng_http_handler_alloc(3http), nng_http_server_get_data(3http),
nng_http_server_add_handler(3http), nng(7)

NAME

nng_http_handler_set_host - set host for HTTP handler

SYNOPSIS

```
#include <nng/nng.h>
#include <nng/supplemental/http/http.h>

int nng_http_handler_set_host(nng_http_handler *handler, const char *host);
```

DESCRIPTION

The nng_http_handler_set_host() function is used to limit the scope of the *handler* so that it will only be called when the specified *host* matches the value of the Host: HTTP header.

> 💡 This can be used to create servers with multiple handlers for virtual hosting.

The value of the *host* can include a colon and port, and should match exactly the value of the Host header sent by the client. (Canonicalization of the host name is performed though.)

> 💡 As the server framework does not support listening on multiple ports, the port number can be elided. The matching test only considers the hostname or IP address, and ignores any trailing port number.

RETURN VALUES

This function returns 0 on success, and non-zero otherwise.

ERRORS

NNG_ENOMEM	Insufficient free memory to perform the operation.
NNG_ENOTSUP	No support for HTTP in the library.

SEE ALSO

nng_http_handler_alloc(3http), nng_http_server_add_handler(3http), nng(7)

NAME

nng_http_handler_set_method - set HTTP handler method

SYNOPSIS

```
#include <nng/nng.h>
#include <nng/supplemental/http/http.h>

int nng_http_handler_set_method(nng_http_handler *handler, const char *method);
```

DESCRIPTION

The nng_http_handler_set_method() function sets the *method* that the *handler* will be called for, such as
"GET" or "POST". (By default the "GET" method is handled.) If *method* is NULL, then the request method
is not examined, and the handler will be executed regardless of the method.

> 🛈 The server will automatically call "GET" handlers if the client sends a "HEAD" request, and will
> suppress HTTP body data in the responses sent for such requests.

> 🛈 No validation of the *method* is performed, but HTTP specifications insist that the actual method
> sent over the wire be capitalized.

The handler may always examine the actual method used using the nng_http_req_get_method()
function.

RETURN VALUES

This function returns 0 on success, and non-zero otherwise.

ERRORS

NNG_ENOMEM	Insufficient free memory exists.
NNG_ENOTSUP	No support for HTTP in the library.

SEE ALSO

nng_http_handler_alloc(3http), nng_http_server_add_handler(3http),
nng_http_req_get_method(3http), nng(7)

NAME

nng_http_handler_set_tree - set HTTP handler to match trees

SYNOPSIS

```
#include <nng/nng.h>
#include <nng/supplemental/http/http.h>

int nng_http_handler_set_tree(nng_http_handler *handler);
```

DESCRIPTION

The nng_http_handler_set_tree() function causes the *handler* to be matched if the Request URI sent by the client is a logical child of the path for *handler*.

> 💡 This method is useful when constructing API handlers where a single service address (path) supports dynamically generated children.

RETURN VALUES

This function returns 0 on success, and non-zero otherwise.

ERRORS

NNG_ENOMEM	Insufficient free memory exists.
NNG_ENOTSUP	No support for HTTP in the library.

SEE ALSO

nng_http_handler_alloc(3http), nng_http_server_add_handler(3http), nng_http_req_get_method(3http), nng(7)

NAME

nng_http_hijack - hijack HTTP server connection

SYNOPSIS

```
#include <nng/nng.h>
#include <nng/supplemental/http/http.h>

void nng_http_hijack(nng_http_conn *conn);
```

DESCRIPTION

The nng_http_hijack() function hijacks the connection *conn*, causing it to be disassociated from the HTTP server where it was created.

The purpose of this function is the creation of HTTP upgraders (such as WebSocket), where the underlying HTTP connection will be taken over for some other purpose, and should not be used any further by the server.

This function is most useful when called from a handler function. (See nng_http_handler_alloc().)

> 🛈 It is the responsibility of the caller to dispose of the underlying connection when it is no longer needed. Furthermore, the HTTP server will no longer send any responses to the hijacked connection, so the caller should do that as well if appropriate. (See nng_http_conn_write_res().)

> 💡 This function is intended to facilitate uses cases that involve changing the protocol from HTTP, such as WebSocket. Most applications will never need to use this function.

RETURN VALUES

None.

ERRORS

NNG_ECLOSED	The connection was closed.
NNG_ENOMEM	Insufficient free memory exists.
NNG_ENOTSUP	HTTP not supported.

SEE ALSO

nng_strerror(3), nng_http_conn_write_res(3http), nng_http_handler_alloc(3http), nng(7)

NAME

nng_http_req_add_header - add HTTP request header

SYNOPSIS

```
#include <nng/nng.h>
#include <nng/supplemental/http/http.h>

int nng_http_req_add_header(nng_http_req *req, const char *key,
    const char *val);
```

DESCRIPTION

The nng_http_req_add_header() adds an HTTP header for the request *req* and the *key* to the *val*. The *key* and *val* are copied.

If a header with the value of *key* already exists, then a comma and whitespace separate are appended to it, followed by *val*.

If no such header already exists, then one is created with the value *val*.

> The HTTP specification requires that duplicate headers be treated identically to a single header with multiple comma-delimited values.

> See nng_http_req_set_header() if replacement of an existing header rather than appending to it is desired.

The value of *key* is case insensitive, and should not include the final colon in an HTTP header. For example, specifying Host or hOSt are equivalent, whereas the value Host: is not a legal header key.

RETURN VALUES

This function returns 0 on success, and non-zero otherwise.

ERRORS

NNG_ENOMEM	Insufficient memory to perform the operation.
NNG_ENOTSUP	No support for HTTP in the library.

SEE ALSO

nng_http_req_alloc(3http), nng_http_req_del_header(3http), nng_http_req_get_header(3http), nng_http_req_set_header(3http), nng(7)

NAME

nng_http_req_alloc - allocate HTTP request structure

SYNOPSIS

```
#include <nng/nng.h>
#include <nng/supplemental/http/http.h>

int nng_http_req_alloc(nng_http_req **reqp, const nng_url *url);
```

DESCRIPTION

The nng_http_req_alloc() function allocates a new HTTP request structure and stores a pointer to it in *reqp*. The request will be initialized to perform an HTTP/1.1 GET operation using the URL specified in *url*.

> 💡 It is possible to specify NULL for the URL. In this case the URI for the request must be specified by a subsequent call to nng_http_req_set_uri().

RETURN VALUES

This function returns 0 on success, and non-zero otherwise.

ERRORS

NNG_ENOMEM	Insufficient free memory exists to allocate a message.
NNG_ENOTSUP	HTTP support not configured.

SEE ALSO

nng_http_conn_read_req(3http), nng_http_conn_write_req(3http), nng_http_req_add_header(3http), nng_http_req_copy_data(3http), nng_http_req_del_header(3http), nng_http_req_free(3http), nng_http_req_get_header(3http), nng_http_req_get_method(3http), nng_http_req_get_uri(3http), nng_http_req_get_version(3http), nng_http_req_reset(3http), nng_http_req_set_data(3http), nng_http_req_set_method(3http), nng_http_req_set_uri(3http), nng_http_req_set_version(3http), nng_http_res_alloc(3http), nng_url_parse(3) nng_strerror(3), nng(7)

NAME

nng_http_req_copy_data - copy HTTP request body

SYNOPSIS

```
#include <nng/nng.h>
#include <nng/supplemental/http/http.h>

int nng_http_req_copy_data(nng_http_req *req, const void *body, size_t size);
```

DESCRIPTION

The nng_http_req_copy_data() makes a copy of *body* (of size *size*) and sets the HTTP body for the request *req* to it. The copy will be deallocated automatically when *req* is freed.

The copied body data will be automatically sent with the request when it is sent using nng_http_conn_write_req().

This also updates the relevant Content-Length header of *req*.

i   The current framework does not support sending data via chunked transfer-encoding.

♀   To avoid copying data, the nng_http_req_set_data() may be used instead.

♀   It is a good idea to also set the Content-Type header.

RETURN VALUES

This function returns 0 on success, and non-zero otherwise.

ERRORS

NNG_ENOMEM	Insufficient memory to perform the operation.
NNG_ENOTSUP	No support for HTTP in the library.

SEE ALSO

nng_http_conn_write_req(3http), nng_http_req_alloc(3http), nng_http_req_set_data(3http), nng_http_req_set_header(3http), nng(7)

NAME

nng_http_req_del_header - delete HTTP request header

SYNOPSIS

```
#include <nng/nng.h>
#include <nng/supplemental/http/http.h>

int nng_http_req_del_header(nng_http_req *req, const char *key);
```

DESCRIPTION

The `nng_http_req_del_header()` removes all HTTP headers with the associated *key* from the request structure *req*.

The value of *key* is case insensitive, and should not include the final colon in an HTTP header. For example, specifying Host or hOSt are equivalent, whereas the value Host: is not a legal header key.

RETURN VALUES

This function returns 0 on success, and non-zero otherwise.

ERRORS

NNG_ENOENT   No header with the key *key* was present.

NNG_ENOTSUP   No support for HTTP in the library.

SEE ALSO

nng_http_req_alloc(3http), nng_http_req_add_header(3http), nng_http_req_del_header(3http), nng_http_req_get_header(3http), nng(7)

NAME

nng_http_req_free - free HTTP request structure

SYNOPSIS

```
#include <nng/nng.h>
#include <nng/supplemental/http/http.h>

void nng_http_req_free(nng_http_req *req);
```

DESCRIPTION

The nng_http_req_free() function deallocates the HTTP request structure *req* entirely.

> 💡 Instead of freeing and reallocating request structures, it is possible to reuse *req* with nng_http_req_reset().

RETURN VALUES

None.

ERRORS

None.

SEE ALSO

nng_http_req_alloc(3http), nng_http_req_reset(3http), nng(7)

NAME

nng_http_req_get_data - get HTTP request body

SYNOPSIS

```
#include <nng/nng.h>
#include <nng/supplemental/http/http.h>

void nng_http_req_get_data(nng_http_req *req, void **bodyp, size_t *sizep);
```

DESCRIPTION

The nng_http_req_get_data() gets the HTTP body associated with the request *req*, storing a pointer to the buffer at the location referenced by *bodyp*, and the length of the associated buffer at the location referenced by *sizep*.

ℹ️   The buffer returned is owned by *req*, and will automatically freed when the request is freed.

RETURN VALUES

None.

ERRORS

None.

SEE ALSO

nng_http_req_alloc(3http), nng_http_req_copy_data(3http), nng_http_req_copy_data(3http), nng(7)

NAME

nng_http_req_get_header - return HTTP request header

SYNOPSIS

```
#include <nng/nng.h>
#include <nng/supplemental/http/http.h>

const char *nng_http_req_get_header(nng_http_req *req, const char *key);
```

DESCRIPTION

The nng_http_req_get_header() looks for an HTTP header *key* in the request *req*, and returns the associated value if found, or NULL if not found.

The value of *key* is case insensitive, and should not include the final colon in an HTTP header. For example, specifying Host or hOSt are equivalent, whereas the value Host: will not find anything.

RETURN VALUES

HTTP header value for *key*, if it exists, or NULL otherwise.

ERRORS

None.

SEE ALSO

nng_http_req_alloc(3http), nng_http_req_add_header(3http), nng_http_req_set_header(3http), nng(7)

NAME

nng_http_req_get_method - return HTTP request method

SYNOPSIS

```
#include <nng/nng.h>
#include <nng/supplemental/http/http.h>

const char *nng_http_req_get_method(nng_http_req *req);
```

DESCRIPTION

The nng_http_req_get_method() returns the HTTP method associated with the request *req*. The value will be a string, such as "GET" or "POST".

RETURN VALUES

Request method as a string.

ERRORS

None.

SEE ALSO

nng_http_req_alloc(3http), nng_http_req_set_method(3http), nng(7)

NAME

nng_http_req_get_uri - return HTTP request URI

SYNOPSIS

```
#include <nng/nng.h>
#include <nng/supplemental/http/http.h>

const char *nng_http_req_get_uri(nng_http_req *req);
```

DESCRIPTION

The nng_http_req_get_uri() returns the URI (path) associated with the HTTP request *req*. The value returned includes the path, as well as any query information or fragment. The value will look like a file system path with those optional components appended, such as /api/get_info.cgi?name=garrett.

RETURN VALUES

Request URI as a string.

ERRORS

None.

SEE ALSO

nng_http_req_alloc(3http), nng_http_req_set_uri(3http), nng(7)

NAME

nng_http_req_get_version - return HTTP request protocol version

SYNOPSIS

```
#include <nng/nng.h>
#include <nng/supplemental/http/http.h>

const char *nng_http_req_get_version(nng_http_req *req);
```

DESCRIPTION

The nng_http_req_get_version() returns a string representing the HTTP protocol version associated with the request *req*, such as "HTTP/1.1".

RETURN VALUES

Request version as a string.

ERRORS

None.

SEE ALSO

nng_http_req_alloc(3http), nng_http_req_set_version(3http), nng(7)

NAME

nng_http_req_reset - reset HTTP request structure

SYNOPSIS

```
#include <nng/nng.h>
#include <nng/supplemental/http/http.h>

void nng_http_req_reset(nng_http_req *req);
```

DESCRIPTION

The nng_http_req_reset() function resets the request *req* so that it is just as if it had been freshly allocated with nng_http_req_alloc() with a NULL URL.

ℹ   Before using this with an HTTP operation, the URI must be set using nng_http_req_set_uri().

RETURN VALUES

None.

ERRORS

None.

SEE ALSO

nng_http_req_alloc(3http), nng_http_req_set_uri(3http), nng(7)

NAME

nng_http_req_set_data - set HTTP request body

SYNOPSIS

```
#include <nng/nng.h>
#include <nng/supplemental/http/http.h>

int nng_http_req_set_data(nng_http_req *req, const void *body, size_t size);
```

DESCRIPTION

The nng_http_req_set_data() sets the HTTP body associated with the request *req* to *body*, and the size of the body to *size*. This body data will be automatically sent with the request when it is sent using nng_http_conn_write_req().

This also updates the relevant Content-Length header of *req*.

ℹ️   The current framework does not support sending data via chunked transfer-encoding.

The *body* is **not** copied, and the caller must ensure that it is available until the *req* is deallocated.

💡   To have a local copy allocated with *req* that will be automatically deallocated when *req* is freed, see
      nng_http_req_copy_data().

💡   It is a good idea to also set the Content-Type header.

RETURN VALUES

This function returns 0 on success, and non-zero otherwise.

ERRORS

NNG_ENOMEM   Insufficient memory to perform the operation.

NNG_ENOTSUP   No support for HTTP in the library.

SEE ALSO

nng_http_conn_write_req(3http), nng_http_req_alloc(3http), nng_http_req_copy_data(3http),
nng_http_req_set_header(3http), nng(7)

NAME

nng_http_req_set_header - set HTTP request header

SYNOPSIS

```
#include <nng/nng.h>
#include <nng/supplemental/http/http.h>

int nng_http_req_set_header(nng_http_req *req, const char *key,
    const char *val);
```

DESCRIPTION

The nng_http_req_set_header() sets the HTTP header for the request *req* and the *key* to the *val*. The *key* and *val* are copied. Any previous header with the same *key* is replaced.

> 💡 See nng_http_req_add_header() to add additional headers with the same *key* without replacing them.

The value of *key* is case insensitive, and should not include the final colon in an HTTP header. For example, specifying Host or hOSt are equivalent, whereas the value Host: is not a legal header key.

RETURN VALUES

This function returns 0 on success, and non-zero otherwise.

ERRORS

NNG_ENOMEM	Insufficient memory to perform the operation.
NNG_ENOTSUP	No support for HTTP in the library.

SEE ALSO

nng_http_req_alloc(3http), nng_http_req_add_header(3http), nng_http_req_del_header(3http), nng_http_req_get_header(3http), nng(7)

NAME

nng_http_req_set_method - set HTTP request method

SYNOPSIS

```
#include <nng/nng.h>
#include <nng/supplemental/http/http.h>

int nng_http_req_set_method(nng_http_req *req, const char *method);
```

DESCRIPTION

The nng_http_req_set_method() sets the HTTP method associated with the request *req* to *method*. The *method* must be a string, such as "GET" or "POST", and the HTTP specifications indicate that it must be upper case.

The default value method for newly allocated requests is "GET".

A local copy of the *method* is made in the request *req*.

RETURN VALUES

This function returns 0 on success, and non-zero otherwise.

ERRORS

NNG_ENOMEM	Insufficient memory to perform the operation.
NNG_ENOTSUP	No support for HTTP in the library.

SEE ALSO

nng_http_req_alloc(3http), nng_http_req_get_method(3http), nng(7)

NAME

nng_http_req_set_uri - set HTTP request URI

SYNOPSIS

```
#include <nng/nng.h>
#include <nng/supplemental/http/http.h>

int nng_http_req_set_uri(nng_http_req *req, const char *uri);
```

DESCRIPTION

The nng_http_req_set_uri() sets the Request-URI associated with the request *req* to *uri*. The *uri* should contain precisely the string that will be sent to the HTTP server in the request, including any query information or fragment.

A local copy of the *uri* is made in the request *req*.

🛈   No validation or canonicalization of the *uri* is performed.

💡   The nng_url_parse() function can be used to perform validation and canonicalization. The u_requri member will contain a suitable value that can be used with this function.

RETURN VALUES

This function returns 0 on success, and non-zero otherwise.

ERRORS

NNG_ENOMEM	Insufficient memory to perform the operation.
NNG_ENOTSUP	No support for HTTP in the library.

SEE ALSO

nng_http_req_alloc(3http), nng_http_req_get_uri(3http), nng_url_parse(3), nng(7)

NAME

nng_http_req_set_version - set HTTP request protocol version

SYNOPSIS

```
#include <nng/nng.h>
#include <nng/supplemental/http/http.h>

int nng_http_req_set_version(nng_http_req *req, const char *version);
```

DESCRIPTION

The nng_http_req_set_version() sets the HTTP protocol version associated with the request *req* to *version*. The *version* must be a string containing a valid HTTP protocol version, such as "HTTP/1.0". The default value is "HTTP/1.1".

A local copy of the *version* is made in the request *req*.

> ℹ️   No validation of the version supplied is performed.

> ℹ️   The library does not contain support for versions of HTTP other than "HTTP/1.0" and "HTTP/1.1". Specifying any other version may result in unspecified behavior.

RETURN VALUES

This function returns 0 on success, and non-zero otherwise.

ERRORS

NNG_ENOMEM	Insufficient memory to perform the operation.
NNG_ENOTSUP	No support for HTTP in the library.

SEE ALSO

nng_http_req_alloc(3http), nng_http_req_get_version(3http), nng(7)

NAME

nng_http_res_add_header - add HTTP response header

SYNOPSIS

```
#include <nng/nng.h>
#include <nng/supplemental/http/http.h>

int nng_http_res_add_header(nng_http_res *res, const char *key,
    const char *val);
```

DESCRIPTION

The nng_http_res_add_header() adds an HTTP header for the response *res* and the *key* to the *val*. The *key* and *val* are copied.

If a header with the value of *key* already exists, then a comma and whitespace separate are appended to it, followed by *val*.

If no such header already exists, then one is created with the value *val*.

> 💡 The HTTP specification requires that duplicate headers be treated identically to a single header with multiple comma-delimited values.

> 💡 See nng_http_res_set_header() if replacement of an existing header rather than appending to it is desired.

The value of *key* is case insensitive, and should not include the final colon in an HTTP header. For example, specifying Host or hOSt are equivalent, whereas the value Host: is not a legal header key.

RETURN VALUES

This function returns 0 on success, and non-zero otherwise.

ERRORS

NNG_ENOMEM	Insufficient memory to perform the operation.
NNG_ENOTSUP	No support for HTTP in the library.

SEE ALSO

nng_http_res_alloc(3http), nng_http_res_del_header(3http), nng_http_res_get_header(3http), nng_http_res_set_header(3http), nng(7)

NAME

nng_http_res_alloc - allocate HTTP response structure

SYNOPSIS

```
#include <nng/nng.h>
#include <nng/supplemental/http/http.h>

int nng_http_res_alloc(nng_http_res **resp);
```

DESCRIPTION

The nng_http_res_alloc() function allocates a new HTTP response structure and stores a pointer to it in *resp*. The response will be initialized with status code 200 (NNG_HTTP_STATUS_OK), and a reason phrase of `"OK"`, and HTTP protocol version `"HTTP/1.1"`.

> 💡 When an error response is needed, consider using nng_http_res_alloc_error() instead.

RETURN VALUES

This function returns 0 on success, and non-zero otherwise.

ERRORS

NNG_ENOMEM	Insufficient free memory exists to allocate a message.
NNG_ENOTSUP	HTTP support not configured.

SEE ALSO

nng_http_conn_read_res(3http), nng_http_conn_write_res(3http), nng_http_req_alloc(3http), nng_http_res_alloc_error(3http), nng_http_res_add_header(3http), nng_http_res_copy_data(3http), nng_http_res_del_header(3http), nng_http_res_free(3http), nng_http_res_get_header(3http), nng_http_res_get_reason(3http), nng_http_res_get_status(3http), nng_http_res_get_version(3http), nng_http_res_reset(3http), nng_http_res_set_data(3http), nng_http_res_set_reason(3http), nng_http_res_set_status(3http), nng_http_res_set_version(3http), nng_strerror(3), nng(7)

NAME

nng_http_res_alloc_error - allocate HTTP error response

SYNOPSIS

```
#include <nng/nng.h>
#include <nng/supplemental/http/http.h>

int nng_http_res_alloc_error(nng_http_res **resp, uint16_t status);
```

DESCRIPTION

The nng_http_res_alloc_error() function allocates a new HTTP response structure and stores a pointer to it in *resp*. The response will be initialized with the status code *status*, a corresponding reason phrase, and a simple HTML page containing the same information will be generated and attached to the response. (Relevant HTTP headers will be set as well, such as Content-Type and Content-Length.) The HTTP protocol version is also set to "HTTP/1.1".

> 💡   This is the simplest way to generate an error response.

RETURN VALUES

This function returns 0 on success, and non-zero otherwise.

ERRORS

NNG_ENOMEM	Insufficient free memory exists to allocate a message.
NNG_ENOTSUP	HTTP support not configured.

SEE ALSO

nng_http_res_alloc(3http), nng_http_res_free(3http), nng_http_res_set_reason(3http), nng_http_res_set_status(3http), nng_strerror(3), nng(7)

NAME

nng_http_res_copy_data - copy HTTP response body

SYNOPSIS

```
#include <nng/nng.h>
#include <nng/supplemental/http/http.h>

int nng_http_res_copy_data(nng_http_res *res, const void *body, size_t size);
```

DESCRIPTION

The nng_http_res_copy_data() makes a copy of *body* (of size *size*) and sets the HTTP body for the response *res* to it. The copy will be deallocated automatically when *res* is freed.

The copied body data will be automatically sent with the response when it is sent using nng_http_conn_write_res().

This also updates the relevant Content-Length header of *res*.

> ℹ The current framework does not support sending data via chunked transfer-encoding.

> 💡 To avoid copying data, the nng_http_res_set_data() may be used instead.

> 💡 It is a good idea to also set the Content-Type header.

RETURN VALUES

This function returns 0 on success, and non-zero otherwise.

ERRORS

NNG_ENOMEM	Insufficient memory to perform the operation.
NNG_ENOTSUP	No support for HTTP in the library.

SEE ALSO

nng_http_conn_write_res(3http), nng_http_res_alloc(3http), nng_http_res_set_data(3http), nng_http_res_set_header(3http), nng(7)

NAME

nng_http_res_set_header - set HTTP response header

SYNOPSIS

```
#include <nng/nng.h>
#include <nng/supplemental/http/http.h>

int nng_http_res_set_header(nng_http_res *res, const char *key);
```

DESCRIPTION

The nng_http_res_del_header() removes all HTTP headers with the associated *key* from the response structure *res*.

The value of *key* is case insensitive, and should not include the final colon in an HTTP header. For example, specifying Host or h0St are equivalent, whereas the value Host: is not a legal header key.

RETURN VALUES

This function returns 0 on success, and non-zero otherwise.

ERRORS

NNG_ENOENT	No header with the key *key* was present.
NNG_ENOTSUP	No support for HTTP in the library.

SEE ALSO

nng_http_res_alloc(3http), nng_http_res_add_header(3http), nng_http_res_del_header(3http), nng_http_res_get_header(3http), nng(7)

NAME

nng_http_res_free - free HTTP response structure

SYNOPSIS

```
#include <nng/nng.h>
#include <nng/supplemental/http/http.h>

void nng_http_res_free(nng_http_res *req);
```

DESCRIPTION

The nng_http_res_free() function deallocates the HTTP response structure *res* entirely.

> 💡 Instead of freeing and reallocating response structures, it is possible to reuse *res* with nng_http_res_reset().

RETURN VALUES

None.

ERRORS

None.

SEE ALSO

nng_http_res_alloc(3http), nng_http_res_reset(3http), nng(7)

NAME

nng_http_res_get_data - get HTTP response body

SYNOPSIS

```
#include <nng/nng.h>
#include <nng/supplemental/http/http.h>

void nng_http_res_get_data(nng_http_res *res, void **bodyp, size_t *sizep);
```

DESCRIPTION

The nng_http_res_get_data() gets the HTTP body associated with the request *res*, storing a pointer to the buffer at the location referenced by *bodyp*, and the length of the associated buffer at the location referenced by *sizep*.

> ℹ️ The buffer returned is owned by *res*, and will automatically freed when the request is freed.

RETURN VALUES

None.

ERRORS

None.

SEE ALSO

nng_http_req_alloc(3http), nng_http_req_copy_data(3http), nng_http_req_copy_data(3http), nng(7)

NAME

nng_http_res_get_header - return HTTP response header

SYNOPSIS

```
#include <nng/nng.h>
#include <nng/supplemental/http/http.h>

const char *nng_http_res_get_header(nng_http_res *res, const char *key);
```

DESCRIPTION

The nng_http_res_get_header() looks for an HTTP header *key* in the response *res*, and returns the associated value if found, or NULL if not found.

The value of *key* is case insensitive, and should not include the final colon in an HTTP header. For example, specifying Host or hOSt are equivalent, whereas the value Host: will not find anything.

RETURN VALUES

HTTP header value for *key*, if it exists, or NULL otherwise.

ERRORS

None.

SEE ALSO

nng_http_res_alloc(3http), nng_http_res_add_header(3http), nng_http_res_set_header(3http), nng(7)

NAME

nng_http_res_get_reason - return HTTP response reason

SYNOPSIS

```
#include <nng/nng.h>
#include <nng/supplemental/http/http.h>

const char *nng_http_res_get_reason(nng_http_res *res);
```

DESCRIPTION

The nng_http_res_get_reason() returns a string representing the "reason phrase" associated with the response *res*. This is a human-readable explanation of the status code that would be obtained from nng_http_res_get_status().

RETURN VALUES

Reason as a string.

ERRORS

None.

SEE ALSO

nng_http_res_alloc(3http), nng_http_res_get_status(3http), nng_http_res_set_reason(3http), nng(7)

NAME

nng_http_res_get_status - return HTTP status code

SYNOPSIS

```
#include <nng/nng.h>
#include <nng/supplemental/http/http.h>

uint16_t nng_http_res_get_status(nng_http_res *res);
```

DESCRIPTION

The nng_http_res_get_status() returns a numeric code corresponding to the HTTP status of the response *res*.

For convenience, a number of predefined symbols corresponding to well-known HTTP status codes are available.

```
enum {
    NNG_HTTP_STATUS_CONTINUE                  = 100,
    NNG_HTTP_STATUS_SWITCHING                 = 101,
    NNG_HTTP_STATUS_PROCESSING                = 102,
    NNG_HTTP_STATUS_OK                        = 200,
    NNG_HTTP_STATUS_CREATED                   = 201,
    NNG_HTTP_STATUS_ACCEPTED                  = 202,
    NNG_HTTP_STATUS_NOT_AUTHORITATIVE         = 203,
    NNG_HTTP_STATUS_NO_CONTENT                = 204,
    NNG_HTTP_STATUS_RESET_CONTENT             = 205,
    NNG_HTTP_STATUS_PARTIAL_CONTENT           = 206,
    NNG_HTTP_STATUS_MULTI_STATUS              = 207,
    NNG_HTTP_STATUS_ALREADY_REPORTED          = 208,
    NNG_HTTP_STATUS_IM_USED                   = 226,
    NNG_HTTP_STATUS_MULTIPLE_CHOICES          = 300,
    NNG_HTTP_STATUS_STATUS_MOVED_PERMANENTLY  = 301,
    NNG_HTTP_STATUS_FOUND                     = 302,
    NNG_HTTP_STATUS_SEE_OTHER                 = 303,
    NNG_HTTP_STATUS_NOT_MODIFIED              = 304,
    NNG_HTTP_STATUS_USE_PROXY                 = 305,
    NNG_HTTP_STATUS_TEMPORARY_REDIRECT        = 307,
    NNG_HTTP_STATUS_PERMANENT_REDIRECT        = 308,
    NNG_HTTP_STATUS_BAD_REQUEST               = 400,
    NNG_HTTP_STATUS_UNAUTHORIZED              = 401,
    NNG_HTTP_STATUS_PAYMENT_REQUIRED          = 402,
    NNG_HTTP_STATUS_FORBIDDEN                 = 403,
    NNG_HTTP_STATUS_NOT_FOUND                 = 404,
    NNG_HTTP_STATUS_METHOD_NOT_ALLOWED        = 405,
    NNG_HTTP_STATUS_NOT_ACCEPTABLE            = 406,
    NNG_HTTP_STATUS_PROXY_AUTH_REQUIRED       = 407,
    NNG_HTTP_STATUS_REQUEST_TIMEOUT           = 408,
    NNG_HTTP_STATUS_CONFLICT                  = 409,
```

```
        NNG_HTTP_STATUS_GONE                    = 410,
        NNG_HTTP_STATUS_LENGTH_REQUIRED         = 411,
        NNG_HTTP_STATUS_PRECONDITION_FAILED     = 412,
        NNG_HTTP_STATUS_PAYLOAD_TOO_LARGE       = 413,
        NNG_HTTP_STATUS_ENTITY_TOO_LONG         = 414,
        NNG_HTTP_STATUS_UNSUPPORTED_MEDIA_TYPE  = 415,
        NNG_HTTP_STATUS_RANGE_NOT_SATISFIABLE   = 416,
        NNG_HTTP_STATUS_EXPECTATION_FAILED      = 417,
        NNG_HTTP_STATUS_TEAPOT                  = 418,
        NNG_HTTP_STATUS_UNPROCESSABLE_ENTITY    = 422,
        NNG_HTTP_STATUS_LOCKED                  = 423,
        NNG_HTTP_STATUS_FAILED_DEPENDENCY       = 424,
        NNG_HTTP_STATUS_UPGRADE_REQUIRED        = 426,
        NNG_HTTP_STATUS_PRECONDITION_REQUIRED   = 428,
        NNG_HTTP_STATUS_TOO_MANY_REQUESTS       = 429,
        NNG_HTTP_STATUS_HEADERS_TOO_LARGE       = 431,
        NNG_HTTP_STATUS_UNAVAIL_LEGAL_REASONS   = 451,
        NNG_HTTP_STATUS_INTERNAL_SERVER_ERROR   = 500,
        NNG_HTTP_STATUS_NOT_IMPLEMENTED         = 501,
        NNG_HTTP_STATUS_BAD_GATEWAY             = 502,
        NNG_HTTP_STATUS_SERVICE_UNAVAILABLE     = 503,
        NNG_HTTP_STATUS_GATEWAY_TIMEOUT         = 504,
        NNG_HTTP_STATUS_HTTP_VERSION_NOT_SUPP   = 505,
        NNG_HTTP_STATUS_VARIANT_ALSO_NEGOTIATES = 506,
        NNG_HTTP_STATUS_INSUFFICIENT_STORAGE    = 507,
        NNG_HTTP_STATUS_LOOP_DETECTED           = 508,
        NNG_HTTP_STATUS_NOT_EXTENDED            = 510,
        NNG_HTTP_STATUS_NETWORK_AUTH_REQUIRED   = 511,
}
```

> 💡 When displaying status information to users (or logging such information), consider also including the "reason phrase" obtained with nng_http_res_get_reason().

RETURN VALUES

HTTP status code.

ERRORS

None.

SEE ALSO

nng_http_res_alloc(3http), nng_http_res_get_reason(3http), nng_http_res_set_status(3http), nng(7)

NAME

nng_http_res_get_version - return HTTP response protocol version

SYNOPSIS

```
#include <nng/nng.h>
#include <nng/supplemental/http/http.h>

const char *nng_http_res_get_version(nng_http_res *res);
```

DESCRIPTION

The nng_http_res_get_version() returns a string representing the HTTP protocol version associated with the request *res*, such as "HTTP/1.1".

RETURN VALUES

Response version as a string.

ERRORS

None.

SEE ALSO

nng_http_res_alloc(3http), nng_http_res_set_version(3http), nng(7)

NAME

nng_http_res_reset - reset HTTP response structure

SYNOPSIS

```
#include <nng/nng.h>
#include <nng/supplemental/http/http.h>

void nng_http_res_reset(nng_http_res *res);
```

DESCRIPTION

The nng_http_res_reset() function resets the response *res* so that it is just as if it had been freshly allocated with nng_http_res_alloc().

RETURN VALUES

None.

ERRORS

None.

SEE ALSO

nng_http_res_alloc(3http), nng(7)

NAME

nng_http_res_set_data - set HTTP response body

SYNOPSIS

```
#include <nng/nng.h>
#include <nng/supplemental/http/http.h>

int nng_http_res_set_data(nng_http_res *res, const void *body, size_t size);
```

DESCRIPTION

The nng_http_res_set_data() sets the HTTP body associated with the response *res* to *body*, and the size of the body to *size*. This body data will be automatically sent with the response when it is sent using nng_http_conn_write_res().

This also updates the relevant Content-Length header of *res*.

> ℹ The current framework does not support sending data via chunked transfer-encoding.

The *body* is **not** copied, and the caller must ensure that it is available until the *res* is deallocated.

> 💡 To have a local copy allocated with *res* that will be automatically deallocated when *res* is freed, see nng_http_res_copy_data().

> 💡 It is a good idea to also set the Content-Type header.

RETURN VALUES

This function returns 0 on success, and non-zero otherwise.

ERRORS

NNG_ENOMEM	Insufficient memory to perform the operation.
NNG_ENOTSUP	No support for HTTP in the library.

SEE ALSO

nng_http_conn_write_res(3http), nng_http_res_alloc(3http), nng_http_res_copy_data(3http), nng_http_res_set_header(3http), nng(7)

NAME

nng_http_res_set_header - set HTTP response header

SYNOPSIS

```
#include <nng/nng.h>
#include <nng/supplemental/http/http.h>

int nng_http_res_set_header(nng_http_res *res, const char *key,
    const char *val);
```

DESCRIPTION

The nng_http_res_set_header() sets the HTTP header for the response *res* and the *key* to the *val*. The *key* and *val* are copied. Any previous header with the same *key* is replaced.

> 💡 See nng_http_res_add_header() to add additional headers with the same *key* without replacing them.

The value of *key* is case insensitive, and should not include the final colon in an HTTP header. For example, specifying Host or hOSt are equivalent, whereas the value Host: is not a legal header key.

RETURN VALUES

This function returns 0 on success, and non-zero otherwise.

ERRORS

NNG_ENOMEM	Insufficient memory to perform the operation.
NNG_ENOTSUP	No support for HTTP in the library.

SEE ALSO

nng_http_res_alloc(3http), nng_http_res_add_header(3http), nng_http_res_del_header(3http), nng_http_res_get_header(3http), nng(7)

NAME

nng_http_res_set_reason - set HTTP response reason

SYNOPSIS

```
#include <nng/nng.h>
#include <nng/supplemental/http/http.h>

int nng_http_res_set_reason(nng_http_res *res, const char *reason);
```

DESCRIPTION

The nng_http_res_set_reason() sets the human readable "reason phrase" associated with the response *res* to *reason*.

If the value of *reason* is NULL (the default), then a default reason phrase is supplied based upon the value of the status code (see nng_http_res_set_status()).

> 💡 The *reason* is never parsed automatically, but it can be a hint for humans to help them understand the nature of any erroneous result.

A local copy of the *reason* is made in the response *res*.

RETURN VALUES

This function returns 0 on success, and non-zero otherwise.

ERRORS

NNG_ENOMEM	Insufficient memory to perform the operation.
NNG_ENOTSUP	No support for HTTP in the library.

SEE ALSO

nng_http_res_alloc(3http), nng_http_req_get_reason(3http), nng_http_req_set_status(3http), nng(7)

NAME

nng_http_res_set_status - set HTTP response status

SYNOPSIS

```
#include <nng/nng.h>
#include <nng/supplemental/http/http.h>

int nng_http_res_set_status(nng_http_res *res, uint16_t status);
```

DESCRIPTION

The nng_http_res_set_status() sets the numeric HTTP status code associated with the response *res* to *status*. The default value for a newly allocated response is 200 (NNG_HTTP_STATUS_OK).

The *status* is not verified, so the caller should take care to ensure that only a valid code is supplied.

For convenience, a number of predefined symbols are available.

```
enum {
    NNG_HTTP_STATUS_CONTINUE                = 100,
    NNG_HTTP_STATUS_SWITCHING               = 101,
    NNG_HTTP_STATUS_PROCESSING              = 102,
    NNG_HTTP_STATUS_OK                      = 200,
    NNG_HTTP_STATUS_CREATED                 = 201,
    NNG_HTTP_STATUS_ACCEPTED                = 202,
    NNG_HTTP_STATUS_NOT_AUTHORITATIVE       = 203,
    NNG_HTTP_STATUS_NO_CONTENT              = 204,
    NNG_HTTP_STATUS_RESET_CONTENT           = 205,
    NNG_HTTP_STATUS_PARTIAL_CONTENT         = 206,
    NNG_HTTP_STATUS_MULTI_STATUS            = 207,
    NNG_HTTP_STATUS_ALREADY_REPORTED        = 208,
    NNG_HTTP_STATUS_IM_USED                 = 226,
    NNG_HTTP_STATUS_MULTIPLE_CHOICES        = 300,
    NNG_HTTP_STATUS_STATUS_MOVED_PERMANENTLY = 301,
    NNG_HTTP_STATUS_FOUND                   = 302,
    NNG_HTTP_STATUS_SEE_OTHER               = 303,
    NNG_HTTP_STATUS_NOT_MODIFIED            = 304,
    NNG_HTTP_STATUS_USE_PROXY               = 305,
    NNG_HTTP_STATUS_TEMPORARY_REDIRECT      = 307,
    NNG_HTTP_STATUS_PERMANENT_REDIRECT      = 308,
    NNG_HTTP_STATUS_BAD_REQUEST             = 400,
    NNG_HTTP_STATUS_UNAUTHORIZED            = 401,
    NNG_HTTP_STATUS_PAYMENT_REQUIRED        = 402,
    NNG_HTTP_STATUS_FORBIDDEN               = 403,
    NNG_HTTP_STATUS_NOT_FOUND               = 404,
    NNG_HTTP_STATUS_METHOD_NOT_ALLOWED      = 405,
    NNG_HTTP_STATUS_NOT_ACCEPTABLE          = 406,
    NNG_HTTP_STATUS_PROXY_AUTH_REQUIRED     = 407,
    NNG_HTTP_STATUS_REQUEST_TIMEOUT         = 408,
```

```
      NNG_HTTP_STATUS_CONFLICT                    = 409,
      NNG_HTTP_STATUS_GONE                        = 410,
      NNG_HTTP_STATUS_LENGTH_REQUIRED             = 411,
      NNG_HTTP_STATUS_PRECONDITION_FAILED         = 412,
      NNG_HTTP_STATUS_PAYLOAD_TOO_LARGE           = 413,
      NNG_HTTP_STATUS_ENTITY_TOO_LONG             = 414,
      NNG_HTTP_STATUS_UNSUPPORTED_MEDIA_TYPE      = 415,
      NNG_HTTP_STATUS_RANGE_NOT_SATISFIABLE       = 416,
      NNG_HTTP_STATUS_EXPECTATION_FAILED          = 417,
      NNG_HTTP_STATUS_TEAPOT                      = 418,
      NNG_HTTP_STATUS_UNPROCESSABLE_ENTITY        = 422,
      NNG_HTTP_STATUS_LOCKED                      = 423,
      NNG_HTTP_STATUS_FAILED_DEPENDENCY           = 424,
      NNG_HTTP_STATUS_UPGRADE_REQUIRED            = 426,
      NNG_HTTP_STATUS_PRECONDITION_REQUIRED       = 428,
      NNG_HTTP_STATUS_TOO_MANY_REQUESTS           = 429,
      NNG_HTTP_STATUS_HEADERS_TOO_LARGE           = 431,
      NNG_HTTP_STATUS_UNAVAIL_LEGAL_REASONS       = 451,
      NNG_HTTP_STATUS_INTERNAL_SERVER_ERROR       = 500,
      NNG_HTTP_STATUS_NOT_IMPLEMENTED             = 501,
      NNG_HTTP_STATUS_BAD_GATEWAY                 = 502,
      NNG_HTTP_STATUS_SERVICE_UNAVAILABLE         = 503,
      NNG_HTTP_STATUS_GATEWAY_TIMEOUT             = 504,
      NNG_HTTP_STATUS_HTTP_VERSION_NOT_SUPP       = 505,
      NNG_HTTP_STATUS_VARIANT_ALSO_NEGOTIATES     = 506,
      NNG_HTTP_STATUS_INSUFFICIENT_STORAGE        = 507,
      NNG_HTTP_STATUS_LOOP_DETECTED               = 508,
      NNG_HTTP_STATUS_NOT_EXTENDED                = 510,
      NNG_HTTP_STATUS_NETWORK_AUTH_REQUIRED       = 511,
  };
```

Please see the relevant HTTP RFCs for the semantics and correct use of these status codes.

> 💡 It is a good idea to also set the "reason phrase" with `nng_http_set_reason()`. This will help any humans who may have to diagnose a failure.

RETURN VALUES

This function returns 0 on success, and non-zero otherwise.

ERRORS

NNG_ENOTSUP   No support for HTTP in the library.

SEE ALSO

nng_http_res_alloc(3http), nng_http_req_get_status(3http), nng_http_req_set_reason(3http), nng(7)

NAME

nng_http_res_set_version - set HTTP response protocol version

SYNOPSIS

```
#include <nng/nng.h>
#include <nng/supplemental/http/http.h>

int nng_http_res_set_version(nng_http_res *res, const char *version);
```

DESCRIPTION

The nng_http_res_set_version() sets the HTTP protocol version associated with the response *res* to *version*. The *version* must be a string containing a valid HTTP protocol version, such as "HTTP/1.0". The default value is "HTTP/1.1".

A local copy of the *version* is made in the response *res*.

ⓘ   No validation of the version supplied is performed.

ⓘ   The library does not contain support for versions of HTTP other than "HTTP/1.0" and "HTTP/1.1". Specifying any other version may result in unspecified behavior.

RETURN VALUES

This function returns 0 on success, and non-zero otherwise.

ERRORS

NNG_ENOMEM	Insufficient memory to perform the operation.
NNG_ENOTSUP	No support for HTTP in the library.

SEE ALSO

nng_http_res_alloc(3http), nng_http_req_get_version(3http), nng(7)

NAME

nng_http_server_add_handler - add HTTP server handler

SYNOPSIS

```
#include <nng/nng.h>
#include <nng/supplemental/http/http.h>

int nng_http_server_add_handler(nng_http_server *s, nng_http_handler *h);
```

DESCRIPTION

The nng_http_server_add_handler() adds the handler *h* to the server instance *s*.

If another handler is already added to the server that would conflict with handler *h*, then the operation will fail with NNG_EADDRINUSE.

If a handler is added to a server, and the server is subsequently deallocated, the handler and any of its resources will also be deallocated.

Handlers that are added to a server may be subsequently removed using the nng_http_server_del_handler() function.

RETURN VALUES

This function returns 0 on success, and non-zero otherwise.

ERRORS

NNG_EADDRINUSE	Handler conflicts with another handler.
NNG_ENOMEM	Insufficient free memory exists.
NNG_ENOTSUP	HTTP not supported.

SEE ALSO

nng_http_handler_alloc(3http), nng_http_server_del_handler(3http), nng_http_server_hold(3http), nng_strerror(3), nng(7)

NAME

nng_http_server_del_handler - delete HTTP server handler

SYNOPSIS

```
#include <nng/nng.h>
#include <nng/supplemental/http/http.h>

int nng_http_server_del_handler(nng_http_server *s, nng_http_handler *h);
```

DESCRIPTION

The nng_http_server_del_handler() removes the handler *h* from the server instance *s*.

Once a handler has been deleted from a server, it is the responsibility of the caller to dispose of the handler, or add it to another server instance.

RETURN VALUES

This function returns 0 on success, and non-zero otherwise.

ERRORS

NNG_ENOENT	Handler is not registered with server.
NNG_ENOTSUP	HTTP not supported.

SEE ALSO

nng_http_handler_free(3http), nng_http_server_add_handler(3http), nng_strerror(3), nng(7)

NAME

nng_http_server_get_tls - get HTTP server TLS configuration

SYNOPSIS

```
#include <nng/nng.h>
#include <nng/supplemental/http/http.h>

int nng_http_server_get_tls(nng_http_server *s, nng_tls_config **cfgp);
```

DESCRIPTION

The nng_http_server_get_tls() obtains the TLS configuration of server *s* and saves a pointer to it in the address referenced by *cfgp*.

The object will be returned with an extra hold (see nng_tls_config_hold()) placed on it on behalf of the caller. The caller should free this hold by calling nng_tls_config_free() with it is done with the TLS configuration.

RETURN VALUES

This function returns 0 on success, and non-zero otherwise.

ERRORS

NNG_EINVAL	TLS not configured on server.
NNG_ENOMEM	Insufficient free memory exists.
NNG_ENOTSUP	Either HTTP or TLS not supported.

SEE ALSO

nng_http_server_hold(3http), nng_http_server_set_tls(3http), nng_http_server_start(3http), nng_tls_config_alloc(3tls), nng_tls_config_free(3tls), nng_tls_config_hold(3tls), nng_strerror(3), nng(7)

NAME

nng_http_server_hold - get and hold HTTP server instance

SYNOPSIS

```
#include <nng/nng.h>
#include <nng/supplemental/http/http.h>

int nng_http_server_hold(nng_http_server **serverp, const nng_url *url);
```

DESCRIPTION

The nng_http_server_hold() acquires an instance of an HTTP server suitable for use in serving the URL identified by *url*, and stores a pointer to it at the location pointed to by *serverp*.

This function first looks to see if an existing HTTP server instance exists, that is suitable for this. If so, it increments the reference count on it and uses that. Otherwise, it will attempt to create a new server instance with an initial reference count of one (1).

The server instance is not started, and can have additional configuration applied to it before it is later started with nng_http_server_start().

> The URL matching logic in determining servers is unable to distinguish between different aliases for the same local IP address. This may create problems when using URLs for virtual hosting. It is recommended to use canonical IP addresses or names in the *url* to avoid confusion.

RETURN VALUES

This function returns 0 on success, and non-zero otherwise.

ERRORS

NNG_ENOMEM	Insufficient free memory exists.
NNG_ENOTSUP	HTTP not supported.

SEE ALSO

nng_http_server_add_handler(3http), nng_http_server_release(3http), nng_http_server_stop(3http), nng_url_parse(3) nng_strerror(3), nng(7)

NAME

nng_http_server_release - release HTTP server instance

SYNOPSIS

```
#include <nng/nng.h>
#include <nng/supplemental/http/http.h>

void nng_http_server_release(nng_http_server *server);
```

DESCRIPTION

The nng_http_server_release() releases an instance of an HTTP *server* that was previously held with nng_http_server_hold().

This effectively drops the reference count on the server instance. When the reference count drops to zero, then the *server* and all resources associated with it (e.g. HTTP handlers, connections, etc.) are deallocated. (If the server is "running" when this occurs, then the server is stopped.)

⚠ It is an error to release an instance of a server that has not previously been held, or to attempt to release an instance more times than it has been held.

RETURN VALUES

None.

ERRORS

None.

SEE ALSO

nng_http_server_hold(3http), nng_http_server_stop(3http), nng(7)

NAME

nng_http_server_res_error - use HTTP server error page

SYNOPSIS

```
#include <nng/nng.h>
#include <nng/supplemental/http/http.h>

int nng_http_server_res_error(nng_http_server *server,
        nng_http_res *response);
```

DESCRIPTION

The nng_http_server_res_error() sets the body of *response* to *server*'s error page, which may have been customized using the nng_http_server_error_file() or nng_http_server_error_page() functions.

The status code of the *response* should have already been set, either implicitly by allocating it with nng_http_res_alloc_error(), or by calling nng_http_res_set_status().

Any content body previously set for *response* will be overridden by this function.

RETURN VALUES

This function returns 0 on success, and non-zero otherwise.

ERRORS

NNG_ENOMEM	Insufficient free memory exists.
NNG_ENOTSUP	HTTP not supported.

SEE ALSO

nng_http_res_alloc_error(3http), nng_http_server_hold(3http), nng_http_server_set_error_file(3http), nng_http_server_set_error_page(3http), nng_strerror(3), nng(7)

NAME

nng_http_server_set_error_file - set custom HTTP error file

SYNOPSIS

```
#include <nng/nng.h>
#include <nng/supplemental/http/http.h>

int nng_http_server_set_error_file(nng_http_server *server,
        uint16_t code, const char *path);
```

DESCRIPTION

The nng_http_server_set_error_file() sets an error page to be used for HTTP status *code* on the server instance *server*. The body content of the HTTP responses will contain the file contents of the file located at *path*, which should be an HTML file.

The custom HTML content will be used when the server is returning an internally generated error response, or is returning an error response that was allocated with the nng_http_res_alloc_error() function. This HTML content will also be used if the application calls the nng_http_server_res_error(). The last custom error page set for *code* by either this function or nng_http_server_error_page() will be used.

> ⓘ Error responses that have their body content changed after allocation, or that are written directly by the application, will not use the body content supplied here.

> ⓘ The file contents of *path* are read when this function is called. Therefore, if the file contents are changed, then this function should be called again to update the error page.

RETURN VALUES

This function returns 0 on success, and non-zero otherwise.

ERRORS

NNG_ENOENT	The file named by *path* does not exist.
NNG_EPERM	No permission to read the file named by *path*.
NNG_ENOMEM	Insufficient free memory exists.
NNG_ENOTSUP	HTTP not supported.

SEE ALSO

nng_http_res_alloc_error(3http), nng_http_server_hold(3http), nng_http_server_res_error(3http), nng_http_server_set_error_page(3http), nng_strerror(3), nng(7)

NAME

nng_http_server_set_error_page - set custom HTTP error page

SYNOPSIS

```
#include <nng/nng.h>
#include <nng/supplemental/http/http.h>

int nng_http_server_set_error_page(nng_http_server *server,
        uint16_t code, const char *html);
```

DESCRIPTION

The nng_http_server_set_error_page() sets an error page to be used for HTTP status *code* on the server instance *server*. The body content of the HTTP responses will contain *html*.

The custom HTML content will be used when the server is returning an internally generated error response, or is returning an error response that was allocated with the nng_http_res_alloc_error() function. This HTML content will also be used if the application calls the nng_http_server_res_error(). The last custom error page set for *code* by either this function or nng_http_server_error_file() will be used.

ℹ️   Error responses that have their body content changed after allocation, or that are written directly by the application, will not use the body content supplied here.

The supplied HTML content is copied by this function, and may be reused after this function returns.

RETURN VALUES

This function returns 0 on success, and non-zero otherwise.

ERRORS

NNG_ENOMEM	Insufficient free memory exists.
NNG_ENOTSUP	HTTP not supported.

SEE ALSO

nng_http_res_alloc_error(3http), nng_http_server_hold(3http), nng_http_server_res_error(3http), nng_http_server_set_error_file(3http), nng_strerror(3), nng(7)

NAME

nng_http_server_set_tls - set HTTP server TLS configuration

SYNOPSIS

```
#include <nng/nng.h>
#include <nng/supplemental/http/http.h>

int nng_http_server_set_tls(nng_http_server *s, nng_tls_config *cfg);
```

DESCRIPTION

The nng_http_server_set_tls() sets the TLS configuration of server *s* to *cfg*.

This change overwrites any previous TLS configuration.

> ⚠️   This also invalidates any previously obtained values from nng_http_server_get_tls().

If the server is already running (i.e. it has been started with nng_http_server_start()) then this will fail with NNG_EBUSY.

> 💡   Generally, the *cfg* must have a configured private key, set with nng_tls_config_own_cert() or similar.

RETURN VALUES

This function returns 0 on success, and non-zero otherwise.

ERRORS

NNG_EBUSY	Server instance is running.
NNG_ENOMEM	Insufficient free memory exists.
NNG_ENOTSUP	Either HTTP or TLS not supported.

SEE ALSO

nng_http_server_get_tls(3http), nng_http_server_hold(3http), nng_http_server_start(3http), nng_tls_config_alloc(3tls), nng_strerror(3), nng(7)

NAME

nng_http_server_start - start HTTP server

SYNOPSIS

```
#include <nng/nng.h>
#include <nng/supplemental/http/http.h>

int nng_http_server_start(nng_http_server *server);
```

DESCRIPTION

The nng_http_server_start() starts the HTTP server instance *server*. This causes it to bind to the appropriate TCP port, and start accepting connections and handling HTTP requests.

RETURN VALUES

This function returns 0 on success, and non-zero otherwise.

ERRORS

NNG_EADDRINUSE	The TCP port is unavailable.
NNG_EADDRINVAL	The server is configured with an invalid address.
NNG_ENOMEM	Insufficient free memory exists.
NNG_ENOTSUP	HTTP not supported.

SEE ALSO

nng_http_server_hold(3http), nng_http_server_release(3http), nng_http_server_stop(3http), nng_url_parse(3) nng_strerror(3), nng(7)

NAME

nng_http_server_stop - stop HTTP server

SYNOPSIS

```
#include <nng/nng.h>
#include <nng/supplemental/http/http.h>

void nng_http_server_stop(nng_http_server *server);
```

DESCRIPTION

The nng_http_server_stop() undoes the effect of nng_http_server_start().

Each call by nng_http_server_start() acts as reference count, and should be matched by a call to nng_http_server_stop(). When the reference count drops to zero, then the server is actually stopped, and existing open connections to it are closed.

This function does not wait for the connections to close.

> ℹ️ Once the server instance is actually stopped, it cannot be started again, and any future calls to nng_http_server_hold() will return a new instance of the server. It is expected that the caller will follow this function call with a call to nng_http_server_release().

RETURN VALUES

None.

ERRORS

None.

SEE ALSO

nng_http_server_hold(3http), nng_http_server_release(3http), nng_http_server_start(3http), nng(7)

Section 3supp

Supplemental Functions

NAME

nng_clock - get time

SYNOPSIS

```
#include <nng/nng.h>
#include <nng/supplemental/util/platform.h>

typedef uint64_t nng_time;

nng_time nng_clock(void);
```

DESCRIPTION

The nng_clock() returns the number of elapsed milliseconds since some arbitrary time in the past. The resolution of the clock depends on the underlying timing facilities of the system. This function may be used for timing, but applications should not expect very fine grained values.

> ⚠ The reference time will be the same for a given program, but different programs may have different references.

> 💡 This function is intended mostly to help with setting appropriate timeouts using nng_cv_until(3supp).

RETURN VALUES

Milliseconds since reference time.

ERRORS

None.

SEE ALSO

nng_sleep_aio(3), nng_strerror(3), nng_cv_until(3supp), nng_msleep(3supp), nng_duration(5), nng(7)

NAME

nng_cv_alloc - allocate condition variable

SYNOPSIS

```
#include <nng/nng.h>
#include <nng/supplemental/util/platform.h>

typedef struct nng_cv nng_cv;

int nng_cv_alloc(nng_cv **cvp, nng_mtx *mtx);
```

DESCRIPTION

The nng_cv_alloc() function allocates a condition variable, using the mutex *mtx*, and returns it in *cvp*.

Every condition variable is associated with a mutex, which must be owned when a thread waits for the condition using nng_cv_wait() or nng_cv_until(). The mutex must also be owned when signaling the condition using the nng_cv_wake() or nng_cv_wake1() functions.

RETURN VALUES

This function returns 0 on success, and non-zero otherwise.

ERRORS

NNG_ENOMEM   Insufficient free memory exists.

SEE ALSO

nng_cv_free(3supp), nng_cv_until(3supp), nng_cv_wait(3supp), nng_cv_wake(3supp), nng_cv_wake1(3supp), nng_mtx_alloc(3supp), nng_strerror(3), nng(7)

NAME

nng_cv_free - free condition variable

SYNOPSIS

```
#include <nng/nng.h>
#include <nng/supplemental/util/platform.h>

void nng_cv_free(nng_cv *cv);
```

DESCRIPTION

The nng_cv_free() function frees the condition variable *cv*.

RETURN VALUES

None.

ERRORS

None.

SEE ALSO

nng_cv_alloc(3supp), nng(7)

NAME

nng_cv_until - wait for condition or timeout

SYNOPSIS

```
#include <nng/nng.h>
#include <nng/supplemental/util/platform.h>

int nng_cv_until(nng_cv *cv, nng_time when);
```

DESCRIPTION

The nng_cv_until() waits until either the condition variable *cv* is signaled by another thread calling either nng_cv_wake() or nng_cv_wake1(), or the system clock (as tracked by nng_clock()) reaches *when*.

The caller must have have ownership of the mutex that was used when *cv* was allocated. This function will drop the ownership of that mutex, and reacquire it atomically just before returning to the caller. (The waiting is done without holding the mutex.)

ℹ️ Any condition may be used or checked, but the condition must be checked, as it is possible for this function to wake up "spuriously". The best way to do this is inside a loop that repeats until the condition tests for true.

EXAMPLE

The following example demonstrates use of this function:

Example 1: Waiting for the condition

```
nng_mtx_lock(m);  // assume cv was allocated using m
while (!condition_true) {
    if (nng_cv_wait(cv) == NNG_ETIMEDOUT) {
        printf("Time out reached!\n");
        break;
    }
}
// condition_true is true
nng_mtx_unlock(m);
```

Example 2: Signaling the condition

```
nng_mtx_lock(m);
condition_true = true;
nng_cv_wake(cv);
nng_mtx_unlock(m);
```

RETURN VALUES

None.

ERRORS

None.

SEE ALSO

nng_cv_alloc(3supp), nng_cv_wait(3supp), nng_cv_wake(3supp), nng_cv_wake1(3supp),
nng_mtx_alloc(3supp), nng_mtx_lock(3supp), nng_mtx_unlock(3supp), nng(7)

NAME

nng_cv_wait - wait for condition

SYNOPSIS

```
#include <nng/nng.h>
#include <nng/supplemental/util/platform.h>

void nng_cv_wait(nng_cv *cv);
```

DESCRIPTION

The nng_cv_wait() waits for the condition variable *cv* to be signaled by another thread calling either nng_cv_wake() or nng_cv_wake1().

The caller must have have ownership of the mutex that was used when *cv* was allocated. This function will drop the ownership of that mutex, and reacquire it atomically just before returning to the caller. (The waiting is done without holding the mutex.)

> ℹ Any condition may be used or checked, but the condition must be checked, as it is possible for this function to wake up "spuriously". The best way to do this is inside a loop that repeats until the condition tests for true.

EXAMPLE

The following example demonstrates use of this function:

Example 1: Waiting for the condition

```
nng_mtx_lock(m);  // assume cv was allocated using m
while (!condition_true) {
    nng_cv_wait(cv);
}
// condition_true is true
nng_mtx_unlock(m);
```

Example 2: Signaling the condition

```
nng_mtx_lock(m);
condition_true = true;
cv_wake(cv);
nng_mtx_unlock(m);
```

RETURN VALUES

None.

ERRORS

None.

SEE ALSO

nng_cv_alloc(3supp), nng_cv_until(3supp), nng_cv_wake(3supp), nng_cv_wake1(3supp),
nng_mtx_alloc(3supp), nng_mtx_lock(3supp), nng_mtx_unlock(3supp), nng(7)

NAME

nng_cv_wake - wake all waiters

SYNOPSIS

```
#include <nng/nng.h>
#include <nng/supplemental/util/platform.h>

void nng_cv_wake(nng_cv *cv);
```

DESCRIPTION

The nng_cv_wake() wakes any threads waiting for the condition variable *cv* to be signaled in the nng_cv_wait() or nng_cv_until() functions.

The caller must have have ownership of the mutex that was used when *cv* was allocated.

> ℹ️ The caller should already have set the condition that the waiters will check, while holding the mutex.

> 💡 This function wakes all threads, which is generally safer but can lead to a problem known as the "thundering herd" when there are many waiters, as they are all woken simultaneously. See nng_cv_wake1() for a solution to this problem.

RETURN VALUES

None.

ERRORS

None.

SEE ALSO

nng_cv_alloc(3supp), nng_cv_until(3supp), nng_cv_wait(3supp), nng_cv_wake1(3supp), nng_mtx_alloc(3supp), nng_mtx_lock(3supp), nng_mtx_unlock(3supp), nng(7)

NAME

nng_cv_wake1 - wake one waiter

SYNOPSIS

```
#include <nng/nng.h>
#include <nng/supplemental/util/platform.h>

void nng_cv_wake1(nng_cv *cv);
```

DESCRIPTION

The nng_cv_wake1() wakes at most one thread waiting for the condition variable *cv* to be signaled in the nng_cv_wait() or nng_cv_until() functions.

The caller must have have ownership of the mutex that was used when *cv* was allocated.

ℹ️ The caller should already have set the condition that the waiters will check, while holding the mutex.

💡 While this function avoids the "thundering herd" problem, the caller cannot predict which waiter will be woken, and so the design must ensure that it is sufficient that *any* waiter be woken. When in doubt, it is safer to use nng_cv_wake().

RETURN VALUES

None.

ERRORS

None.

SEE ALSO

nng_cv_alloc(3supp), nng_cv_until(3supp), nng_cv_wait(3supp), nng_cv_wake(3supp), nng_mtx_alloc(3supp), nng_mtx_lock(3supp), nng_mtx_unlock(3supp), nng(7)

NAME

nng_msleep - sleep milliseconds

SYNOPSIS

```
#include <nng/nng.h>
#include <nng/supplemental/util/platform.h>

void nng_msleep(nng_duration msec);
```

DESCRIPTION

The nng_msleep() blocks the caller for at least *msec* milliseconds.

> 🛈 This function may block for longer than requested. The actual wait time is determined by the capabilities of the underlying system.

RETURN VALUES

None.

ERRORS

None.

SEE ALSO

nng_sleep_aio(3), nng_strerror(3), nng_clock(3supp), nng_duration(5), nng(7)

NAME

nng_mtx_alloc - allocate mutex

SYNOPSIS

```
#include <nng/nng.h>
#include <nng/supplemental/util/platform.h>

typedef struct nng_mtx nng_mtx;

int nng_mtx_alloc(nng_mtx **mtxp);
```

DESCRIPTION

The nng_mtx_alloc() function allocates mutex and returns it in *mtxp*.

The mutex objects created by this function are suitable only for simple lock and unlock operations, and are not recursive. Every effort has been made to use light-weight underlying primitives when available.

Mutex (mutual exclusion) objects can be thought of as binary semaphores, where only a single thread of execution is permitted to "own" the semaphore.

Furthermore, a mutex can only be unlocked by the thread that locked it.

RETURN VALUES

This function returns 0 on success, and non-zero otherwise.

ERRORS

NNG_ENOMEM   Insufficient free memory exists.

SEE ALSO

nng_cv_alloc(3supp), nng_mtx_free(3supp), nng_mtx_lock(3supp), nng_mtx_unlock(3supp), nng_strerror(3), nng(7)

NAME

nng_mtx_free - free mutex

SYNOPSIS

```
#include <nng/nng.h>
#include <nng/supplemental/util/platform.h>

void nng_mtx_free(nng_mtx *mtx);
```

DESCRIPTION

The nng_mtx_free() function frees the mutex *mtx*. The mutex must not be locked when this function is called.

RETURN VALUES

None.

ERRORS

None.

SEE ALSO

nng_mtx_alloc(3supp), nng(7)

NAME

nng_mtx_lock - lock mutex

SYNOPSIS

```
#include <nng/nng.h>
#include <nng/supplemental/util/platform.h>

void nng_mtx_lock(nng_mtx *mtx);
```

DESCRIPTION

The nng_mtx_lock() acquires exclusive ownership of the mutex *mtx*. If the lock is already owned, this function will wait until the current owner releases it with nng_mtx_unlock().

If multiple threads are waiting for the lock, the order of acquisition is not specified.

> **ⓘ** A mutex can *only* be unlocked by the thread that locked it.

> **⚠** Mutex locks are *not* recursive; attempts to reacquire the same mutex may result in deadlock or aborting the current program. It is a programming error for the owner of a mutex to attempt to reacquire it.

nng offers neither a "trylock" operation, nor recursive mutexes. This is by design, as *nng* itself does not use such things, and most often the need for them is the result of poor design. If such capabilities are needed, they may be synthesized fairly easily from mutexes and condition variables.

RETURN VALUES

None.

ERRORS

None.

SEE ALSO

nng_cv_alloc(3supp), nng_mtx_alloc(3supp), nng_mtx_unlock(3supp), nng(7)

NAME

nng_mtx_lock - lock mutex

SYNOPSIS

```
#include <nng/nng.h>
#include <nng/supplemental/util/platform.h>

void nng_mtx_unlock(nng_mtx *mtx);
```

DESCRIPTION

The `nng_mtx_unlock()` relinquishes ownership of the mutex *mtx* that was previously acquired via `nng_mtx_lock()`.

> ⚠️ A mutex can *only* be unlocked by the thread that locked it. Attempting to unlock a mutex that is not owned by the caller will result in undefined behavior.

RETURN VALUES

None.

ERRORS

None.

SEE ALSO

nng_mtx_alloc(3supp), nng_mtx_lock(3supp), nng(7)

NAME

nng_opts_parse - parse command line options

SYNOPSIS

```
#include <nng/nng.h>
#include <nng/supplemental/util/options.h>

typedef struct nng_optspec {
    const char *o_name; // Long style name (may be NULL for short only)
    int         o_short; // Short option (no clustering!)
    int         o_val;   // Value stored on a good parse (>0)
    bool        o_arg;   // Option takes an argument if true
} nng_optspec;

int nng_opts_parse(int argc, char *const *argv, const nng_optspec *spec, int *val, char
**arg, int *idx);
```

DESCRIPTION

The nng_opts_parse() is function is a supplemental function intended to facilitate parsing command line arguments. This function exists largely to stand in for getopt() from POSIX systems, but it is available everywhere that *NNG* is, and it includes some capabilities missing from getopt().

The function parses arguments from main() (using *argc* and *argv*), starting at the index referenced by *idx*. (New invocations typically set the value pointed to by *idx* to 1.)

Options are parsed as specified by *spec* (see Option Specification.) The value of the parsed option will be stored at the address indicated by *val*, and the value of *idx* will be incremented to reflect the next option to parse.

> 💡 For using this to parse command-line like strings that do not include the command name itself, set the value referenced by *idx* to zero instead of one.

If the option had an argument, a pointer to that is returned at the address referenced by *arg*.

This function should be called repeatedly, until it returns either -1 (indicating the end of options is reached) or a non-zero error code is returned.

Option Specification

The calling program must first create an array of nng_optspec structures describing the options to be supported. This structure has the following members:

o_name

> The long style name for the option, such as "verbose". This will be parsed on the command line when it is prefixed with two dashes. It may be NULL if only a short option is to be supported.

o_short

> This is a single letter (at present only ASCII letters are supported). These options appear as just a

single letter, and are prefixed with a single dash on the command line. The use of a slash in lieu of the dash is *not* supported, in order to avoid confusion with path name arguments. This value may be set to 0 if no short option is needed.

o_val

This is a numeric value that is unique to this option. This value is assigned by the application program, and must be non-zero for a valid option. If this is zero, then it indicates the end of the specifications, and the rest of this structure is ignored. The value will be returned to the caller in *val* by nng_opts_parse() when this option is parsed from the command line.

o_arg

This value should be set to true if the option should take an argument.

Long Options

Long options are parsed from the *argv* array, and are indicated when the element being scanned starts with two dashes. For example, the "verbose" option would be specified as --verbose on the command line. If a long option takes an argument, it can either immediately follow the option as the next element in *argv*, or it can be appended to the option, separated from the option by an equals sign (=) or a colon (:).

Short Options

Short options appear by themselves in an *argv* element, prefixed by a dash (-). If the short option takes an argument, it can either be appended in the same element of *argv*, or may appear in the next *argv* element.

ℹ Option clustering, where multiple options can be crammed together in a single *argv* element, is not supported by this function (yet).

Prefix Matching

When using long options, the parser will match if it is equal to a prefix of the o_name member of a option specification, provided that it do so unambiguously (meaning it must not match any other option specification.)

EXAMPLE

The following program fragment demonstrates this function.

```
enum { OPT_LOGFILE, OPT_VERBOSE };
char *logfile; // options to be set
bool verbose;

static nng_optspec specs[] = {
    {
        .o_name = "logfile",
        .o_short = 'D',
        .o_val = OPT_LOGFILE,
        .o_arg = true,
    }, {
        .o_name = "verbose",
        .o_short = 'V',
        .o_val = OPT_VERBOSE,
        .o_arg = false,
    }, {
        .o_val = 0; // Terminate array
    }
};

for (int idx = 1;;) {
    int rv, opt;
    char *arg;
    rv = nng_opts_parse(argc, argv, specs, &opt, &arg, &idx);
    if (rv != 0) {
        break;
    }
    switch (opt) {
    case OPT_LOGFILE:
        logfile = arg;
        break;
    case OPT_VERBOSE:
        verbose = true;
        break;
    }
}
if (rv != -1) {
    printf("Options error: %s\n", nng_strerror(rv));
    exit(1);
}
```

RETURN VALUES

This function returns 0 if an option parsed correctly, -1 if no more options are available to be parsed, or an error number otherwise.

ERRORS

NNG_EAMBIGUOUS	Parsed option matches more than one specification.
NNG_ENOARG	Option requires an argument, but one is not present.

NNG_EINVAL   An invalid (unknown) argument is present.

SEE ALSO

nng_strerror(3), nng(7)

NAME

nng_random - get random number

SYNOPSIS

```
#include <nng/nng.h>
#include <nng/supplemental/util/platform.h>

uint32_t nng_random(void);
```

DESCRIPTION

The nng_random() returns a random number. The value returned is suitable for use with cryptographic functions such as key generation. The value is obtained using platform specific cryptographically strong random number facilities when available.

RETURN VALUES

Random number.

ERRORS

None.

SEE ALSO

nng(7)

NAME

nng_thread_create - create thread

SYNOPSIS

```
#include <nng/nng.h>
#include <nng/supplemental/util/platform.h>

typedef struct nng_thread nng_thread;

int nng_thread_create(nng_thread **thrp, void (*func)(void *), void *arg);
```

DESCRIPTION

The nng_thread_create() function creates a single thread of execution, running *func* with the argument *arg*. The thread is started immediately. A pointer to the thread object is returned in *thrp*.

The intention of this program is to facilitate writing parallel programs. Threads created by this program will be based upon the underlying threading mechanism of the system that *NNG* is running on. This may include use of so-called "green threads" or coroutines.

Using threads created by this function can make it easy to write programs that use simple sequential execution, using functions in the *NNG* suite that would otherwise normally "block".

When the thread is no longer needed, the nng_thread_destroy() function should be used to reap it. (This function will block waiting for *func* to return.)

> ⚠ Thread objects created by this function may not be "real" threads capable of performing blocking I/O operations using normal blocking system calls. If use of blocking system calls is required (not including APIs provided by the *NNG* library itself of course), then real OS-specific threads should be created instead (such as with pthread_create() or similar functions.)

> ⚠ Thread objects created by this function cannot be passed to any system threading functions.

> 💡 The system may impose limits on the number of threads that can be created. Typically applications should not create more than a few dozen of these. If greater concurrency or scalability is needed, consider instead using an asynchronous model using nng_aio structures.

> 💡 Threads can be synchronized using mutexes and condition variables.

RETURN VALUES

This function returns 0 on success, and non-zero otherwise.

ERRORS

NNG_ENOMEM   Insufficient free memory exists.

SEE ALSO

nng_strerror(3), nng_cv_alloc(3supp), nng_mtx_alloc(3supp), nng_thread_destroy(3supp), nng_aio(5), nng(7)

NAME

nng_thread_destroy - reap thread

SYNOPSIS

```
#include <nng/nng.h>
#include <nng/supplemental/util/platform.h>

void nng_thread_destroy(nng_thread *thread);
```

DESCRIPTION

The nng_thread_destroy() function reaps the *thread*. It waits for the thread function to return, and then deallocates the resources for the thread.

⚠   Do not call this function from the thread function itself, or a deadlock will occur.

RETURN VALUES

None.

ERRORS

None.

SEE ALSO

nng_thread_create(3supp), nng(7)

Section 3tls

Supplemental TLS Functions

NAME

nng_tls_config_alloc - allocate TLS configuration object

SYNOPSIS

```
#include <nng/nng.h>
#include <nng/supplemental/tls/tls.h>

typedef enum nng_tls_mode {
    NNG_TLS_MODE_CLIENT,
    NNG_TLS_MODE_SERVER
} nng_tls_mode;

int nng_tls_config_alloc(nng_tls_config **cfgp, nng_tls_mode mode);
```

DESCRIPTION

The nng_tls_config_alloc() function creates a newly initialized Transport Layer Security [https://tools.ietf.org/html/rfc5246]) configuration object, and stores a pointer to it in the value pointed to by *cfgp*.

This object is initialized for use when acting as either a client (NNG_TLS_MODE_CLIENT) or as a server (NNG_TLS_MODE_SERVER), depending on the value of *mode*.

A TLS object can be further modified by functions that set the security keys used, peer certificates, protocol policies, and so forth.

A single TLS configuration object can be used with multiple TLS streams or services. The underlying system uses reference counting to ensure that object is not inadvertently freed while in use.

A configuration object created with nng_tls_config_alloc() starts with a reference count of one. The reference count may be incremented using nng_tls_config_hold() and may be decremented with nng_tls_config_free().

Also note that a TLS configuration object becomes "read-only" after it is first used with a service. After this points, attempts to apply further changes to the configuration will result in NNG_EBUSY.

RETURN VALUES

This function returns 0 on success, and non-zero otherwise.

ERRORS

NNG_ENOMEM	Insufficient memory is available.
NNG_EINVAL	An invalid *mode* was specified.

SEE ALSO

nng_strerror(3), nng_tls_config_auth_mode(3tls), nng_tls_config_ca_chain(3tls),
nng_tls_config_own_cert(3tls), nng_tls_config_free(3tls), nng_tls_config_hold(3tls),
nng_tls_config_server_name(3tls), nng(7)

NAME

nng_tls_config_auth_mode - configure authentication mode

SYNOPSIS

```
#include <nng/nng.h>
#include <nng/supplemental/tls/tls.h>

typedef enum nng_tls_auth_mode {
        NNG_TLS_AUTH_MODE_NONE,
        NNG_TLS_AUTH_MODE_OPTIONAL,
        NNG_TLS_AUTH_MODE_REQUIRED
} nng_tls_auth_mode;

int nng_tls_config_auth_mode(nng_tls_config *cfg, nng_tls_auth_mode mode);
```

DESCRIPTION

The nng_tls_config_auth_mode() function configures the authentication mode to be used for TLS sessions using this configuration object.

The possible modes are:

NNG_TLS_AUTH_MODE_NONE
No authentication of the TLS peer is performed. This is the default for TLS servers, which most typically do not authenticate their clients.

NNG_TLS_AUTH_MODE_OPTIONAL
If a certificate is presented by the peer, then it is validated. However, if the peer does not present a valid certificate, then the session is allowed to proceed without authentication.

NNG_TLS_AUTH_MODE_REQUIRED
A check is made to ensure that the peer has presented a valid certificate used for the session. If the peer's certificate is invalid or missing, then the session is refused. This is the default for clients.

RETURN VALUES

This function returns 0 on success, and non-zero otherwise.

ERRORS

NNG_ENOMEM	Insufficient memory is available.
NNG_EINVAL	An invalid *mode* was specified.
NNG_EBUSY	The configuration *cfg* is already in use, and cannot be modified.

SEE ALSO

nng_strerror(3), nng_tls_config_alloc(3tls), nng_tls_config_ca_chain(3tls), nng_tls_config_ca_file(3tls), nng_tls_config_server_name(3tls), nng(7)

NAME

nng_tls_config_ca_chain - configure certificate authority certificate chain

SYNOPSIS

```
#include <nng/nng.h>
#include <nng/supplemental/tls/tls.h>

int nng_tls_config_ca_chain(nng_tls_config *cfg, const char *chain, const char *crl);
```

DESCRIPTION

The nng_tls_config_ca_chain() function configures a certificate or certificate chain to be used when validating peers using the configuration *cfg*.

> ℹ️ Certificates **must** be configured when using the authentication mode NNG_TLS_AUTH_MODE_REQUIRED.

> 💡 This function may be called multiple times, to add additional chains to a configuration, without affecting those added previously.

The certificates located in *chain* must be a zero-terminated C string in PEM [https://tools.ietf.org/html/rfc7468] format. Multiple certificates may appear concatenated together, with the leaf certificate listed first.

The *crl* may be NULL, or may also be a C string containing a PEM format certificate revocation list for the associated authority.

RETURN VALUES

This function returns 0 on success, and non-zero otherwise.

ERRORS

NNG_ENOMEM	Insufficient memory is available.
NNG_EBUSY	The configuration *cfg* is already in use, and cannot be modified.
NNG_EINVAL	An invalid *chain* or *crl* was supplied.

SEE ALSO

nng_strerror(3), nng_tls_config_alloc(.3tls), nng_tls_config_auth_mode(.3tls), nng_tls_config_ca_file(.3tls), nng(7)

NAME

nng_tls_config_ca_file - load certificate authority from file

SYNOPSIS

```
#include <nng/nng.h>
#include <nng/supplemental/tls/tls.h>

int nng_tls_config_ca_file(nng_tls_config *cfg, const char *path);
```

DESCRIPTION

The `nng_tls_config_ca_file()` function configures the certificate authority certificate chain and optional revocation list by loading the certificates (and revocation list if present) from a single named file. The file must at least one X.509 certificate in PEM [https://tools.ietf.org/html/rfc7468] format, and may contain multiple such certificates, as well as zero or more PEM CRL objects. This information is used to validate certificates that are presented by peers, when using the configuration *cfg*.

🛈   Certificates **must** be configured when using the authentication mode `NNG_TLS_AUTH_MODE_REQUIRED`.

💡   This function may be called multiple times, to add additional chains to a configuration, without affecting those added previously.

RETURN VALUES

This function returns 0 on success, and non-zero otherwise.

ERRORS

NNG_ENOMEM	Insufficient memory is available.
NNG_EBUSY	The configuration *cfg* is already in use, and cannot be modified.
NNG_EINVAL	The contents of *path* are invalid or do not contain a valid PEM certificate.
NNG_ENOENT	The file *path* does not exist.
NNG_EPERM	The file *path* is not readable.

SEE ALSO

nng_strerror(3), nng_tls_config_alloc(3tls), nng_tls_config_auth_mode(3tls), nng_tls_config_ca_chain(3tls), nng(7)

NAME

nng_tls_config_cert_key_file - load own certificate and key from file

SYNOPSIS

```
#include <nng/nng.h>
#include <nng/supplemental/tls/tls.h>

int nng_tls_config_cert_key_file(nng_tls_config *cfg, const char *path,
    const char *pass);
```

DESCRIPTION

The nng_tls_config_cert_key_file() function loads a certificate (or certificate chain) and a private key from the file named by *path*.

The file must contain both the PEM [https://tools.ietf.org/html/rfc7468] encoded certificate and associated private key, which will be used when establishing TLS sessions using *cfg*. It may contain additional certificates leading to a validation chain, with the leaf certificate first. There is no need to include the self-signed root, as the peer will need to have that already in order to perform its own validation.

The private key may be encrypted with a password, in which can be supplied in *pass*. The value NULL should be supplied for *pass* if the key is not encrypted.

On servers, it is possible to call this function multiple times for the same configuration. This can be useful for specifying different parameters to be used for different cryptographic algorithms.

RETURN VALUES

This function returns 0 on success, and non-zero otherwise.

ERRORS

NNG_ENOMEM	Insufficient memory is available.
NNG_EBUSY	The configuration *cfg* is already in use, and cannot be modified.
NNG_EINVAL	The contents of *path* are invalid.
NNG_ENOENT	The file named by *path* does not exist.
NNG_EPERM	The file named by *path* cannot be opened.

SEE ALSO

nng_strerror(3), nng_tls_config_alloc(3tls), nng_tls_config_own_cert(3tls), nng(7)

NAME

nng_tls_config_free - deallocate a TLS configuration object

SYNOPSIS

```
#include <nng/nng.h>
#include <nng/supplemental/tls/tls.h>

void nng_tls_config_free(nng_tls_config *cfg);
```

DESCRIPTION

The nng_tls_config_free() decrements the reference count on the TLS configuration object pointed to by *cfg*, and if the resulting reference count is zero, then deallocates the configuration object.

RETURN VALUES

None.

ERRORS

None.

SEE ALSO

nng_tls_config_alloc(3tls), nng(7)

NAME

nng_tls_config_hold - hold TLS configuration object

SYNOPSIS

```
#include <nng/nng.h>
#include <nng/supplemental/tls/tls.h>

void nng_tls_config_alloc(nng_tls_config *cfg);
```

DESCRIPTION

The nng_tls_config_hold() increments the reference count on the configuration object named by *cfg*, thereby preventing it from being freed while in use.

The hold can be released by calling nng_tls_config_free().

Multiple holds can be placed on a configuration object; the object will not be freed until the last hold is released.

RETURN VALUES

None.

ERRORS

None.

SEE ALSO

nng_tls_config_alloc(3tls), nng_tls_config_free(3tls), nng(7)

NAME

nng_tls_config_own_cert - configure own certificate and key

SYNOPSIS

```
#include <nng/nng.h>
#include <nng/supplemental/tls/tls.h>

int nng_tls_config_own_cert(nng_tls_config *cfg, const char *cert,
    const char *key, const char *pass);
```

DESCRIPTION

The nng_tls_config_own_cert() function configures a certificate *cert* identifying the local side of a TLS connection used with *cfg*, along with an associated private or secret key *key*. The certificate may be a chain, with the leaf signer first and the root at the end. The self-signed certificate at the end can be omitted. (The client should already have it, and will have to in order to validate this certificate anyway).

The *key* may be encrypted with a password, in which can be supplied in *pass*. The value NULL should be supplied for *pass* if the key is not encrypted.

On servers, it is possible to call this function multiple times for the same configuration. This can be useful for specifying different parameters to be used for different cryptographic algorithms.

The certificate located in *cert* and *key* must be NUL (\0) terminated C strings containing PEM [https://tools.ietf.org/html/rfc7468] formatted material.

RETURN VALUES

This function returns 0 on success, and non-zero otherwise.

ERRORS

NNG_ENOMEM	Insufficient memory is available.
NNG_EBUSY	The configuration *cfg* is already in use, and cannot be modified.
NNG_EINVAL	An invalid *cert* or *key* was supplied.

SEE ALSO

nng_strerror(3), nng_tls_config_alloc(3tls), nng_tls_config_cert_key_file(3tls), nng(7)

NAME

nng_tls_config_server_name - configure remote server name

SYNOPSIS

```
#include <nng/nng.h>
#include <nng/supplemental/tls/tls.h>

int nng_tls_config_server_name(nng_tls_config *cfg, const char *name);
```

DESCRIPTION

The nng_tls_config_server_name() function configures the remote server name to be used by a client when connection to a server. The supplied *name* is used when comparing the identity in the server's certificate. Furthermore, when Server Name Indication (SNI) is used, the *name* may be sent to the server as a hint to tell it which of several possible certificates should be used.

> This function is only useful in configuring client behavior.

RETURN VALUES

This function returns 0 on success, and non-zero otherwise.

ERRORS

NNG_ENOMEM	Insufficient memory is available.
NNG_EBUSY	The configuration *cfg* is already in use, and cannot be modified.

SEE ALSO

nng_strerror(3), nng_tls_config_alloc(3tls), nng_tls_config_auth_mode(3tls), nng(7)

Section 5

Macros and Types

NAME

nng_aio - asynchronous I/O handle

SYNOPSIS

```
#include <nng/nng.h>

typedef struct nng_aio nng_aio;
```

DESCRIPTION

An nng_aio is an opaque structure used in conjunction with asynchronous I/O operations. Every asynchronous operation uses one of these structures, each of which can only be used with a single operation at a time.

Asynchronous operations are performed without blocking calling application threads. Instead the application registers a "callback" function to be executed when the operation is complete (whether successfully or not). This callback will be executed exactly once.

The asynchronous I/O framework in *nng* also supports cancellation of operations that are already in progress (see nng_aio_cancel()), as well setting a maximum timeout for them to complete within (see nng_aio_set_timeout()).

It is also possible to initiate an asynchronous operation, and wait for it to complete using nng_aio_wait().

These structures are created using the nng_aio_alloc(), and destroyed using nng_aio_free().

SEE ALSO

nng_aio_abort(3), nng_aio_alloc(3), nng_aio_cancel(3), nng_aio_count(3), nng_aio_free(3), nng_aio_get_input(3), nng_aio_get_msg(3), nng_aio_get_output(3), nng_aio_result(3), nng_aio_set_input(3), nng_aio_set_iov(3), nng_aio_set_msg(3), nng_aio_set_timeout(3), nng_aio_stop(3), nng_aio_wait(3), nng_strerror(3), nng_aio(5), nng(7)

NAME

nng_ctx - protocol context

SYNOPSIS

```
#include <nng/nng.h>

typedef struct nng_ctx_s nng_ctx
```

DESCRIPTION

An nng_ctx is a handle to an underlying "context" object, which keeps the protocol state for some stateful protocols. The purpose of a separate context object is to permit applications to share a single socket, with its various underlying dialers, listeners, and pipes, while still benefiting from separate state tracking.

For example, a *req* context will contain the request ID of any sent request, a timer to retry the request on failure, and so forth. A separate context on the same socket can have similar data, but corresponding to a completely different request.

> ⚠ The nng_ctx structure is always passed by value (both for input parameters and return values), and should be treated opaquely. Passing structures this way ensures gives the compiler a chance to perform accurate type checks in functions passing values of this type.

All contexts share the same socket, and so some options, as well as the underlying transport details, will be common to all contexts on that socket.

> ⓘ Not every protocol supports separate contexts. See the protocol-specific documentation for further details about whether contexts are supported, and details about what options are supported for contexts.

Protocols that make use of contexts will also have a "default" context that is used when the socket global operations are used. Operations using the global context will generally not interfere with any other contexts, except that certain socket options may affect socket global behavior.

Historically, applications wanting to use a stateful protocol concurrently would have to resort to raw mode sockets, which bypasses much of the various protocol handling, leaving it to up to the application to do so. Contexts make it possible to still benefit from advanced protocol handling, including timeouts, retries, and matching requests to responses, while doing so concurrently.

> ⓘ Raw mode sockets do not support contexts, since there is generally no state tracked for them, and thus contexts make no sense.

> ♀ Contexts are an excellent mechanism to use when building concurrent applications, and should be used in lieu of raw mode sockets when possible.

> ⚠ Use of file descriptor polling (with descriptors obtained using the NNG_OPT_RECVFD or NNG_OPT_SENDFD options) while contexts are in use on the same socket is not supported, and may lead to unpredictable behavior. These asynchronous methods should not be mixed on the same socket.

Initialization

A context may be initialized using the macro NNG_CTX_INITIALIZER before it is opened, to prevent confusion with valid open contexts.

EXAMPLE

The following program fragment demonstrates the use of contexts to implement a concurrent *rep* service that simply echos messages back to the sender.

```c
struct echo_context {
    nng_ctx ctx;
    nng_aio *aio;
    enum { INIT, RECV, SEND } state;
};

void
echo(void *arg)
{
    struct echo_context *ec = arg;

    switch (ec->state) {
    case INIT:
        ec->state = RECV;
        nng_ctx_recv(ec->ctx, ec->aio);
        return;
    case RECV:
        if (nng_aio_result(ec->aio) != 0) {
            // ... handle error
        }
        // We reuse the message on the ec->aio
        ec->state = SEND;
        nng_ctx_send(ec->ctx, ec->aio);
        return;
    case SEND:
        if (nng_aio_result(ec->aio) != 0) {
            // ... handle error
        }
        ec->state = RECV;
        nng_ctx_recv(ec->ctx, ec->aio);
        return;
    }
}
```

Given the above fragment, the following example shows setting up the service. It assumes that the socket has already been created and any transports set up as well with functions such as nng_dial() or nng_listen().

```
#define CONCURRENCY 1024

echo_context ecs[CONCURRENCY];

void
start_echo_service(nng_socket rep_socket)
{
    for (int i = 0; i < CONCURRENCY; i++) {
        // error checks elided for clarity
        nng_ctx_open(ec[i].ctx, rep_socket)
        nng_aio_alloc(ec[i].aio, echo, &e[i]);
        ec[i].state = INIT;
        echo(&ec[i]); // start it running
    }
}
```

SEE ALSO

libnng(3), nng_ctx_close(3), nng_ctx_open(3), nng_ctx_getopt(3), nng_ctx_id(3), nng_ctx_recv(3), nng_ctx_send(3), nng_ctx_setopt(3), nng_dialer(5), nng_listener(5), nng_socket(5), nng_options(5), nng(7)

NAME

nng_dialer - dialer

SYNOPSIS

```
#include <nng/nng.h>

typedef struct nng_dialer_s nng_dialer;
```

DESCRIPTION

An nng_dialer is a handle to a "dialer" object, which is responsible for creating a single nng_pipe at a time by establishing an outgoing connection.

If the connection is broken, or fails, the dialer object will automatically attempt to reconnect, and will keep doing so until the dialer or socket is destroyed.

Dialer objects are created by the nng_dialer_create() or nng_dial() functions, and are always "owned" by a single nng_socket.

> ⚠ The nng_dialer structure is always passed by value (both for input parameters and return values), and should be treated opaquely. Passing structures this way ensures gives the compiler a chance to perform accurate type checks in functions passing values of this type.

> 💡 A given nng_socket may have multiple dialer objects, multiple listener objects, or even some of both.

> 💡 The client/server relationship described by dialer/listener is completely orthogonal to any similar relationship in the protocols. For example, a *rep* socket may use a dialer to connect to a listener on an *req* socket. This orthogonality can lead to innovative solutions to otherwise challenging communications problems.

Dialer objects may be destroyed by the nng_dialer_close() function. They are also closed when their "owning" socket is closed.

Initialization

A dialer may be initialized using the macro NNG_DIALER_INITIALIZER before it is opened, to prevent confusion with valid open dialers.

SEE ALSO

nng_dial(3), nng_dialer_close(3), nng_dialer_create(3), nng_dialer_getopt(3), nng_dialer_id(3), nng_dialer_setopt(3), nng_dialer_start(3), nng_listener(5), nng_pipe(5), nng_socket(5), nng(7)

NAME

nng_duration - relative time in milliseconds

SYNOPSIS

```
#include <nng/nng.h>

typedef int32_t nng_duration;

#define NNG_DURATION_INFINITE (-1)
#define NNG_DURATION_DEFAULT  (-2)
#define NNG_DURATION_ZERO     (0)
```

DESCRIPTION

An nng_duration is a relative time, measured in milliseconds. This type is most often used in conjunction with timers and timeouts.

A couple of special values have been set aside, and carry special meanings.

NNG_DURATION_DEFAULT
Indicates a context-specific default value should be used.

NNG_DURATION_INFINITE
Effectively an infinite duration; used most often to disable timeouts.

NNG_DURATION_ZERO
Zero length duration; used to perform a single polling operation.

SEE ALSO

nng_options(5), nng(7)

NAME

nng_iov - scatter/gather element

SYNOPSIS

```
#include <nng/nng.h>

typedef struct {
    void * iov_buf;
    size_t iov_len;
} nng_iov;
```

DESCRIPTION

An nng_iov structure represents a single element in a scatter/gather array. Some operations can use arrays of these to access different regions of memory in a single operation. For example, it may be useful to send a message with header data from one part of memory, and a user payload from another.

The operations that do this typically store an array of these in an nng_aio structure using the nng_aio_set_iov() function.

The following structure members are present:

iov_buf
  This is a pointer to the first byte within the memory being referenced by this scatter/gather element.

iov_len
  This is the size in bytes of this scatter/gather element.

SEE ALSO

nng_aio_set_iov(3), nng_aio(5), nng(7)

NAME

nng_listener - listener

SYNOPSIS

```
#include <nng/nng.h>

typedef struct nng_listener_s nng_listener;
```

DESCRIPTION

An nng_listener is a handle to a "listener" object, which is responsible for creating nng_pipe objects by accepting incoming connections. A given listener object may create many pipes at the same time, much like an HTTP server can have many connections to multiple clients simultaneously.

Listener objects are created by the nng_listener_create() or nng_listen() functions, and are always "owned" by a single nng_socket.

> ⚠ The nng_listener structure is always passed by value (both for input parameters and return values), and should be treated opaquely. Passing structures this way ensures gives the compiler a chance to perform accurate type checks in functions passing values of this type.

> 💡 A given nng_socket may have multiple listener objects, multiple dialer objects, or even some of both.

> 💡 The client/server relationship described by dialer/listener is completely orthogonal to any similar relationship in the protocols. For example, a *rep* socket may use a dialer to connect to a listener on an *req* socket. This orthogonality can lead to innovative solutions to otherwise challenging communications problems.

Listener objects may be destroyed by the nng_listener_close() function. They are also closed when their "owning" socket is closed.

Initialization

A listener may be initialized using the macro NNG_LISTENER_INITIALIZER before it is opened, to prevent confusion with valid open listener.

SEE ALSO

nng_listen(3), nng_listener_close(3), nng_listener_create(3), nng_listener_getopt(3), nng_listener_id(3), nng_listener_setopt(3), nng_listener_start(3), nng_dialer(5), nng_pipe(5), nng_socket(5), nng(7)

NAME

nng_msg - message

SYNOPSIS

```
#include <nng/nng.h>

typedef struct nng_msg nng_msg;
```

DESCRIPTION

An nng_msg represents a single message sent between Scalability Protocols peers. Messages internally have a body, containing the application supplied payload, and a header, containing protocol specific routing and similar related information.

> Using the message-oriented functions in the *nng* API is a good way to reduce the likelihood of data copies and improve application performance.

Messages are allocated using the nng_msg_alloc() function, and are deallocated using the nng_msg_free() function.

In addition there are other functions used to access message contents, including adding data to either the beginning or end of the message, automatic data conversion, and removing data from the beginning or end. These functions are designed to try to avoid copying message contents by making use of scratch areas at the beginning and end of the message.

SEE ALSO

nng_aio_get_msg(3), nng_aio_set_msg(3), nng_msg_alloc(3), nng_msg_body(3), nng_msg_dup(3), nng_msg_free(3), nng_msg_header(3), nng_msg_header_len(3), nng_msg_len(3), nng_msg_realloc(3), nng_recvmsg(3), nng_sendmsg(3), nng_strerror(3), nng(7)

NAME

nng_options - socket, dialer, listener, and pipe options

SYNOPSIS

```
#include <nng/nng.h>

#define NNG_OPT_SOCKNAME      "socket-name"
#define NNG_OPT_RAW           "raw"
#define NNG_OPT_PROTO         "protocol"
#define NNG_OPT_PROTONAME     "protocol-name"
#define NNG_OPT_PEER          "peer"
#define NNG_OPT_PEERNAME      "peer-name"
#define NNG_OPT_RECVBUF       "recv-buffer"
#define NNG_OPT_SENDBUF       "send-buffer"
#define NNG_OPT_RECVFD        "recv-fd"
#define NNG_OPT_SENDFD        "send-fd"
#define NNG_OPT_RECVTIMEO     "recv-timeout"
#define NNG_OPT_SENDTIMEO     "send-timeout"
#define NNG_OPT_LOCADDR       "local-address"
#define NNG_OPT_REMADDR       "remote-address"
#define NNG_OPT_URL           "url"
#define NNG_OPT_MAXTTL        "ttl-max"
#define NNG_OPT_RECVMAXSZ     "recv-size-max"
#define NNG_OPT_RECONNMINT    "reconnect-time-min"
#define NNG_OPT_RECONNMAXT    "reconnect-time-max"
#define NNG_OPT_TCP_NODELAY   "tcp-nodelay"
#define NNG_OPT_TCP_KEEPALIVE "tcp-keepalive"
```

DESCRIPTION

This page documents the various standard options that can be set or retrieved on objects in the *nng* library.

Sockets (nng_socket objects) use the functions nng_getopt() and nng_setopt() to set and retrieve option values.

Dialers (nng_dialer objects) use the functions nng_dialer_getopt() and nng_dialer_setopt() to set and retrieve option values.

Listeners (nng_listener objects) use the functions nng_listener_getopt() and nng_listener_setopt() to set and retrieve option values.

Pipes (nng_pipe objects) can only retrieve option values using the nng_pipe_getopt() function.

In addition to the options listed here, transports and protocols will generally have some of their own options, which will be documented with the transport or protocol.

Options

In the following list of options, the name of the option is supplied, along with the data type of the underlying value. Some options are only meaningful or supported in certain contexts; for example there is no single meaningful address for a socket, since sockets can have multiple dialers and endpoints associated with them. An attempt has been made to include details about such restrictions in the description of the option.

NNG_OPT_LOCADDR

(nng_sockaddr) This read-only option may be used on listeners, dialers and connected pipes, and represents the local address used for communication. Not all transports support this option, and some transports may support it listeners but not dialers.

NNG_OPT_RAW

(bool) This read-only option indicates whether the socket is in "raw" mode. If true, the socket is in "raw" mode, and if false the socket is in "cooked" mode. Raw mode sockets generally do not have any protocol-specific semantics applied to them; instead the application is expected to perform such semantics itself. (For example, in "cooked" mode a *rep* socket would automatically copy message headers from a received message to the corresponding reply, whereas in "raw" mode this is not done.) See Raw Mode for more details.

NNG_OPT_RECONNMINT

(nng_duration) This is the minimum amount of time (milliseconds) to wait before attempting to establish a connection after a previous attempt has failed. This can be set on a socket, but it can also be overridden on an individual dialer. The option is irrelevant for listeners.

NNG_OPT_RECONNMAXT

(nng_duration) This is the maximum amount of time (milliseconds) to wait before attempting to establish a connection after a previous attempt has failed. If this is non-zero, then the time between successive connection attempts will start at the value of NNG_OPT_RECONNMINT, and grow exponentially, until it reaches this value. If this value is zero, then no exponential back-off between connection attempts is done, and each attempt will wait the time specified by NNG_OPT_RECONNMINT. This can be set on a socket, but it can also be overridden on an individual dialer. The option is irrelevant for listeners.

NNG_OPT_RECVBUF

(int) This is the depth of the socket's receive buffer as a number of messages. Messages received by a transport may be buffered until the application has accepted them for delivery.

NNG_OPT_RECVFD

(int) This read-only option is used to obtain an integer file descriptor suitable for use with poll() [http://pubs.opengroup.org/onlinepubs/7908799/xsh/poll.html], select() [http://pubs.opengroup.org/onlinepubs/7908799/xsh/select.html], (or on Windows systems WSAPoll() [https://msdn.microsoft.com/en-us/library/windows/desktop/ms741669(v=vs.85).aspx]) and similar functions. This descriptor will be **readable** when a message is available for receiving on the socket. When no message is ready for receiving, then this file descriptor will **not** be readable.

⚠ Applications should never attempt to read or write to the returned file descriptor.

💡 While this option may help applications integrate into existing polling loops, it is more efficient, and often easier, to use the asynchronous I/O objects instead. See nng_aio_alloc().

NNG_OPT_RECVMAXSZ

(size_t) This is the maximum message size that the will be accepted from a remote peer. If a peer attempts to send a message larger than this, then the message will be discarded. If the value of this is zero, then no limit on message sizes is enforced. This option exists to prevent certain kinds of denial-of-service attacks, where a malicious agent can claim to want to send an extraordinarily large message, without sending any data. This option can be set for the socket, but may be overridden for on a per-dialer or per-listener basis.

> **ⓘ**   Some transports may have further message size restrictions!

NNG_OPT_RECVTIMEO

(nng_duration) This is the socket receive timeout in milliseconds. When no message is available for receiving at the socket for this period of time, receive operations will fail with a return value of NNG_ETIMEDOUT.

NNG_OPT_REMADDR

(nng_sockaddr) This read-only option may be used on dialers and connected pipes, and represents the address of a remote peer. Not all transports support this option.

NNG_OPT_SENDBUF

(int) This is the depth of the socket send buffer as a number of messages. Messages sent by an application may be buffered by the socket until a transport is ready to accept them for delivery. This value must be an integer between 0 and 8192, inclusive.

> **ⓘ**   Not all protocols support buffering sent messages; generally multicast protocols like *pub* will simply discard messages when they cannot be delivered immediately.

NNG_OPT_SENDFD

(int) This read-only option is used to obtain an integer file descriptor suitable for use with poll() [http://pubs.opengroup.org/onlinepubs/7908799/xsh/poll.html], select() [http://pubs.opengroup.org/onlinepubs/7908799/xsh/select.html], (or on Windows systems WSAPoll() [https://msdn.microsoft.com/en-us/library/windows/desktop/ms741669(v=vs.85).aspx]) and similar functions. This descriptor will be **readable** when the socket is able to accept a message for sending without blocking. When the socket is no longer able to accept such messages without blocking, the descriptor will **not** be readable.

> **⚠**   Applications should never attempt to read or write to the returned file descriptor.

> **♀**   While this option may help applications integrate into existing polling loops, it is more efficient, and often easier, to use the asynchronous I/O objects instead. See nng_aio_alloc().

NNG_OPT_SENDTIMEO

(nng_duration) This is the socket send timeout in milliseconds. When a message cannot be queued for delivery by the socket for this period of time (such as if send buffers are full), the operation will fail with a return value of NNG_ETIMEDOUT.

NNG_OPT_SOCKNAME

(string) This the socket name. By default this is a string corresponding to the value of the socket. The string must fit within 64-bytes, including the terminating NUL byte, but it can be changed for other application uses.

NNG_OPT_MAXTTL

(int) This is the maximum number of "hops" a message may traverse (see nng_device()). The intention here is to prevent forwarding loops in device chains. When this is supported, it can have a value between 1 and 255, inclusive.

ⓘ Not all protocols support this option. Those that do generally have a default value of 8.

♀ Each node along a forwarding path may have its own value for the maximum time-to-live, and performs its own checks before forwarding a message. Therefore it is helpful if all nodes in the topology use the same value for this option.

NNG_OPT_URL

(string) This read-only option is used to obtain the URL with which a listener or dialer was configured. Accordingly it can only be used with dialers, listeners, and pipes.

ⓘ Some transports will canonify URLs before returning them to the application.

NNG_OPT_PROTO

(int) This read-only option is used to obtain the 16-bit number for the socket's protocol.

NNG_OPT_PEER

(int) This read-only option is used to obtain the 16-bit number of the peer protocol for the socket.

NNG_OPT_PROTONAME

(string) This read-only option is used to obtain the name of the socket's protocol.

NNG_OPT_PEERNAME

(string) This read-only option is used to obtain the name of the peer protocol for the socket.

NNG_OPT_TCP_NODELAY

(bool) This option is used to disable (or enable) the use of Nagle's algorithm for TCP connections. When true (the default), messages are sent immediately by the underlying TCP stream without waiting to gather more data. When false, Nagle's algorithm is enabled, and the TCP stream may wait briefly in attempt to coalesce messages. Nagle's algorithm is useful on low-bandwidth connections to reduce overhead, but it comes at a cost to latency.

ⓘ This setting may apply to transports that are built on top of TCP. See the transport documentation for each transport for details.

NNG_OPT_TCP_KEEPALIVE

(bool) This option is used to enable the sending of keep-alive messages on the underlying TCP stream. This option is false by default. When enabled, if no messages are seen for a period of time, then a zero length TCP message is sent with the ACK flag set in an attempt to tickle some traffic from the peer. If none is still seen (after some platform-specific number of retries and timeouts), then the remote peer is presumed dead, and the connection is closed.

ⓘ This setting may apply to transports that are built on top of TCP. See the transport documentation for each transport for details.

♀ This option has two purposes. First, it can be used to detect dead peers on an otherwise quiescent network. Second, it can be used to keep connection table entries in NAT and other middleware from being expiring due to lack of activity.

SEE ALSO

nng_dialer_getopt(3), nng_dialer_setopt(3), nng_getopt(3), nng_listener_getopt(3), nng_listener_setopt(3), nng_pipe_getopt(3), nng_setopt(3), nng(7)

NAME

nng_pipe - communications pipe

SYNOPSIS

```
#include <nng/nng.h>

typedef struct nng_pipe_s nng_pipe;
```

DESCRIPTION

An nng_pipe is a handle to a "pipe", which can be thought of as a single connection. (In most cases this is actually the case — the pipe is an abstraction for a single TCP or IPC connection.) Pipes are associated with either the listener or dialer that created them, and therefore are also automatically associated with a single socket.

> **⚠** The nng_pipe structure is always passed by value (both for input parameters and return values), and should be treated opaquely. Passing structures this way ensures gives the compiler a chance to perform accurate type checks in functions passing values of this type.

> **♀** Most applications should never concern themselves with individual pipes. However it is possible to access a pipe when more information about the source of a message is needed, or when more control is required over message delivery.

Pipe objects are created by dialers (nng_dialer objects) and listeners (nng_listener objects), which can be thought of as "owning" the pipe.

Pipe objects may be destroyed by the nng_pipe_close() function. They are also closed when their "owning" dialer or listener is closed, or when the remote peer closes the underlying connection.

Initialization

A pipe may be initialized using the macro NNG_PIPE_INITIALIZER before it is opened, to prevent confusion with valid open pipes.

For example:

```
nng_pipe p = NNG_PIPE_INITIALIZER;
```

SEE ALSO

nng_msg_get_pipe(3), nng_pipe_close(3), nng_pipe_getopt(3), nng_pipe_dialer(3), nng_pipe_id(3), nng_pipe_listener(3), nng_pipe_socket(3), nng_dialer(5), nng_listener(5), nng_options(5), nng(7)

NAME

nng_sockaddr - socket address

SYNOPSIS

```
#include <nng/nng.h>

typedef union nng_sockaddr {
    uint16_t            s_family;
    nng_sockaddr_ipc    s_ipc;
    nng_sockaddr_inproc s_inproc;
    nng_sockaddr_in     s_in;
    nng_sockaddr_in6    s_in6;
    nng_sockaddr_zt     s_zt;
} nng_sockaddr;

enum sockaddr_family {
    NNG_AF_UNSPEC = 0,
    NNG_AF_INPROC = 1,
    NNG_AF_IPC    = 2,
    NNG_AF_INET   = 3,
    NNG_AF_INET6  = 4,
    NNG_AF_ZT     = 5,
};
```

DESCRIPTION

An nng_sockaddr is a structure used for representing the addresses used by underlying transports, such as TCP/IP addresses, IPC paths, and so forth.

> The name sockaddr is based on its similarity with POSIX struct sockaddr, but in the *nng* library, these addresses are more closely affiliated with instances of nng_pipe than of nng_socket. The naming confusion is unfortunate.

This structure is actually a union, with different members for different types of addresses.

Every member structure has as its first element a uint16_t field containing the "address family". This overlaps the s_family member of the union, and indicates which specific member should be used.

The values of s_family are as follows:

NNG_AF_UNSPEC   Invalid address, no other valid fields.

NNG_AF_INPROC   Address for intraprocess communication (nng_inproc(7)). The s_inproc member is valid.

NNG_AF_IPC   Address for interprocess communication (nng_ipc(7)). The s_path member is valid.

NNG_AF_INET   Address for TCP/IP (v4) communication. The s_in member is valid.

NNG_AF_INET6	Address for TCP/IP (v6) communication. The s_in6 member is valid.
NNG_AF_ZT	Address for ZeroTier transport (nng_zerotier(7)). The s_zt member is valid.

Please see the manual pages for each individual type for more information.

SEE ALSO

nng_sockaddr_in(5), nng_sockaddr_in6(5), nng_sockaddr_inproc(5), nng_sockaddr_ipc(5), nng_sockaddr_zt(5), nng(7)

NAME

nng_sockaddr_in - IPv4 socket address

SYNOPSIS

```
#include <nng/nng.h>

enum sockaddr_family {
    NNG_AF_INET = 3,
};

typedef struct {
    uint16_t sa_family;
    uint16_t sa_port;
    uint32_t sa_addr;
} nng_sockaddr_in;
```

DESCRIPTION

An nng_sockaddr_in is the flavor of nng_sockaddr used to represent TCP (and sometimes UDP) addresses, including the Internet Protocol (IP) address and port number.

This structure is used with IPv4 addresses. A different structure, nng_sockaddr_in6, is used for IPv6 addresses.

The following structure members are present:

sa_family
   This field will always have the value NNG_AF_INET.

sa_port
   This field holds the TCP or UDP port number, in network byte-order. A zero value here is used when no specific port number is indicated.

sa_addr
   This field holds the IP address in network-byte order.

> 💡 The sa_port and sa_addr fields are in network-byte order to facilitate their use with system APIs such as inet_ntop(). Most platforms use some form of BSD-derived network API, which uses network-byte order in the various structures (such as sockaddr_in).

> ⚠ This field appears similar to BSD sockaddr_in, but it is *not* the same, and they may not be used interchangeably.

SEE ALSO

nng_sockaddr(5), nng_sockaddr_in6(5), nng_tcp(7), nng(7)

NAME

nng_sockaddr_in - IPv6 socket address

SYNOPSIS

```
#include <nng/nng.h>

enum sockaddr_family {
    NNG_AF_INET6 = 4,
};

typedef struct {
    uint16_t sa_family;
    uint16_t sa_port;
    uint8_t  sa_addr[16];
} nng_sockaddr_in6;
```

DESCRIPTION

An nng_sockaddr_in6 is the flavor of nng_sockaddr used to represent TCP (and sometimes UDP) addresses, including the Internet Protocol (IP) address and port number.

This structure is used with IPv6 addresses. A different structure, nng_sockaddr_in, is used for IPv4 addresses.

The following structure members are present:

sa_family
This field will always have the value NNG_AF_INET6.

sa_port
This field holds the TCP or UDP port number, in network byte-order. A zero value here is used when no specific port number is indicated.

sa_addr
This field holds the IP address in network-byte order.

> The sa_port and sa_addr fields are in network-byte order to facilitate their use with system APIs such as inet_ntop(). Most platforms use some form of BSD-derived network API, which uses network-byte order in the various structures (such as sockaddr_in6).

> This field appears similar to BSD sockaddr_in6, but it is *not* the same, and they may not be used interchangeably.

SEE ALSO

nng_sockaddr(5), nng_sockaddr_in(5), nng_tcp(7), nng(7)

NAME

nng_sockaddr_inproc - inproc socket address

SYNOPSIS

```
#include <nng/nng.h>

enum sockaddr_family {
    NNG_AF_INPROC = 1,
};

typedef struct {
    uint16_t sa_family;
    uint16_t sa_name[128];
} nng_sockaddr_inproc;
```

DESCRIPTION

An nng_sockaddr_inproc is the flavor of nng_sockaddr used to represent addresses associated with intra-process communication using the *inproc* transport.

The following structure members are present:

sa_family

This field will always have the value NNG_AF_INPROC.

sa_name

This field holds an arbitrary C string, which is the "name" of the address. The string must be NUL terminated, but no other restrictions exist.

💡 In order to ensure maximum compatibility, applications should avoid hard coding the size of the sa_name member explicitly, but use the sizeof operator to determine its actual size at compile time. Furthermore, the size is guaranteed to be at least 128.

SEE ALSO

nng_sockaddr(5), nng_inproc(7) nng(7)

NAME

nng_sockaddr_ipc - IPC socket address

SYNOPSIS

```
#include <nng/nng.h>

enum sockaddr_family {
    NNG_AF_IPC = 2,
};

typedef struct {
    uint16_t sa_family;
    uint16_t sa_path[128];
} nng_sockaddr_ipc;
```

DESCRIPTION

An nng_sockaddr_ipc is the flavor of nng_sockaddr used to represent addresses associated with IPC communication using the *ipc* transport.

The following structure members are present:

sa_family
This field will always have the value NNG_AF_IPC.

sa_path
This field holds the C string corresponding to path name where the IPC socket is located. For systems using UNIX domain sockets, this will be an absolute path name in the file system, where the UNIX domain socket is located. For Windows systems, this is the path name of the Named Pipe, without the leading \\.pipe\ portion, which will be automatically added.

> **ⓘ** At this time, there is no support for Linux "abstract sockets".

> **♡** In order to ensure maximum compatibility, applications should avoid hard coding the size of the sa_path member explicitly, but use the sizeof operator to determine its actual size at compile time. Furthermore, the size is guaranteed to be at least 128, but paths of this length may not be supported on all systems.

> **ⓘ** If compatibility with legacy *nanomsg* applications is required, then pathnames must not be longer than 122 bytes, including the final NUL byte. This is because legacy versions of *nanomsg* cannot express URLs longer than 128 bytes, including the ipc:// prefix.

SEE ALSO

nng_sockaddr(5), nng_ipc(7) nng(7)

NAME

nng_sockaddr_zt - ZeroTier socket address

SYNOPSIS

```
#include <nng/nng.h>

enum sockaddr_family {
    NNG_AF_ZT = 5,
};

typedef struct {
    uint16_t sa_family;
    uint64_t sa_nwid;
    uint64_t sa_nodeid;
    uint32_t sa_port;
} nng_sockaddr_zt;
```

DESCRIPTION

An nng_sockaddr_zt is the flavor of nng_sockaddr used to represent ZeroTier addresses, including the port number used by the *zt* transport.

> ⚠️ The ZeroTier transport, and the details of this structure, are still considered experimental, and subject to change.

The following structure members are present:

sa_family

This field will always have the value NNG_AF_ZT.

sa_nwid

This field holds the ZeroTier network number (or ID). This value is in native byte order.

sa_nodeid

This field holds the ZeroTier node ID. This value is in native byte order, and only the lower 40 bits are significant. (ZeroTier node numbers are 40 bits long.) A zero value here is used for a wild-card to indicate that the caller's own node number be used.

sa_port

This field holds the "port number" used by the *zt* transport to distinguish different sockets. This value in native byte order. A zero value here indicates that a port number should be chosen randomly from the ephemeral ports. Only the lower 24 bits of the port number are used.

> ℹ️ ZeroTier port numbers are in **native** byte order, and are larger than TCP/IP port numbers. They are also not part of the ZeroTier protocol itself, but defined by the Scalability Protocols binding for them.

SEE ALSO

nng_sockaddr(5), nng_zerotier(7), nng(7)

NAME

nng_socket - socket handle

SYNOPSIS

```
#include <nng/nng.h>

typedef struct nng_socket_s nng_socket;
```

DESCRIPTION

An nng_socket is a handle to an underlying "socket" object. All communication between the application and remote Scalability Protocol peers is done through sockets. A given socket can have multiple dialers (nng_dialer) and/or listeners (nng_listener), and multiple pipes (nng_pipe), and may be connected to multiple transports at the same time. However, a given socket will have exactly one "protocol" associated with it, and is responsible for any state machines or other protocol-specific logic.

> ⚠ The nng_socket structure is always passed by value (both for input parameters and return values), and should be treated opaquely. Passing structures this way ensures gives the compiler a chance to perform accurate type checks in functions passing values of this type.

Each nng_socket is created by a protocol-specific constructor, such as nng_rep_open(). When the socket is no longer needed, it can be closed with nng_close().

Initialization

A socket may be initialized using the macro NNG_SOCKET_INITIALIZER before it is opened, to prevent confusion with valid open sockets.

For example:

```
nng_socket s = NNG_SOCKET_INITIALIZER;
```

SEE ALSO

libnng(3), nng_close(3), nng_getopt(3), nng_setopt(3), nng_socket_id(3), nng_dialer(5), nng_listener(5), nng_options(5), nng(7)

NAME

nng_stat - statistic

SYNOPSIS

```
#include <nng/nng.h>

typedef struct nng_stat nng_stat;
```

DESCRIPTION

An nng_stat represents a statistic. All statistics have names (nng_stat_name()) and descriptions (nng_stat_desc()), and are typed (nng_stat_type()).

Most statistics are numeric, and thus carry a value (nng_stat_value()) and frequently also a unit that the value measures (nng_stat_unit()).

Some statistics however, are simply strings (nng_stat_string()), and thus carry no numeric value.

Statistics are organized as a tree, and any given statistic can have siblings (nng_stat_next()). Note however that generally only NNG_STAT_SCOPE statistics, which are act as placeholders in the tree (and carry no value), will have children (nng_stat_child()).

A tree of statistics is collected using nng_stats_get(), and can be freed when no longer needed with nng_stats_free(). This collection process is generally performed in a way to minimize impact to running operations, but there is still some impact caused by collection of statistics.

The time when a statistic's value is captured can be obtained using nng_stat_timestap(), which is useful for measuring rates of change in certain statistics.

> ℹ The presence, names, and meanings of any given statistic are subject to change at any time. These statistics are provided as an aid for debugging, and should generally not be relied upon for programmatic behaviors.

> ℹ Statistics may be disabled by build-time configuration options, in order to reduce program size and run-time overheads.

SEE ALSO

libnng(3), nng_stats_free(3), nng_stats_get(3), nng_stat_child(3), nng_stat_desc(3), nng_stat_name(3), nng_stat_next(3), nng_stat_string(3), nng_stat_timestamp(3), nng_stat_type(3), nng_stat_unit(3), nng_stat_value(3), nng(7)

Section 7

Protocols and Transports

NAME

nng - nanomsg next generation

SYNOPSIS

cc ['flags'] 'files' **-lnng** ['libraries']

DESCRIPTION

The *nng* library provides a common messaging framework intended to solve common communication problems in distributed applications. It offers a number of *protocols*, and also a number of *transports*.

The *protocols* implement the semantics associated with particular communications scenarios, such as RPC style services, service discovery, publish/subscribe, and so forth.

The *transports* provide support for underlying transport methods, such as TCP, IPC, websockets, and so forth.

The *nng* library is designed to permit easy creation of new *transports* and, to a lesser extent, new *protocols*.

The *nng* library is wire compatible with the SP protocols described in the nanomsg project; projects using *libnanomsg* [https://github.com/nanomsg/nanomsg] can inter-operate with nng as well as other conforming implementations. (One such implementation is *mangos* [https://github.com/go-mangos/mangos].) Applications using *nng* which wish to communicate with older libraries must ensure that they only use protocols or transports offered by the earlier library.

The *nng* library also offers a compatible API, permitting legacy code to be recompiled or relinked against *nng*. When doing this, support for certain enhancements or features will likely be absent, requiring the application developer to use the new-style API.

The *nng* library is implemented in pure C; if you need bindings for other languages please check the website [http://nanomsg.org/].

Protocols

nng_bus(7)	Bus protocol
nng_pair(7)	Pair protocol
nng_pub(7)	Publisher side of publish/subscribe protocol
nng_pull(7)	Pull side of pipeline protocol
nng_push(7)	Push side of pipeline protocol
nng_sub(7)	Subscriber side of publish/subscribe protocol
nng_rep(7)	Reply side of request/reply protocol
nng_req(7)	Request side of request/reply protocol
nng_respondent(7)	Respondent side of survey protocol
nng_surveyor(7)	Surveyor side of survey protocol

Transports

nng_inproc(7)	Intra-process transport
nng_ipc(7)	Inter-process transport
nng_tls(7)	TLSv1.2 over TCP transport
nng_tcp(7)	TCP (and TCPv6) transport
nng_ws(7)	WebSocket transport
nng_zerotier(7)	ZeroTier transport

Conceptual Overview

nng presents a *socket* view of networking. The sockets are constructed using protocol-specific functions, as a given socket implements precisely one *nng* protocol.

Each socket can be used to send and receive messages (if the protocol) supports it, and implements the appropriate protocol semantics. For example, *sub* sockets automatically filter incoming messages to discard those for topics that have not been subscribed.

nng sockets are message oriented, so that messages are either delivered wholly, or not at all. Partial delivery is not possible. Furthermore, *nng* does not provide any other delivery or ordering guarantees; messages may be dropped or reordered (Some protocols, such as *req* may offer stronger guarantees by performing their own retry and validation schemes.)

Each socket can have zero, one, or many "endpoints", which are either *listeners* or *dialers*. (A given socket may freely choose whether it uses listeners, dialers, or both.) These "endpoints" provide access to underlying transports, such as TCP, etc.

Each endpoint is associated with a URL, which is a service address. For dialers, this will be the service address that will be contacted, whereas for listeners this is where the listener will accept new connections.

Endpoints do not themselves transport data. They are instead responsible for the creation of *pipes*, which can be thought of as message-oriented connected streams. Pipes frequently correspond to a single underlying byte stream. For example both IPC and TCP transports implement their pipes using a 1:1 relationship with a connected operating system socket.

Endpoints create pipes as needed. Listeners will create them when a new client connection request arrives, and dialers will generally create one, then wait for it to disconnect before reconnecting.

Most applications should not have to worry about endpoints or pipes at all; the socket abstraction should provide all the functionality needed other than in a few specific circumstances.

Raw Mode

Most applications will use *nng* sockets in "cooked" mode. This mode provides the full semantics of the protocol. For example, *req* sockets will automatically match a reply to a request, and resend requests periodically if no reply was received.

There are situations, such as with proxies, where it is desirable to bypass these semantics and simply pass messages to and from the socket with no extra semantic handling. This is possible using "raw" mode sockets.

Raw mode sockets are generally constructed with a different function, such as nng_req0_open_raw(). Using these sockets, the application can simply send and receive messages, and is responsible for supplying any additional socket semantics. Typically this means that the application will need to inspect message headers on incoming messages, and supply them on outgoing messages.

> The nng_device() function only works with raw mode sockets, but as it only forwards the messages, no additional application processing is needed.

URLs

The *nng* library uses universal resource locators (URLs) following the format specified in RFC 3986 [https://tools.ietf.org/html/rfc3986], including some schemes that are unique to SP. The URLs used in *nng* are canonicalized as follows, mostly in accordance with RFC 3986 6.2.2 [https://tools.ietf.org/html/rfc3986#section-6.2.2]:

1. The URL is parsed into scheme, userinfo, host, port, path, query and fragment components. (Not all of these members are necessarily present.)

2. The scheme, hostname, and port if present, are converted to lower case.

3. Percent-encoded values for unreserved characters [https://tools.ietf.org/html/rfc3986#section-2.3] converted to their unencoded forms.

4. Additionally URL percent-encoded values for characters in the path and with numeric values larger than 127 (i.e. not ASCII) are decoded.

5. The resulting path is checked for invalid UTF-8 sequences, consisting of surrogate pairs, illegal byte sequences, or overlong encodings. If this check fails, then the entire URL is considered invalid.

6. Path segments consisting of . and .. are resolved as per RFC 3986 6.2.2.3 [https://tools.ietf.org/html/rfc3986#section-6.2.2.3].

7. Further, empty path segments are removed, meaning that duplicate slash (/) separators are removed from the path.

Note that steps 4, 5, and 7 are not specified by RFC 3986, but performing them is believed to improve both the usability and security of *nng* applications, without violating RFC 3986 itself.

> Port numbers may be service names in some instances, but it is recommended that numeric port numbers be used when known. If service names are used, it is recommended that they follow the naming conventions for C identifiers, and not be longer than 32 characters in length. This will maximize compatibility across systems and minimize opportunities for confusion when they are parsed on different systems.

API

The library API is documented at libnng(3).

SEE ALSO

libnng(3), nng_compat(3compat)

NAME

nng_bus - bus protocol

SYNOPSIS

```
#include <nng/protocol/bus0/bus.h>
```

DESCRIPTION

The *bus* protocol provides for building mesh networks where every peer is connected to every other peer. In this protocol, each message sent by a node is sent to every one of its directly connected peers.

> 💡 Messages are only sent to directly connected peers. This means that in the event that a peer is connected indirectly, it will not receive messages. When using this protocol to build mesh networks, it is therefore important that a *fully-connected* mesh network be constructed.

All message delivery in this pattern is best-effort, which means that peers may not receive messages. Furthermore, delivery may occur to some, all, or none of the directly connected peers. (Messages are not delivered when peer nodes are unable to receive.) Hence, send operations will never block; instead if the message cannot be delivered for any reason it is discarded.

> 💡 In order to minimize the likelihood of message loss, this protocol should not be used for high throughput communications. Furthermore, the more traffic *in aggregate* that occurs across the topology, the more likely that message loss is to occur.

Socket Operations

The `nng_bus0_open()` functions create a bus socket. This socket may be used to send and receive messages. Sending messages will attempt to deliver to each directly connected peer.

Protocol Versions

Only version 0 of this protocol is supported. (At the time of writing, no other versions of this protocol have been defined.)

Protocol Options

The *bus* protocol has no protocol-specific options.

Protocol Headers

When using a "raw" *bus* socket, received messages will contain the incoming pipe ID as the sole element in the header. If a message containing such a header is sent using a raw *bus* socket, then, the message will be delivered to all connected pipes *except* the one identified in the header. This behavior is intended for use with device configurations consisting of just a single socket. Such configurations are useful in the creation of rebroadcasters, and this capability prevents a message from being routed back to its source. If no header is present, then a message is sent to all connected pipes.

When using "cooked" *bus* sockets, no message headers are present.

SEE ALSO

nng_bus_open(3), nng(7)

NAME

nng_inproc - intra-process transport

SYNOPSIS

```
#include <nng/transport/inproc/inproc.h>

int nng_inproc_register(void);
```

DESCRIPTION

The *inproc* transport provides communication support between *nng* sockets within the same process. This may be used as an alternative to slower transports when data must be moved within the same process.

This transport tries hard to avoid copying data, and thus is very light-weight.

Registration

The *inproc* transport is generally built-in to the *nng* core, so no extra steps to use it should be necessary.

URI Format

This transport uses URIs using the scheme inproc://, followed by an arbitrary string of text, terminated by a NUL byte.

Multiple URIs can be used within the same application, and they will not interfere with one another.

Two applications may also use the same URI without interfering with each other, and they will be unable to communicate with each other using that URI.

Socket Address

When using an nng_sockaddr structure, the actual structure is of type nng_sockaddr_inproc.

Transport Options

The *inproc* transport has no special options.

SEE ALSO

nng_inproc_register(3), nng_sockaddr_inproc(5), nng(7)

NAME

nng_ipc - IPC transport

SYNOPSIS

```
#include <nng/transport/ipc/ipc.h>

int nng_ipc_register(void);
```

DESCRIPTION

The *ipc* transport provides communication support between *nng* sockets within different processes on the same host. For POSIX platforms, this is implemented using UNIX domain sockets. For Windows, this is implemented using Windows Named Pipes. Other platforms may have different implementation strategies.

Registration

The *ipc* transport is generally built-in to the *nng* core, so no extra steps to use it should be necessary.

URI Format

This transport uses URIs using the scheme ipc://, followed by a path name in the file system where the socket or named pipe should be created.

> 💡 On Windows, all names are prefixed by \\.\pipe\ and do not reside in the normal file system. On POSIX platforms, the path is taken literally, and is relative to the current directory, unless it begins with /, in which case it is relative to the root directory.

> ℹ️ When using relative paths on POSIX systems, the address used and returned in properties like NNG_OPT_LOCADDR and NNG_OPT_URL will also be relative. Consequently, they will only be interpreted the same by processes that have the same working directory. To ensure maximum portability and safety, absolute paths are recommended whenever possible.

> ℹ️ If compatibility with legacy *nanomsg* applications is required, then pathnames must not be longer than 122 bytes, including the final NUL byte. This is because legacy versions of *nanomsg* cannot express URLs longer than 128 bytes, including the ipc:// prefix.

Socket Address

When using an nng_sockaddr structure, the actual structure is of type nng_sockaddr_ipc.

Transport Options

NNG_OPT_IPC_PERMISSIONS
    (int) This write-only option may be applied to a listener to configure the permissions that are used on the UNIX domain socket created by that listener. This property is only supported on POSIX systems. The value is of type int, representing the normal permission bits on a file, such as 0600 (typically meaning read-write to the owner, and no permissions for anyone else.) The default is

system-specific, most often 0644.

⚠ Not all systems validate these permissions. In particular, illumos and Solaris are known to ignore these permission settings when connecting.

ℹ Normally both read and write permission will be necessary for a peer dialer to connect. See your system documentation for UNIX domain sockets for more information.

ℹ The *umask* of the process is **not** applied to these bits.

💡 The best practice for limiting access is to place the socket in a directory writable only by the server, and only readable and searchable by clients. All mainstream POSIX systems will fail to permit a client to connect to a socket located in a directory for which the client lacks search (execute) permission.

💡 Also consider using the NNG_OPT_IPC_PEER_UID property from within a a pipe notification callback (nng_pipe_notify()) to validate peer credentials.

NNG_OPT_IPC_SECURITY_DESCRIPTOR

(PSECURITY_DESCRIPTOR) This write-only option may be used on listeners on Windows platforms to configure the SECURITY_DESCRIPTOR that is used when creating the underlying named pipe. The value is a pointer, PSECURITY_DESCRIPTOR, and may only be applied to listeners that have not been started yet.

NNG_OPT_IPC_PEER_UID

(uint64_t) This read-only option may be read from a pipe to determine the peer user id. This is the effective user id of the peer when either the underlying listen() or connect() calls were made, and is not forgeable. This option is generally only available on POSIX systems.

NNG_OPT_IPC_PEER_GID

(uint64_t) This read-only option may be read from a pipe to determine the peer primary group id. This is the effective group id of the peer when either the underlying listen() or connect() calls were made, and is not forgeable. This option is generally only available on POSIX systems.

NNG_OPT_IPC_PEER_PID

(uint64_t) This read-only option may be read from a pipe to determine the process id of the peer. This option is only available on Windows, Linux, and certain other systems.

ℹ Applications should not assume that the process ID does not change, as it is possible (although unsupported!) for a nefarious process to pass a file descriptor between processes. However, it is not possible for a nefarious application to forge the identity of a well-behaved one using this method.

NNG_OPT_IPC_PEER_ZONEID

(uint64_t) This read-only option may be read from a pipe to determine the zone id of the peer. Zones (and this option) are only supported on Solaris and illumos systems.

SEE ALSO

nng_sockaddr(5), nng(7)

NAME

nng_pair - pair protocol

SYNOPSIS

Version 0

```
#include <nng/protocol/pair0/pair.h>
```

Version 1

```
#include <nng/protocol/pair1/pair.h>
```

DESCRIPTION

The *pair* protocol implements a peer-to-peer pattern, where relationships between peers are one-to-one.

Version 1 of this protocol supports an optional *polyamorous* mode where a peer can maintain multiple partnerships. Using this mode requires some additional sophistication in the application.

Socket Operations

The nng_pair_open() functions create *pair* socket.

Normally, this pattern will block when attempting to send a message if no peer is able to receive the message.

> Even though this mode may appear to be "reliable", because back-pressure prevents discarding messages most of the time, there are topologies involving *devices* (see nng_device()) or raw mode sockets (see NNG_OPT_RAW) where messages may be discarded. Applications that require reliable delivery semantics should consider using *req* sockets, or implement their own acknowledgment layer on top of *pair* sockets.

In order to avoid head-of-line blocking conditions, *polyamorous* mode *pair* sockets (version 1 only) discard messages if they are unable to deliver them to a peer.

Protocol Versions

Version 0 is the legacy version of this protocol. It lacks any header information, and is suitable when building simple one-to-one topologies.

> Use version 0 if you need to communicate with other implementations, including the legacy nanomsg [https://github.com/nanomsg/nanomsg] library or mangos [https://github.com/go-mangos/mangos].

Version 1 of the protocol offers improved protection against loops when used with nng_device(). It also offers *polyamorous* mode for forming multiple partnerships on a single socket.

> Version 1 of this protocol is considered experimental at this time.

Polyamorous Mode

Normally pair sockets are for one-to-one communication, and a given peer will reject new connections if it already has an active connection to another peer.

In *polyamorous* mode, which is only available with version 1, a socket can support many one-to-one connections. In this mode, the application must choose the remote peer to receive an outgoing message by setting the `nng_pipe` to use for the outgoing message with the `nng_msg_set_pipe()` function.

Most often the value of the outgoing pipe will be obtained from an incoming message using the `nng_msg_get_pipe()` function, such as when replying to an incoming message.

In order to prevent head-of-line blocking, if the peer on the given pipe is not able to receive (or the pipe is no longer available, such as if the peer has disconnected), then the message will be discarded with no notification to the sender.

Protocol Options

The following protocol-specific options are available.

NNG_OPT_PAIR1_POLY

(`bool`, version 1 only) This option enables the use of *polyamorous* mode. The value is read-write, and takes an integer Boolean value. The default false value (0) indicates that legacy monogamous mode should be used.

NNG_OPT_MAXTTL

(`int`, version 1 only). Maximum time-to-live.

Protocol Headers

Version 0 of the pair protocol has no protocol-specific headers.

Version 1 of the pair protocol uses a single 32-bit unsigned value. The low-order (big-endian) byte of this value contains a "hop" count, and is used in conjunction with the `NNG_OPT_MAXTTL` option to guard against device forwarding loops. This value is initialized to 1, and incremented each time the message is received by a new node.

SEE ALSO

nng_pair_open(3), nng_options(5), nng(7)

NAME

nng_pub - publisher protocol

SYNOPSIS

```
#include <nng/protocol/pubsub0/pub.h>
```

DESCRIPTION

The *pub* protocol is one half of a publisher/subscriber pattern. In this pattern, a publisher sends data, which is broadcast to all subscribers. The subscribing applications only see the data to which they have subscribed.

The *pub* protocol is the publisher side, and the *sub* protocol is the subscriber side.

> In this implementation, the publisher delivers all messages to all subscribers. The subscribers maintain their own subscriptions, and filter them locally. Thus, this pattern should not be used in an attempt to reduce bandwidth consumption.

The topics that subscribers subscribe to is just the first part of the message body. Applications should construct their messages accordingly.

Socket Operations

The nng_pub0_open() functions create a publisher socket. This socket may be used to send messages, but is unable to receive them. Attempts to receive messages will result in NNG_ENOTSUP.

Protocol Versions

Only version 0 of this protocol is supported. (At the time of writing, no other versions of this protocol have been defined.)

Protocol Options

The *pub* protocol has no protocol-specific options.

Protocol Headers

The *pub* protocol has no protocol-specific headers.

SEE ALSO

nng_pub_open(3), nng_sub(7), nng(7)

NAME

nng_pull - pull protocol

SYNOPSIS

```
#include <nng/protocol/pipeline0/pull.h>
```

DESCRIPTION

The *pull* protocol is one half of a pipeline pattern. The other half is the *push* protocol.

In the pipeline pattern, pushers distribute messages to pullers. Each message sent by a pusher will be sent to one of its peer pullers, chosen in a round-robin fashion from the set of connected peers available for receiving. This property makes this pattern useful in load-balancing scenarios.

Socket Operations

The nng_pull0_open() functions create a puller socket. This socket may be used to receive messages, but is unable to send them. Attempts to send messages will result in NNG_ENOTSUP.

When receiving messages, the *pull* protocol accepts messages as they arrive from peers. If two peers both have a message ready, the order in which messages are handled is undefined.

Protocol Versions

Only version 0 of this protocol is supported. (At the time of writing, no other versions of this protocol have been defined.)

Protocol Options

The *pull* protocol has no protocol-specific options.

Protocol Headers

The *pull* protocol has no protocol-specific headers.

SEE ALSO

nng_pull_open(3), nng_push(7), nng(7),

NAME

nng_push - push protocol

SYNOPSIS

```
#include <nng/protocol/pipeline0/push.h>
```

DESCRIPTION

The *push* protocol is one half of a pipeline pattern. The other side is the *pull* protocol.

In the pipeline pattern, pushers distribute messages to pullers. Each message sent by a pusher will be sent to one of its peer pullers, chosen in a round-robin fashion from the set of connected peers available for receiving. This property makes this pattern useful in load-balancing scenarios.

Socket Operations

The nng_push0_open() call creates a pusher socket. This socket may be used to send messages, but is unable to receive them. Attempts to receive messages will result in NNG_ENOTSUP.

Send operations will observe flow control (back-pressure), so that only peers capable of accepting a message will be considered. If no peer is available to receive a message, then the send operation will wait until one is available, or the operation times out.

> Although the pipeline protocol honors flow control, and attempts to avoid dropping messages, no guarantee of delivery is made. Furthermore, as there is no capability for message acknowledgment, applications that need reliable delivery are encouraged to consider the *req* protocol instead.

Protocol Versions

Only version 0 of this protocol is supported. (At the time of writing, no other versions of this protocol have been defined.)

Protocol Options

The *push* protocol has no protocol-specific options.

Protocol Headers

The *push* protocol has no protocol-specific headers.

SEE ALSO

nng_push(3), nng_pull(7), nng_req(7), nng(7)

NAME

nng_rep - reply protocol

SYNOPSIS

```
#include <nng/protocol/reqrep0/rep.h>
```

DESCRIPTION

The *rep* protocol is one half of a request/reply pattern. In this pattern, a requester sends a message to one replier, who is expected to reply. The request is resent if no reply arrives, until a reply is received or the request times out.

> 💡 This protocol is useful in setting up RPC-like services. It is also "reliable", in that a the requester will keep retrying until a reply is received.

The *rep* protocol is the replier side, and the *req* protocol is the requester side.

Socket Operations

The nng_rep0_open() functions create a replier socket. This socket may be used to receive messages (requests), and then to send replies.

Generally a reply can only be sent after receiving a request.

Send operations will result in NNG_ESTATE if no corresponding request was previously received.

Likewise, only one receive operation may be pending at a time. Any additional concurrent receive operations will result in NNG_ESTATE.

Raw mode sockets ignore all these restrictions.

Context Operations

This protocol supports the creation of contexts for concurrent use cases using nng_ctx_open().

Each context may have at most one outstanding request, and operates independently from the others. The restrictions for order of operations with sockets apply equally well for contexts, except that each context will be treated as if it were a separate socket.

Protocol Versions

Only version 0 of this protocol is supported. (At the time of writing, no other versions of this protocol have been defined.)

Protocol Options

The *rep* protocol has no protocol-specific options.

Protocol Headers

The *rep* protocol uses a *backtrace* in the header. This is more fully documented in the *req* manual.

SEE ALSO

nng_rep_open(3), nng(7), nng_req(7)

NAME

nng_req - request protocol

SYNOPSIS

```
#include <nng/protocol/reqrep0/req.h>
```

DESCRIPTION

The *req* protocol is one half of a request/reply pattern. In this pattern, a requester sends a message to one replier, who is expected to reply. The request is resent if no reply arrives, until a reply is received or the request times out.

> 💡 This protocol is useful in setting up RPC-like services. It is also "reliable", in that a the requester will keep retrying until a reply is received.

> ℹ️ Because requests are resent, it is important that they be idempotent to ensure predictable and repeatable behavior even in the face of duplicated requests, which can occur (for example if a reply message is lost for some reason.)

The requester generally only has one outstanding request at a time unless in "raw" mode (via NNG_OPT_RAW), and it will generally attempt to spread work requests to different peer repliers.

> 💡 This property, when combined with nng_device() can help provide a degree of load-balancing.

The *req* protocol is the requester side, and the *rep* protocol is the replier side.

Socket Operations

The nng_req0_open() functions create a requester socket. This socket may be used to send messages (requests), and then to receive replies.

Generally a reply can only be received after sending a request. (Attempts to receive a message will result in NNG_ESTATE if there is no outstanding request.)

Furthermore, only a single receive operation may be pending at a time. Attempts to post more receive operations concurrently will result in NNG_ESTATE.

Requests may be canceled by sending a different request. This will cause the requester to discard any reply from the earlier request, but it will not stop a replier from processing a request it has already received or terminate a request that has already been placed on the wire.

Raw mode sockets ignore all these restrictions.

Context Operations

This protocol supports the creation of contexts for concurrent use cases using nng_ctx_open().

The NNG_OPT_REQ_RESENDTIME value may be configured differently on contexts created this way.

Each context may have at most one outstanding request, and operates independently from the others.

The restrictions for order of operations with sockets apply equally well for contexts, except that each context will be treated as if it were a separate socket.

Protocol Versions

Only version 0 of this protocol is supported. (At the time of writing, no other versions of this protocol have been defined.)

Protocol Options

The following protocol-specific option is available.

NNG_OPT_REQ_RESENDTIME

(nng_duration) When a new request is started, a timer of this duration is also started. If no reply is received before this timer expires, then the request will be resent. (Requests are also automatically resent if the peer to whom the original request was sent disconnects, or if a peer becomes available while the requester is waiting for an available peer.)

Protocol Headers

This protocol uses a *backtrace* in the header. This form uses a "stack" of 32-bit big-endian identifiers. There **must** be at least one identifier, the *request ID*, which will be the last element in the array, and **must** have the most significant bit set.

There may be additional *peer ID*s preceding the request ID. These will be distinguishable from the request ID by having their most significant bit clear.

When a request message is received by a forwarding node (see nng_device()), the forwarding node prepends a 32-bit peer ID (which **must** have the most significant bit clear), which is the forwarder's way of identifying the directly connected peer from which it received the message. (This peer ID, except for the most significant bit, has meaning only to the forwarding node itself.)

It may help to think of prepending a peer ID as "pushing" a peer ID onto the front of the stack of headers for the message. (It will use the peer ID it popped from the front to determine the next intermediate destination for the reply.)

When a reply message is created, it is created using the same headers that the request contained.

A forwarding node can "pop" the peer ID it originally pushed on the message, stripping it from the front of the message as it does so.

When the reply finally arrives back at the initiating requester, it should have only a single element in the message, which will be the request ID it originally used for the request.

SEE ALSO

nng_ctx_open(3), nng_device(3), nng_req_open(3), nng_ctx(5), nng(7), nng_rep(7)

NAME

nng_respondent - respondent protocol

SYNOPSIS

```
#include <nng/protocol/survey0/respond.h>
```

DESCRIPTION

The *respondent* protocol is one half of a survey pattern. In this pattern, a surveyor sends a survey, which is broadcast to all peer respondents. The respondents then have a chance to reply (but are not obliged to reply). The survey itself is a timed event, so that responses received after the survey has finished are discarded.

> 💡 This protocol is useful in solving voting problems, such as leader election in cluster configurations, as well as certain kinds of service discovery problems.

The *respondent* protocol is the respondent side, and the *surveyor* protocol is the surveyor side.

Socket Operations

The nng_respondent0_open() functions create a respondent socket. This socket may be used to receive messages, and then to send replies. A reply can only be sent after receiving a survey, and generally the reply will be sent to surveyor from whom the last survey was received.

Respondents may discard a survey by simply not replying to it.

Raw mode sockets (set with NNG_OPT_RAW) ignore all these restrictions.

Context Operations

This protocol supports the creation of contexts for concurrent use cases using nng_ctx_open().

Incoming surveys will be routed to and received by only one context. Additional surveys may be received by other contexts in parallel. Replies made using a context will be returned to the the surveyor that issued the survey most recently received by that context. The restrictions for order of operations with sockets apply equally well for contexts, except that each context will be treated as if it were a separate socket.

Protocol Versions

Only version 0 of this protocol is supported. (At the time of writing, no other versions of this protocol have been defined. An earlier and incompatible version of the protocol was used in older pre-releases of nanomsg [http://nanomsg.org], but was not released in any production version.)

Protocol Options

The *respondent* protocol has no protocol-specific options.

Protocol Headers

The *respondent* protocol uses a *backtrace* in the header. This is more fully documented in the *surveyor* manual.

SEE ALSO

nng_respondent_open(3), nng_surveyor(7), nng(7)

NAME

nng_sub - subscriber protocol

SYNOPSIS

```
#include <nng/nng.h>
#include <nng/protocol/pubsub0/sub.h>
```

DESCRIPTION

The *sub* protocol is one half of a publisher/subscriber pattern. In this pattern, a publisher sends data, which is broadcast to all subscribers. The subscribing applications only see the data to which they have subscribed.

The *sub* protocol is the subscriber side, and the *pub* protocol is the publisher side.

> ℹ️ In this implementation, the publisher delivers all messages to all subscribers. The subscribers maintain their own subscriptions, and filter them locally. Thus, this pattern should not be used in an attempt to reduce bandwidth consumption.

The topics that subscribers subscribe to is just the first part of the message body. Applications should construct their messages accordingly.

Socket Operations

The nng_sub0_open() functions create a subscriber socket. This socket may be used to receive messages, but is unable to send them. Attempts to send messages will result in NNG_ENOTSUP.

Protocol Versions

Only version 0 of this protocol is supported. (At the time of writing, no other versions of this protocol have been defined.)

Protocol Options

The following protocol-specific options are available.

NNG_OPT_SUB_SUBSCRIBE

This option registers a topic that the subscriber is interested in. The option is write-only, and takes an array of bytes, of arbitrary size. Each incoming message is checked against the list of subscribed topics. If the body begins with the entire set of bytes in the topic, then the message is accepted. If no topic matches, then the message is discarded.

> 💡 To receive all messages, an empty topic (zero length) can be used.

NNG_OPT_SUB_UNSUBSCRIBE

This option, also read-only, removes a topic from the subscription list. Note that if the topic was not previously subscribed to with NNG_OPT_SUB_SUBSCRIBE then an NNG_ENOENT error will result.

Protocol Headers

The *sub* protocol has no protocol-specific headers.

SEE ALSO

nng_sub_open(3), nng_pub(7), nng(7)

NAME

nng_surveyor - surveyor protocol

SYNOPSIS

```
#include <nng/nng.h>
#include <nng/protocol/survey0/survey.h>
```

DESCRIPTION

The *surveyor* protocol is one half of a survey pattern. In this pattern, a surveyor sends a survey, which is broadcast to all peer respondents. The respondents then have a chance to reply (but are not obliged to reply). The survey itself is a timed event, so that responses received after the survey has finished are discarded.

> 💡 This protocol is useful in solving voting problems, such as leader election in cluster configurations, as well as certain kinds of service discovery problems.

The *surveyor* protocol is the surveyor side, and the *respondent* protocol is the respondent side.

Socket Operations

The `nng_surveyor0_open()` functions create a surveyor socket. This socket may be used to send messages (surveys), and then to receive replies. A reply can only be received after sending a survey. A surveyor can normally expect to receive at most one reply from each responder. (Messages can be duplicated in some topologies, so there is no guarantee of this.)

Attempts to receive on a socket with no outstanding survey will result in NNG_ESTATE. If the survey times out while the surveyor is waiting for replies, then the result will be NNG_ETIMEDOUT.

Only one survey can be outstanding at a time; sending another survey will cancel the prior one, and any responses from respondents from the prior survey that arrive after this will be discarded.

Raw mode sockets ignore all these restrictions.

Context Operations

This protocol supports the creation of contexts for concurrent use cases using `nng_ctx_open()`.

Each context can initiate its own surveys, and it will receive only responses to its own outstanding surveys. Other contexts on the same socket may have overlapping surveys operating at the same time.

Each of these may have their own timeouts established with NNG_OPT_SURVEYOR_SURVEYTIME.

Additionally, sending a survey on a context will only cancel an outstanding survey on the same context.

> ℹ️ Due to the best-effort nature of this protocol, if too may contexts are attempting to perform surveys simultaneously, it is possible for either individual outgoing surveys or incoming responses to be lost.

Protocol Versions

Only version 0 of this protocol is supported. (At the time of writing, no other versions of this protocol have been defined. An earlier and incompatible version of the protocol was used in older pre-releases of nanomsg [http://nanomsg.org], but was not released in any production version.)

Protocol Options

The following protocol-specific options is available.

NNG_OPT_SURVEYOR_SURVEYTIME

(nng_duration) Duration of surveys. When a new survey is started, a timer of this duration is also started. Any responses arriving this time will be discarded. Attempts to receive after the timer expires with no other surveys started will result in NNG_ESTATE. Attempts to receive when this timer expires will result in NNG_ETIMEDOUT.

Protocol Headers

This form uses a "stack" of 32-bit big-endian identifiers. There **must** be at least one identifier, the *survey ID*, which will be the last element in the array, and **must** have the most significant bit set.

There may be additional *peer ID*s preceding the survey ID. These will be distinguishable from the survey ID by having their most significant bit clear.

When a survey message is received by a forwarding node (see nng_device()), the forwarding node prepends a 32-bit peer ID (which **must** have the most significant bit clear), which is the forwarder's way of identifying the directly connected peer from which it received the message. (This peer ID, except for the most significant bit, has meaning only to the forwarding node itself.)

It may help to think of prepending a peer ID as "pushing" a peer ID onto the front of the stack of headers for the message. (It will use the peer ID it popped from the front to determine the next intermediate destination for the response.)

When a response message is created, it is created using the same headers that the survey contained.

A forwarding node can "pop" the peer ID it originally pushed on the message, stripping it from the front of the message as it does so.

When the response finally arrives back at the initiating surveyor, it should have only a single element in the message, which will be the survey ID it originally used for the request.

SEE ALSO

nng_surveyor_open(3), nng_respondent(7), nng(7)

NAME

nng_tcp - TCP/IP transport

SYNOPSIS

```
#include <nng/transport/tcp/tcp.h>

int nng_tcp_register(void);
```

DESCRIPTION

The *tcp* transport provides communication support between *nng* sockets across a TCP/IP network. Both IPv4 and IPv6 are supported when the underlying platform also supports it.

Registration

The *nng_tcp* transport is generally built-in to the *nng* core, so no extra steps to use it should be necessary.

URI Format

This transport uses URIs using the scheme tcp://, followed by an IP address or hostname, followed by a colon and finally a TCP port number. For example, to contact port 80 on the localhost either of the following URIs could be used: tcp://127.0.0.1:80 or tcp://localhost:80.

A URI may be restricted to IPv6 using the scheme tcp6://, and may be restricted to IPv4 using the scheme tcp4://.

> Specifying tcp6:// may not prevent IPv4 hosts from being used with IPv4-in-IPv6 addresses, particularly when using a wildcard hostname with listeners. The details of this varies across operating systems.

> Both tcp6:// and tcp4:// are *nng* extensions, and might not be understood by other implementations.

> We recommend using either numeric IP addresses, or names that are specific to either IPv4 or IPv6 to prevent confusion and surprises.

When specifying IPv6 addresses, the address must be enclosed in square brackets ([]) to avoid confusion with the final colon separating the port.

For example, the same port 80 on the IPv6 loopback address (::1) would be specified as tcp://[::1]:80.

The special value of 0 (INADDR_ANY) can be used for a listener to indicate that it should listen on all interfaces on the host. A short-hand for this form is to either omit the address, or specify the asterisk (*) character. For example, the following three URIs are all equivalent, and could be used to listen to port 9999 on the host:

1. `tcp://0.0.0.0:9999`
2. `tcp://*:9999`
3. `tcp://:9999`

The entire URI must be less than `NNG_MAXADDRLEN` bytes long.

Socket Address

When using an `nng_sockaddr` structure, the actual structure is either of type `nng_sockaddr_in` (for IPv4) or `nng_sockaddr_in6` (for IPv6).

Transport Options

NNG_OPT_TCP_KEEPALIVE

(`bool`) Enable TCP keep-alives, defaults to `false`.

NNG_OPT_TCP_NODELAY

(`bool`) Disable Nagle's algorithm. When enabled (`false`), the underlying TCP stream will attempt to buffer and coalesce messages before sending them on, waiting a short interval to improve buffering and reduce the overhead caused by sending too-small messages. This comes at a cost to latency, and is not recommended with modern high speed networks. Defaults to `true`.

SEE ALSO

nng_sockaddr(5), nng_sockaddr_in(5), nng_sockaddr_in6(5), nng(7)

NAME

nng_tls - TLS transport

SYNOPSIS

```
#include <nng/transport/tls/tls.h>

int nng_tls_register(void);
```

DESCRIPTION

The *tls* transport provides communication support between *nng* sockets across a TCP/IP network using TLS v1.2 [https://tools.ietf.org/html/rfc5246] on top of TCP [https://tools.ietf.org/html/rfc793]. Both IPv4 and IPv6 are supported when the underlying platform also supports it.

The protocol details are documented in TLS Mapping for Scalability Protocols [http://nanomsg.org/rfcs/sp-tls-v1.html].

Registration

Depending upon how the library was built, it may be necessary to register the transport by calling nng_tls_register().

Availability

The *tls* transport depends on the use of an external library. As of this writing, mbedTLS [https://tls.mbed.org/] version 2.0 or later is required.

> 💡 Applications may need to add this library (or libraries) to their link line, particularly when using a statically built *nng* library.

> ℹ️ The mbedTLS library uses different licensing terms than *nng* itself; as of this writing it is offered under either Apache License 2.0 [https://opensource.org/licenses/Apache-2.0] or GNU GPL [https://opensource.org/licenses/gpl-license] terms. You are responsible for understanding and adhering to the license terms of any libraries you make use of.

URI Format

This transport uses URIs using the scheme tls+tcp://, followed by an IP address or hostname, followed by a colon and finally a TCP port number. For example, to contact port 4433 on the localhost either of the following URIs could be used: tls+tcp://127.0.0.1:4433 or tls+tcp://localhost:4433.

A URI may be restricted to IPv6 using the scheme tls+tcp6://, and may be restricted to IPv4 using the scheme tls+tcp4://.

> ℹ️ Specifying tls+tcp6:// may not prevent IPv4 hosts from being used with IPv4-in-IPv6 addresses, particularly when using a wildcard hostname with listeners. The details of this varies across operating systems.

> ℹ   Both `tls+tcp6://` and `tls+tcp4://` are *nng* extensions, and may not be understood by other implementations.

> 💡   We recommend using either numeric IP addresses, or names that are specific to either IPv4 or IPv6 to prevent confusion and surprises.

When specifying IPv6 addresses, the address must be enclosed in square brackets ([]) to avoid confusion with the final colon separating the port.

For example, the same port 4433 on the IPv6 loopback address ('::1') would be specified as `tls+tcp://[::1]:4433`.

> 💡   Certificate validation generally works when using names rather than IP addresses. This transport automatically uses the name supplied in the URL when validating the certificate supplied by the server.

The special value of 0 (`INADDR_ANY`) can be used for a listener to indicate that it should listen on all interfaces on the host. A short-hand for this form is to either omit the address, or specify the asterisk (*) character. For example, the following three URIs are all equivalent, and could be used to listen to port 9999 on the host:

1. `tls+tcp://0.0.0.0:9999`
2. `tls+tcp://*:9999`
3. `tls+tcp://:9999`

The entire URI must be less than NNG_MAXADDRLEN bytes long.

Socket Address

When using an nng_sockaddr structure, the actual structure is either of type nng_sockaddr_in (for IPv4) or nng_sockaddr_in6 (for IPv6).

Transport Options

The following transport options are available. Note that setting these must be done before the transport is started.

NNG_OPT_TCP_KEEPALIVE

(bool) Enable TCP keep-alives, defaults to `false`.

NNG_OPT_TCP_NODELAY

(bool) Disable Nagle's algorithm. When enabled (`false`), the underlying TCP stream will attempt to buffer and coalesce messages before sending them on, waiting a short interval to improve buffering and reduce the overhead caused by sending too-small messages. This comes at a cost to latency, and is not recommended with modern high speed networks. Defaults to `true`.

NNG_OPT_TLS_CONFIG

(nng_tls_config *) The underlying TLS configuration object. A hold is placed on the underlying configuration object before returning it. The caller should release the hold with `nng_tls_config_free()` when it no longer needs the TLS configuration object.

> 💡   Use this option when advanced TLS configuration is required.

NNG_OPT_TLS_CA_FILE

    (string) Write-only option naming a file containing certificates to use for peer validation. See `nng_tls_config_ca_file()` for more information.

NNG_OPT_TLS_CERT_KEY_FILE

    (string) Write-only option naming a file containing the local certificate and associated private key. The private key used must be unencrypted. See `nng_tls_config_own_cert()` for more information.

NNG_OPT_TLS_AUTH_MODE

    (`int`) Write-only option used to configure the authentication mode used. See `nng_tls_config_auth_mode()` for more details.

NNG_OPT_TLS_VERIFIED

    (`bool`) Whether the remote peer has been properly verified using TLS authentication. May return incorrect results if peer authentication is disabled.

SEE ALSO

nng_tls_config_alloc(3tls) nng_sockaddr_in(5), nng_sockaddr_in6(5), nng(7),

NAME

nng_ws - WebSocket transport

SYNOPSIS

```
#include <nng/transport/websocket/ws.h>

int nng_ws_register(void);
int nng_wss_register(void);
```

DESCRIPTION

The *ws* transport provides communication support between *nng* sockets across a TCP/IP network using WebSockets [https://tools.ietf.org/html/rfc6455]. Both IPv4 and IPv6 are supported when the underlying platform also supports it.

The protocol details are documented in WebSocket Mapping for Scalability Protocols [http://nanomsg.org/rfcs/sp-websocket-v1.html].

Registration

Depending upon how the library was built, it may be necessary to register the transport by calling nng_ws_register().

If TLS support is enabled in the library, secure WebSockets (over TLS v1.2) can be used as well, but the secure transport may have to be registered using the nng_wss_register() function.

URI Format

This transport uses URIs using the scheme ws://, followed by an IP address or hostname, optionally followed by a colon and an TCP port number, optionally followed by a path. (If no port number is specified then port 80 is assumed. If no path is specified then a path of / is assumed.) For example, the URI ws://localhost/app/pubsub would use port 80 on localhost, with the path /app/pubsub.

Secure WebSockets (if enabled) use the scheme wss://, and the default TCP port number of 443. Otherwise the format is the same as for regular WebSockets.

When specifying IPv6 addresses, the address must be enclosed in square brackets ([]) to avoid confusion with the final colon separating the port.

For example, the same path and port on the IPv6 loopback address (::1) would be specified as ws://[::1]/app/pubsub.

> ℹ The value specified as the host, if any, will also be used in the Host: HTTP header during HTTP negotiation.

To listen to all ports on the system, the host name may be elided from the URL on the listener. This will wind up listening to all interfaces on the system, with possible caveats for IPv4 and IPv6 depending on what the underlying system supports. (On most modern systems it will map to the special IPv6 address ::, and both IPv4 and IPv6 connections will be permitted, with IPv4 addresses mapped to IPv6 addresses.)

Socket Address

When using an `nng_sockaddr` structure, the actual structure is either of type `nng_sockaddr_in` (for IPv4) or `nng_sockaddr_in6` (for IPv6).

Server Instances

This transport makes use of shared HTTP server instances, permitting multiple sockets or listeners to be configured with the same hostname and port. When creating a new listener, it is registered with an existing HTTP server instance if one can be found. Note that the matching algorithm is somewhat simple, using only a string based hostname or IP address and port to match. Therefore it is recommended to use only IP addresses or the empty string as the hostname in listener URLs.

Likewise, when sharing a server instance, it may not be possible to alter TLS configuration if the server is already running, as there is only a single TLS configuration context for the entire server instance.

All sharing of server instances is only typically possible within the same process.

The server may also be used by other things (for example to serve static content), in the same process.

Transport Options

The following transport options are available. Note that setting these must be done before the transport is started.

> 🛈   The TLS specific options (beginning with `NNG_OPT_TLS_`) are only available for `wss://` endpoints.

NNG_OPT_WS_REQUEST_HEADERS

(string) Concentation of multiple lines terminated by CRLF sequences, that can be used to add further headers to the HTTP request sent when connecting. This option can be set on dialers, and retrieved from pipes.

NNG_OPT_WS_RESPONSE_HEADERS

(string) Concatenation of multiple lines terminated by CRLF sequences, that can be used to add further headers to the HTTP response sent when connecting. This option can be set on listeners, and retrieved from pipes.

NNG_OPT_TLS_CONFIG

(`nng_tls_config *`) The underlying TLS configuration object for `wss://` endpoints. A hold is placed on the underlying configuration object before returning it. The caller should release the object with `nng_tls_config_free()` when it no longer needs the TLS configuration.

> 💡   Use this option when advanced TLS configuration is required.

NNG_OPT_TLS_CA_FILE

(string) Write-only option naming a file containing certificates to use for peer validation. See `nng_tls_config_ca_file()` for more information.

NNG_OPT_TLS_CERT_KEY_FILE

(string) Write-only option naming a file containing the local certificate and associated private key.

The private key used must be unencrypted. See `nng_tls_config_own_cert()` for more information.

NNG_OPT_TLS_AUTH_MODE

(`int`) Write-only option used to configure the authentication mode used. See `nng_tls_config_auth_mode()` for more details.

NNG_OPT_TLS_VERIFIED

(`bool`) Whether the remote peer has been properly verified using TLS authentication. May return incorrect results if peer authentication is disabled.

SEE ALSO

nng_tls_config_alloc(3tls), nng_sockaddr(5), nng_sockaddr_in(5), nng_sockaddr_in6(5), nng(7)

NAME

nng_zerotier - ZeroTier transport

SYNOPSIS

```
#include <nng/transport/zerotier/zerotier.h>

int nng_zt_register(void);
```

DESCRIPTION

The *zt* transport provides communication support for *nng* applications over a ZeroTier [http://www.zerotier.com] network, using a Virtual Layer 2 packet facility.

⚠ This transport is experimental. To utilize it at present, the library must be built with support, and linked against a suitable libzerotiercore library. Further information about building with this support are in the build documentation included with the distribution.

⚠ The libzerotiercore library at present is covered under different license terms than the rest of *nng*. Please be careful to review and adhere to the licensing terms.

⚠ The ZeroTier transport can take a long time to establish an initial connection — up to even a minute in extreme cases, while the network topology is configured. Consequently, this transport is not recommended for use cases involving short-lived programs, but is better for long-running programs such as background daemons or agents.

While ZeroTier makes use of the host's IP stack (and UDP in particular), this transport does not use or require an IP stack on the virtual network; thereby mitigating any considerations about IP address management.

This service uses Ethernet type 901 to transport packets. Network rules must permit this Ethernet type to pass in order to have a functional network.

🛈 This document assumes that the reader is familiar with ZeroTier concepts and administration.

Registration

Depending upon how the library was built, it may be necessary to register the transport by calling nng_zt_register(). This function returns zero on success, or an nng error value if the transport cannot be initialized for any reason.

URI Format

This transport uses URIs using the scheme zt://, followed by a node number (ten hexadecimal digits) followed by a . delimited, and then a network address (sixteen hexadecimal digits), followed by a colon (:) and service or port number (decimal value, up to 24-bits). For example, the URI zt://fedcba9876.0123456789abdef:999 indicates that node fedcba9876 on network 0123456789abcdef is listening on port 999.

The special value * can be used in lieu of a node number to represent the node's own node number.

Listeners may use port 0 to indicate that a suitable port number be selected automatically. Applications using this must determine the selected port number using the `nng_listener_getopt()` function.

Socket Address

When using an `nng_sockaddr` structure, the actual structure is of type `nng_sockaddr_zt`.

Node Presence

By default this transport creates an "ephemeral" node, and used the same ephemeral node for any additional endpoints created. As this node is ephemeral, the keys associated with it and all associated data are located in memory and are discarded upon application termination. If a persistent node is desired, please see the `NNG_OPT_ZT_HOME` option.

It is possible for a single application to join multiple networks using the same node, or using separate nodes.

Network Status

A ZeroTier node can be in one of the following states, which can be obtained with the `NNG_OPT_ZT_NETWORK_STATUS` option:

NNG_ZT_STATUS_UP
> The ZeroTier network is up. This is the only state where it is possible to communicate with peers, and the only state where the network name (`NNG_OPT_ZT_NETWORK_NAME`) is available.

NNG_ZT_STATUS_CONFIG
> The ZeroTier node is still configuring, network services are not available.

NNG_ZT_STATUS_DENIED
> The node does not have permission to join the ZeroTier network.

NNG_ZT_STATUS_NOTFOUND
> The ZeroTier network is not found.

NNG_ZT_STATUS_ERROR
> Some other ZeroTier error has occurred; the network is not available.

NNG_ZT_STATUS_OBSOLETE
> The node is running obsolete software; the network is not available.

NNG_ZT_STATUS_UNKNOWN
> The network is in an unknown state. This should not happen, as it indicates that the ZeroTier software is reporting an unexpected status. The network is most likely not available.

Transport Options

The following transport options are available:

NNG_OPT_ZT_HOME

(string) This option represents the "home directory", where the transport can store (and reuse) persistent state, such as key materials, node identity, and federation membership. This option must be set before the ZeroTier transport is first used. If this value is empty, then an ephemeral ZeroTier node is created, and no persistent state is used. The default is to use an ephemeral node.

> ℹ️ If this option is set to different values on different sockets, dialers, or listeners, then separate nodes will be created. It is perfectly valid for an application to have multiple node identities in this fashion.

NNG_OPT_ZT_NWID

(uint64_t) The 64-bit ZeroTier network number (native byte order).

NNG_OPT_ZT_NODE

(uint64_t) The ZeroTier 40-bit node address (native byte order).

NNG_OPT_ZT_NETWORK_STATUS

(int) The ZeroTier network status. See Network Status for an explanation of this option.

NNG_OPT_ZT_NETWORK_NAME

(string) The name of the network as established by the ZeroTier network administrator.

NNG_OPT_ZT_CONN_TIME

(nng_duration) The time to wait between sending connection attempts, only used with dialers. The default is 500 msec.

NNG_OPT_ZT_CONN_TRIES

(int) The maximum number of attempts to try to establish a connection before reporting a timeout, and is only used with dialers. The default is 240, which results in a 2 minute timeout if NNG_OPT_ZT_CONN_TIME is at its default of 500. If the value is set to 0, then connection attempts will keep retrying forever.

NNG_OPT_ZT_PING_TIME

(nng_duration) If no traffic has been received from the ZeroTier peer after this period of time, then a "ping" message is sent to check if the peer is still alive.

NNG_OPT_ZT_PING_TRIES

(int) If this number of consecutive "ping" requests are sent to the peer with no response (and no other intervening traffic), then the peer is assumed to be dead and the connection is closed.

NNG_OPT_ZT_MTU

(size_t) The ZeroTier virtual network MTU (read-only) as configured on the network; this is the Virtual Layer 2 MTU. The headers used by this transport and the protocols consume some of this for each message sent over the network. (The transport uses 20-bytes of this, and each protocol may consume additional space, typically not more than 16-bytes.)

NNG_OPT_ZT_ORBIT

(uint64_t[2]) Write-only array of two uint64_t values, indicating the ID of a ZeroTier "moon", and the node ID of the root server for that moon. (The ID may be zero if the moon ID is the same as its root server ID, which is conventional.)

NNG_OPT_ZT_DEORBIT

(uint64_t) Write-only option indicating the moon ID to "deorbit". If the node is not already orbiting the moon, then this has no effect.

SEE ALSO

nng_sockaddr_zt(5), nng(7)

Appendix A: Software License

This manual documents NNG™, which is distributed under a the MIT License. Furthermore, the individual manual pages in this reference manual are also available separately under the terms of the MIT License. Finally, any code samples in this book are also hereby licensed under the MIT License.

> ⚠️ This book itself is a collection, and is distributed under very different terms. Please see the copyright page at the front of the book for details.

The MIT License

Index

www.ingramcontent.com/pod-product-compliance
Lightning Source LLC
Chambersburg PA
CBHW082127210326
41599CB00031B/5897